# Reviews of English Language Proficiency Tests

J. Charles Alderson
Karl J. Krahnke
Charles W. Stansfield

Editors

Teachers of English to Speakers of Other Languages

**Staff Editor:** Julia Frank-McNeil
Editorial Assistants: Juana E. Hopkins
Christopher R. Byrne

Library of Congress Catalog No. 87-050894
ISBN 0-939791-31-5

Typeset in Linotype Caledonia by
Graftec Corporation, Washington, DC
and lithographed by
Pantagraph Printing, Bloomington, IL

# Acknowledgements

The editors would like to express their gratitude to a number of people for making this publication possible. Most importantly, Donna Ilyin, who originally conceived the project. Without her energy and dedication the project could never have been undertaken. Early in the history of the project, a number of committees around the United States participated in choosing and evaluating tests. While there are too many who participated to mention here, their contributions were invaluable, even though their work may not appear in the final form of the publication. Maria Parish-Johnson and Sayuri Madusa assisted in correspondence and typing. Educational Testing Service provided support for the typing of the manuscript as well as substantial phone and postage expenses. James E. Alatis, a number of recent TESOL Presidents and Executive Boards, TESOL Publication Committee Chairs, H. Douglas Brown, and Julia Frank-McNeil have given unflagging support to the project.

# Preface

This work provides descriptive and evaluative information on the major English as a second language and English as a foreign language (ESL/EFL) tests in current use throughout the world. Tests were selected for review on the basis of two criteria: (a) The test must be commercially available, and (b) the test must be relatively widely used. The first criterion is fairly straightforward. One exception is the Interagency Language Roundtable Oral Proficiency Interview (ILR), which is not actually a published test but a carefully defined and widely used procedure. Commercial availability does not apply to many British tests, as Charles Alderson notes in his introduction to British tests. In addition, the criterion of commerical availability excludes many tests that have been developed and used in local programs or school districts in the United States and only occasionally made available to others.

The second criterion was more difficult to apply since it was impossible to define "widely used." The editors gradually compiled a list of tests on the basis of informal discussions with a number of test users. The list was circulated among testing professionals, in particular those active in ESL/EFL testing, over a period of several years to determine whether tests should be added or deleted. The final result is the product of this process, and although several tests may have been added or omitted, the selection represents the major published tests available and in use at the time of publication of this collection.

A number of compromises were inevitable. The first is with the *number of tests included*. Far more ESL/EFL tests are in use than are reviewed in this volume. The selection criteria excluded all but a fraction of the tests actually in use in the world.

Second, the *quality and content of the reviews* is variable. Reviewing a test is not a precise procedure. While some features of a test are easily observable and confirmable, others are matters of opinion or depend on extensive experience. Reviewers have individual strengths, weaknesses, and interests, and their reviews cannot help but reflect them. To achieve the highest possible quality reviews, the editors have solicited qualified and objective reviewers, and have subjected the reviews themselves to further review.

A third concern is the *timeliness of the reviews*. This collection includes tests that were known to the editors at the time of the completion of the project. New tests or new editions of tests may have become available since that time, and it may be possible to correct this problem in a future edition of this collection. Because tests are frequently being revised and updated, users are urged to contact test publishers for the most recent information on the tests.

## The Editing Process for this Volume

The reviews in this volume have been carefully prepared. Reviewers were cautioned to examine the test materials in depth. Many reviewers already had experience with the test. Others gained experience by administering it to one or more examinees on a trial basis, although they were not required to do so.

The editors generally divided their work as follows. Karl Krahnke took charge of obtaining the North American tests from the publishers. He selected competent reviewers and invited them to write reviews, sent out test materials, and received the completed reviews. Charles Alderson performed these tasks for the British and Australian tests. In addition, he critiqued and edited the reviews submitted to him. Charles Stansfield received the reviews from Krahnke and Alderson, edited them, and verified the information they contained, according to the procedures outlined next.

A unique aspect of this collection, compared with similar collections, such as the test reviews that appear in the *Mental Measurements Yearbook*, is that the reviewers' opinions or comments underwent independent evaluation. A review written by one author was sent to another author for comment. These comments resulted in challenges to statements in a number of cases. Similarly, each review, sometimes in revised form, was sent to the test author or publisher, who was invited to comment also. This produced many points of contention, with some of the publishers providing written replies longer than the reviews themselves. Much of the information supplied by test authors and publishers simply corrected minor inaccuracies in price or other information that is subject to frequent change. However, in other cases, the publishers expressed fundamental differences of opinion with reviewers. While a serious effort was made to resolve these disputes by examining test materials and other supporting documentation, it was not possible to do so to everyone's satisfaction in all cases. In such cases, Stansfield decided on the final version of the review, after considering both the reviewer's freedom to make critical statements about a test and the publisher's desire to have accurate, appropriate statements about the test published. While this process resulted in more balanced and more accurate reviews, the reader should keep in mind that different reviewers could reach different conclusions about the validity of a test. Thus, while the reviews may be helpful, they do not necessarily reflect the conclusions about a test's validity that any user would draw after examining a set of test materials or administering a particular instrument to a group of students.

## Organization of the Volume

This volume is organized into separate reviews of the major tests of ESL and EFL that are currently used in the United States, Canada, the United Kingdom, and Australia—the major population centers of the English-speaking world. The tests are of two kinds: off-the-shelf and secure. Off-the-shelf tests are available for purchase from publishers by a teacher. Such tests are used on multiple occasions and whenever needed. Secure tests are returned to the publisher after use. Instead of purchasing the test, the institution or the examinee may pay a fee for the right to administer it. The test reviews are arranged in alphabetical order.

Each review begins with a Synopsis that presents basic information on the test in summary format. The reader should read the Synopsis first, since the reviewers were encouraged not to repeat in their reviews information that was included in the Synopsis. The information is presented in telegraphic form in the following order:

> Complete title
> Acronym, or commonly used short form
>   of title
> Date of publication
> Intended examinee population
> Intended purpose of test
> Scoring method (by parts or sections of test)
> Type of administration (individual or group)
> Length of test
> Test components (i.e., date of publication
>   and number of pages)
> Cost of components (1985-1986)
> Author(s)
> Publisher, including complete address
>   and phone number

Although the information contained in the Synopsis has been verified by the publisher or by comparing it with test publications, certain types of information (i.e., product availability, components, price, and publisher's address and phone number) change frequently. The reader will want to take this into account before placing an order for a test based on information obtained from this volume.

Following the Synopsis, some reviews contain one or more entries in a Test References section. These are references added by Stansfield and are not mentioned by the reviewer, nor are they included in the technical or administrative manual for the test. Rather, they are intended to provide more comprehensive information about the test and often refer to other published reviews or studies of the test that the reader may consult. The fact that less than half of the reviews contain a Test References section is indicative of the paucity of independent analyses of language proficiency tests.

A description of the test and a discussion of its reliability, validity, and related issues are contained in the Review. Each Review is from 900 to 2,500 words in length; the average length is approximately 1,500 words.

Following the Review are the Reviewer's References. As the name implies, these are references cited by the reviewer in the body of the Review. The reader is encouraged to consult both the Test References and Reviewer's References sections for additional information relevant to each test.

## How to Use this Volume

This volume may be used in several ways. One is to provide information to test users about tests they may already be using, and the second is to provide test users with information to assist them in choosing tests to use for their specific testing needs. Of course, a collection of reviews such as this may be put to a number of other uses. For example, the work provides feedback to test writers and publishers, informs test users about the qualities and criteria they should consider in choosing and using tests, and informs the consumers of test results about the quality and significance of the information they are being provided by tests. In general, the editors hope that the reviews contained in this volume will lead, at least in some small way, to an improvement in both the tests available for ESL/EFL assessment, and the uses made of such tests and their results.

Regarding the primary purposes for using this volume, however, actual or prospective test users should first carefully characterize the type of test takers they will be testing, their purposes for testing them, and the use that will be made of the results of the testing. Only then can they consult specific reviews to determine if a specific (or any) test is appropriate to their needs.

When consulting specific reviews, the test user should first refer to the information on intended examinee population to determine if the stated population for which the test is designed is identical or similar to the population the user wishes to test. The user should also refer to the information on intended purpose of test to determine if the application suggested by the publisher is similar or identical to the user's purpose for testing. (The usual purposes for testing are reviewed later in this Introduction for those who are not familiar with them.)

After determining whether the test is appropriate to the user's purpose and students, the body of the review may be examined to verify whether the intended purpose and population for the test are legitimate. This information may be found in comments about the population on which the test was normed and on the statistics generated during the norming process. In general, the quality of a test can only be determined for the type of test takers on which the test was normed. Tests should be applied with caution to other populations. Test users who cannot interpret the technical information relating to a test are encouraged to consult a specialist in testing (usually available in any school system, college, or university) for assistance.

Next, the test user should consider the practical aspects of the test: administration time and type, training requirements of administrators, cost, and so on. Close attention should be paid to any experience in actually using the test the reviewer reports. Such experience can often uncover strengths or weaknesses in a test that strictly objective information may not reveal.

Test users are encouraged to correspond with publishers to obtain additional information about a test or to inform the publisher of problems in administering a test or interpreting its results. Without constructive feedback, publishers may be unable to improve their products. Test users should also share experiences and discuss problems with each other.

Finally, potential users should examine a copy of a test before making a commitment to use it. Special attention should be given to the accompanying documentation. A good test should have extensive supporting documentation, such as a user's manual or a technical manual. While there may be good tests that lack such documentation, it is difficult to determine their quality or how best to interpret their results.

## Uses and Misuses of Testing

Testing plays a major and sometimes dominant role in language teaching. Most second or foreign language teaching involves some sort of test or examination. Tests are used at the beginning of instruction to determine readiness, during instruction to determine student progress, and at the end of instruction to determine its effectiveness. Tests may be used for research, diagnosis, or even for practice in taking tests. Tests are even rightly or wrongly used as the basis for curriculum, such as when instruction is keyed to preparing students to perform well on a specific test.

Although tests are a universal ingredient in ESL/EFL teaching, they are often poorly understood, misused, or misapplied. One of the most frequently asked questions of second language teaching professionals is "What test do you use for . . . ?" or "What is the best test for . . . ?" Many ESL/EFL teachers seem to believe that one or more tests must exist that will solve all their administrative and instructional problems, but that they simply have not heard about them. This sentiment reflects the difficulty teachers and administrators have in finding, understanding, and evaluating information on ESL/EFL tests. It also reflects the understandable lack of training and experience that many language teaching professionals have in the field of testing and test use.

The complexities of English language testing and the limited expertise of many users of language tests have lead to the misuse (and occasional abuse) of tests, especially of commercially available tests. Out of a well-meaning desire to solve their testing and teaching problems as efficiently as possible, test users can make the mistake of employing the wrong test for their students or purpose, misinterpreting the results, or misapplying the results.

An example of the first kind of mistake is using a test designed to measure students' success at learning a specific instructional set of materials (achievement) to measure students' overall ability in English (proficiency). Another example is using a test designed for and normed on children learning English as a second language to measure the success of adults in a basic education program. In both cases, using the test will provide the testers with scores, but the utility of the scores will be low because the tests are not valid for the population being tested. Another example of misuse is to apply a test designed for native speakers of English to nonnative speakers.

An example of misinterpretation or misapplication of test results is making a decision about a student's progress or readiness for advancement (e.g., mainstreaming in a school system) on the basis of a small difference in scores on a single English language test. This type of misapplication is especially serious when the test does not discriminate between more and less proficient students, when it measures only a narrow range of language behaviors (e.g., only sound-letter correspondence or only reading), or when performance on the test is generalized to broader aspects of language behavior. Another example of misapplication of test results might be the exclusive use of English language test scores to predict success or failure in some other effort, or in school work in general.

The misuse of language tests is minimized when the test user has two kinds of knowledge. One is a basic knowledge of testing principles, knowledge that is available in a number of publications (see Appendix), from teacher education courses and from workshops. The second kind of knowledge concerns the features and quality of the tests that are available.

This volume addresses a knowledge gap in ESL/EFL testing by providing basic descriptive and evaluative information on many commercially available tests. By having this information available in a consistent format, the informed test user can choose appropriate tests if they exist. This volume cannot, of course, substitute for a course on language testing. The test user is encouraged to obtain that knowledge elsewhere or to consult a language testing specialist when choosing a test for a specific testing situation.

## Purposes of Testing

To assist the user of this collection in choosing appropriate tests, a brief introduction to the most common purposes for testing is provided here. Although space permits only a summary of the purposes, teachers and nonspecialists should find this information useful.

Purposes for language testing fall into four major types: placement, measuring achievement, diagnosis, and measuring proficiency.

### Placement

A test is used for placement when the results determine the level of instruction for which a student is ready. A good placement test should: (a) contain the same types of knowledge or skills that are taught in the instruction program in which the student is being placed, and (b) not include tasks that are so unusual or unfamiliar to the test takers that they may negatively affect the students' performance.

*Measuring Achievement*

An achievement test measures a student's success in learning some specific instructional content and is given after the instruction has taken place. A good achievement test should contain only material that was actually taught. Thus, commercially available tests do not serve as achievement tests, except those that have been prepared to accompany some specific instructional material. None of the tests reviewed in this collection do. Achievement tests are normally prepared by the staff of the instructional program in which they are used.

*Diagnosis*

A diagnostic test measures specific aspects of second language ability, usually for the purpose of determining what the test taker knows and needs to learn. Few truly diagnostic language tests have been published, and none are included in this collection. Tests that measure more broadly defined aspects of second language behavior (e.g., listening comprehension vs. reading ability) may claim to be diagnostic, but they are really tests of relative proficiency in different communicative skills.

*Measuring Proficiency*

Proficiency tests measure the test taker's overall ability in English along a broad scale. Proficiency is usually defined independently of any instructional program: Proficiency is not easily taught since it is a global construct. Proficiency tests may help determine whether the test taker is ready for a job or task requiring English (e.g., working as a government official or entering higher or secondary education), or they may be used to compare the overall success of different instructional programs. Proficiency tests are sometimes subdivided into subskills or modes of language, including speaking, listening, reading, writing, vocabulary, grammar, and sociolinguistic, strategic, and discourse competence, among others. Relative ability in these areas can be determined by a proficiency test.

A number of the tests included in this collection are intended to be proficiency tests. It should be noted, however, that proficiency tests are often poor tests of achievement, since the content of a proficiency test usually has little or no relationship to the content of an instructional program. Proficiency tests may not be appropriate for placement, since they may provide an overall stratification of students, but do not specify their abilities according to the specific instructional content of the courses in which they are placed. The global nature of the construct of proficiency also makes many such tests poor diagnostic instruments because

the results do not specify the knowledge a student has or is lacking. Test users should also avoid using proficiency tests to make strong predictions about a test taker's eventual success in some other endeavor (e.g., an academic program), since language is but one element among many that contribute to success.

## A Final Word

No single publication can answer all the questions that test users have about testing, any more than a single test can serve all testing needs. This collection is a tool that can assist test users in choosing tests that are appropriate to their needs and in evaluating the quality of those tests. Nevertheless, for the testing process to function well, it must be carried out by people with expertise in using a particular test. We hope that this volume will contribute to increased awareness on the part of test users, test writers, and test publishers of the need for quality in ESL/EFL testing. If this goal is realized, the ESL/EFL teaching profession will benefit from an improvement in one of the most important tools used in the ESL/EFL educational arena.

The Editors

## Appendix

Following is a selected list of reference books on ESL/EFL and second language testing.

Allen, J. B. P., & Davies, A. (1977). *Testing and experimental methods: Vol. 4*. London: Oxford.

Carroll, B. J. (1980). *Testing communicative performance*. Oxford: Pergamon.

Carroll, B. J., & Hall, P. J. (1985). *Make your own language tests: A practical guide to writing language performance tests*. Oxford: Pergamon.

Cohen, A. D. (1980). *Testing language ability in the classroom*. Rowley, MA: Newbury.

Harris, D. P. (1969). *Testing English as a second language*. New York: McGraw-Hill.

Heaton, J. B. (1975). *Writing English language tests*. London: Longman.

Jones, R. L., & Spolsky, B. (1975). *Testing language proficiency*. Arlington, VA.: Center for Applied Linguistics.

Maculaitis, J. D. (1982). *The MAC checklist for evaluating, preparing, and/or improving standardized tests*. San Francisco: Alemany

Madsen, H. S. (1983). *Techniques in testing*. Oxford: Oxford.

Oller, J. W., Jr. (1979). *Language tests at school*. London: Longman.

Valette, R. M. (1977). *Modern language testing* (2nd ed.). New York: Harcourt Brace Jovanovitch.

# Table of Contents

# A Brief Introduction to ESL
# Proficiency Testing in North America

Commercially published ESL proficiency tests in the United States may be characterized, when comparing them with tests in the United Kingdom, by the fact that most are designed for elementary and secondary school children rather than adults entering higher education institutions. This situation is basically a response to a U.S. Supreme Court decision (*Lau vs. Nichols,* 1974) in which the court ruled that publicly funded schools must provide special instructional programs for non-English-speaking (NES) and limited-English-speaking (LES) students. (The second group is also sometimes called limited English proficient [LEP].)

As a result, in May 1975 the U.S. Office of Civil Rights of the Department of Education issued a set of guidelines for local school districts enabling them to comply with the decision. These guidelines called for the assessment of language dominance (a comparison of proficiency in two or more languages) of all students with linguistic backgrounds involving a language other than English. One programmatic outcome of the guidelines was the widespread implementation of bilingual education programs in the U.S. Prior to the Lau guidelines, bilingual education was common only in church-operated school settings, in cities (such as Miami) containing a large number of refugees, and on American Indian reservations.

As a result of the requirement that proficiency be assessed, dozens of ESL proficiency tests for school children were developed. Some of these tests included parallel versions in one or more other languages. In most of these cases a Spanish language version was developed and published first, while unpublished versions in other languages were developed by researchers or educators. While a number of the early tests were naively constructed and are out of print today, others have survived critical evaluation and enjoy widespread use. New tests for children at the kindergarten through 12th grade level (K-12) continue to be developed and published commercially. Approximately half of all tests reviewed in this volume fall into this group. Typically, at the kindergarten and early elementary school levels (K-2), these tests assess speaking proficiency only (e.g., the PRE-LAS). Tests used with children in subsequent grades (3-12) may exhibit greater variety in the skills assessed, with some (e.g., the LAB) assessing receptive as well as productive skills and others assessing receptive skills only (e.g., the SLEP).

At the higher (tertiary) education level in the U.S. and Canada, students may take one or more of three common instruments: the TOEFL, one of The University of Michigan tests (e.g., MELAB), or CELT. The TOEFL, a secure test, is accepted as evidence of En-glish proficiency by 2,500 universities in the U.S., Canada, and other countries. Similarly, the MELAB (another secure test) is also accepted as evidence of English proficiency by many universities. Both of the these testing programs make available previously used versions of the test or sections of it to English language teaching programs that wish to use the test in order to determine initial placement within their instructional sequence. In some cases however, scores on these less secure, institutional forms of the test may be accepted by a university admissions officer. A third alternative, the CELT, is a nonsecure instrument that is sold to educators and institutions for ESL program placement. These tests have traditionally involved the assessment of listening, reading, vocabulary, and grammar. More recently, the TOEFL moved toward the inclusion of a direct measure of writing, while the MELAB has included one for some time.

Another test of academic English that might be included in this group is the ALIGU, published by the American Language Institute of Georgetown University. It is given only to applicants for scholarships awarded by the Agency for International Development of the U.S. Department of State. At the request of the program, the ALIGU is not reviewed in this volume.

A number of tests of nonacademic English have been developed for adults with limited educational backgrounds in North America. The development of many of these was spurred by the influx of Asian refugees to the the U.S. after the Vietnam War. Nonetheless, it would be inappropriate to assume that these tests are suitable for Asians only, as this was frequently not the authors' intent. Among these tests of nonacademic English for adults are the HELP, the John and Fred tests, the BEST, DOPT, and so forth.

A number of other tests of general English for adults have appeared recently for use in academic situations that are less demanding than traditional universities. These include the tests developed by Donna Ilyin and her colleagues in the San Francisco Community College District.

As a parallel development, the Interagency Language Roundtable (ILR) procedures produced by agencies of the U.S. government have grown increasingly popular and have influenced the development of other tests in the U.S. and outside the U.S. Many of the oral language tests used in North America today exhibit some characteristics of the ILR scale and procedures. The ILR's influence is also felt in the testing of foreign languages in the U.S. The American Council on the Teaching of Foreign Languages (ACTFL) has taught the ILR procedures to over 1,000 foreign language teachers and has added three additional points to the scale at the lower levels.

## Sources of Information on North American ESL Tests

Readers of this volume are encouraged to consult other sources of information on ESL tests. In the North American context, a number of publications publish reviews or studies of ESL tests. The following brief annotated bibliography is provided to assist the reader in this endeavor.

Mitchell, J. V., Jr. (Ed.). (1985). *The ninth mental measurements yearbook*. Lincoln, NE: Buros Institute of Mental Measurements & the University of Nebraska.

The *Mental Measurements Yearbook* (MMY) is generally considered the most authoritative source of reviews available anywhere. Unfortunately, it does not ordinarily publish reviews of tests outside of North America. Nine MMYs have been published since 1936. Many of the tests reviewed in this volume are also reviewed in the seventh, eighth, and ninth MMYs. A tenth MMY is scheduled to be published in 1990. Although the MMY reviews sometimes assume special training in tests and measurements, the series remains a principal reference on tests of all kinds.

Dieterich, T., & Freeman, C. (1979). *A linguistic guide to English proficiency testing in schools*. Washington, DC: Center for Applied Linguistics.

This volume contains short reviews and information on many of the tests included in this volume. It also contains a detailed discussion of different approaches to language testing that are frequently exhibited by ESL tests.

Stansfield, C. W. (1981). The assessment of language proficiency in bilingual children: An analysis of theories and instrumentation. In R. V. Padilla (Ed.), *Bilingual education technology: Vol. 3. Ethnoperspectives in bilingual education research series*. Ypsilanti, MI: Eastern Michigan University.

This article is a cogent introduction to the field of second language proficiency test construction. After reviewing the choices available to a test developer, the author illustrates how the various approaches are reflected in an instrument. A number of ESL tests are reviewed briefly, with a focus on the contrasting approaches they use.

Erickson, J. G., & Omark, D. R. (Eds.). (1981). *Communicative assessment of the bilingual/bicultural child*. Baltimore, MD: University Park.

This volume contains a number of articles on second language tests for children at the K-12 levels. Chapters 7 and 8 include short reviews or analyses of a number of tests, that is, many of the K-12 North American tests reviewed in this volume.

*The Modern Language Journal* (MLJ). The 1976-1980 volumes of this well-established professional journal contain reviews of language proficiency tests that were available at that time, including some that were not reviewed in this volume because they are currently out of print. *The MLJ* is widely available in academic libraries. Information on subscriptions may be obtained by writing: Journals Divisions, University of Wisconsin Press, 114 North Murray Street, Madison, WI 53715, USA.

In addition to the above sources of information specifically on North American tests, the following publications provide further news and information on tests in the U.S., England, and elsewhere.

*Language Testing*. This new professional journal promises to be a useful source of reviews of tests from around the world. Information on subscriptions may be obtained by writing: Edward Arnold Publishers, 41 Bedford Square, London WC1B 3DQ, England. In the U.S. and Canada, subscription information may be obtained from the North American distributor, Cambridge University Press, 32 East 57th Street, New York, NY 10022, USA.

*Language Testing Update*. This newsletter provides information on new research and developments in the language testing world and occasional reviews of second language tests. Information on subscriptions may be obtained by writing: Institute for English Language Education, University of Lancaster, Lancaster, LA1 4YT, England.

Charles Stansfield

# An Overview of ESL/EFL Testing in Britain

In many respects there are considerable differences in the way British and American tests are produced and validated. In addition, there are also differences in the way tests on the two sides of the Atlantic are made available to the teaching profession and the general public. It seems useful, then, to present a brief overview of British testing as background for the British tests reviewed in this collection. We emphasize that this overview cannot be a full account of British testing practices. Omitted, for example, are the very interesting developments in the graded objectives movement in modern languages in the United Kingdom known as Graded Tests. Instead, we confine ourselves to issues relevant to an understanding of those British tests reviewed in this volume. In addition, it should be noted that very interesting changes are about to take place in British school-leaving examinations (to be known as the General Certificate of Secondary Education [GCSE]) which may eventually have considerable impact on the way ESL/EFL tests are produced, administered, and validated in the U.K.

Most of the British tests reviewed in this collection are produced by examination boards, whose main activities relate to the development and administration of secondary school examinations given at ages 16 and 18, approximately. These examinations are known as O (Ordinary) and A (Advanced) Level examinations. These examination boards also produce ESL/EFL examinations to determine ESL/EFL proficiency and readiness for entry to British universities. The examination boards are usually associated with one or more universities, for example, the University of Cambridge Local Examinations Syndicate, the Oxford Delegacy of Local Examinations, the Joint Matriculation Board (of the northern universities of Manchester, Liverpool, Leeds, Sheffield, and Birmingham). There are also other examining bodies roughly similar to the O and A Level Boards: the regionally organized Certificate of Secondary Education Boards; and vocationally oriented boards, such as the Royal Society of Arts, which has recently produced the highly influential Examination in the Communicative Use of English as a Foreign Language. This overview will concentrate on the latter.

Perhaps the most important point to note is that the examinations produced by these exam boards are not standardized or normed in the usual sense, but are produced and administered for one occasion only. Thus, tests (often known as *papers*) produced for administration in Spring 1987 will never be used again. (There are exceptions to this general rule, but they do not affect the principle.) Indeed, past papers are often made publicly available, sometimes for a small fee.

Due to the constant need to produce new examinations and the lack of emphasis by exam boards on the need for empirical rather than judgmental validation, these examinations are rarely, if ever, tried out on pupils or subjected to the statistical analyses of typical test production procedures. Examination boards do not see the need to pretest and validate their instruments, nor conduct posthoc analyses of their tests' performance. Although the objective items in the tests are usually pretested, the statistics are rarely published. There are significant exceptions to this statement: the joint UCLES/British Council's ELTS test and the Associated Examining Board's Test of English for Educational Purposes (see reviews in this volume). It is hoped that publications such as this might induce examination boards to conform more closely to accepted test production practices. This is not to say that the tests produced are not valid and reliable, but that we have very little empirical evidence of their characteristics.

Rather, the exam boards lay great store by the asserted validity of their examination construction procedures, which rely almost exclusively upon "expert" judgments. The production of a test for any occasion is the responsibility of a chief examiner, selected by the board for "proven" qualities of judgment and track record of reliability of marking the production of sample test questions in past years. This chief examiner will also have recent, if not current, experience teaching the subject for which he or she is producing a test. The chief examiner is aided by a set of assistant examiners and a moderating committee, who produce, scrutinize, edit, and finalize the tests (a process known as *moderation*). In addition, the chief examiner produces marking criteria (sometimes known as *mark schemes*) and is responsible, with senior examiners, for the training and standardizing of markers, and the checking of interrater reliability after the examination has been administered. Even in this process of the checking of interrater reliability, it is extremely unusual for an exam board to calculate or publish statistics of reliability of its markers. It would be a simple matter for the board to calculate and provide the data, and we believe they should be encouraged to do so. The exam boards place great faith in the qualities of their chief examiners and in their selection, moderation, standardization, and grade-awarding procedures. They should, however, be prepared to produce the evidence that their examinations are valid and reliable. (As Gary Buck put it: "It is, after all, normal practice to count one's change in the grocery store, even if the cashier looks honest.")

Finally, it should be noted that most, although not all, of the British tests in this collection are not available commercially for administration at any point in time. The normal procedure is for a school to register its pupils with a particular board for a particular exam on the published date. In EFL, it is usually possible for individual students to enter for examinations on prespecified occasions. There are, however, exceptions to this practice, and these are noted in the relevant synopses of the test reviews.

In conclusion, although we have been critical of British tests, we should emphasize that many of these tests are highly innovative in content and format, and they should not be dismissed lightly by the test-producing or test-using fraternity. Indeed, we believe that other tests could benefit greatly, both from greater attention to the actual examples of tests produced by some exam boards and by attention to the content validation procedures they use. It is also true to say that many tests would benefit from greater attention to the relationship between testing and teaching, for which the British Exam Boards are particularly noted. Some combination of British judgmental validation and American empirical validation seems required.

Charles Alderson

# Association of Recognised Language Schools Oral Examinations in Spoken English

*Reviewed by*

**Terry Tony**
**British Council**
**London**

## Synopsis

Association of Recognised Language Schools Oral Examinations in Spoken English. ARELS Oral Examinations. 1967-84. All foreign students of English at three levels: the Preliminary Certificate (AP) for any age, the Higher Certificate (AH) for over 16 years, and the Diploma (AD) for over 18 years. Designed to measure skills in the use and comprehension of spoken English, especially in everyday, realistic situations. Taped verbal responses scored, by appointed examiners only, on scales which vary according to specified criteria/performance descriptions; total score translated to one of three pass grades or two fail grades for AP, and one of six pass grades or three fail grades for AH and AD. Individual and group according to number of tape recorders available. 40 minutes (AP); 45 minutes (AH & AD). New papers compiled for each series of examinations: three AP and AH, and two AD scheduled examinations per year; other than these, Opportunity Examinations are available. *A Guide for Examination Centres* (booklet, 1978, 18 pp.); *Regulations and Outline Syllabuses* (brochure, 1984, 5 pp.); *Rationale, Development and Methods* (booklet, 1983, 12 pp.). Examinations available to recognized centers only; charge per candidate made up of a basic fee (AP, £12; AH, £17; AD, £21) and a local fee (between £3 and £15 depending on center and number of candidates). Past examinations are available in sets (1 master cassette, 5 keys, 20 candidate papers) at £13 for AP, and £10.50 for AH and AD; or individually at £6 for 1 master cassette, £0.35 for each key, and £0.35 (AP) and £0.18 (AH & AD) for each candidate paper. Reel tapes are available at additional cost; booklets and pamphlets listed above are free of charge; postage and overseas bank charges extra. ARELS Examination Trust, 113 Banbury Road, Oxford OX2 6JX, England, telephone: (0) 865-514272.

## Review

The ARELS Oral Examinations are designed to test a candidate's oral production and listening comprehension in everyday English communication. The focus on these two skills is an attempt to counterbalance the emphasis on reading and writing skills found in most other EFL examinations. A consequence of this focus is the manner in which the examinations are conducted. The instructions, text input, questions and candidate responses are all recorded on tape. This means that the number of candidates able to take the examination at any one time is restricted only by the facilities (number of booths in a language laboratory or number of tape recorders) available. The candidates are only required to have minimal reading and writing skills, as the exam is comprised of visual stimuli, texts for reading aloud, grids for marking answers, and spaces for filling in short written answers, with variations according to level.

The three levels of examinations in order of increasing difficulty are: the ARELS Preliminary Certificate (AP), the ARELS Higher Certificate (AH), and the ARELS Diploma (AD).

The AP is meant to show that a candidate has "sufficient skill to survive in an English-speaking environment." The content is based on the Waystage proposals of the Council of Europe and usually takes the form of an extended role play on one central theme (e.g., a wedding, a visit to a holiday camp, etc.) in which the candidate participates from time to time. There are 15 questions testing three areas of competence.

The first of these is *Social English*. Social English is examined in tasks which require the candidate to read (aloud) and write numbers, letters, and common abbreviations. Candidates must also take the role of one participant in a short conversation, give appropriate responses to situations described on the tape, and finally ask questions. The second area of competence tested is *Audial Comprehension*. The word *audial* is used in place of *aural* because of the possible confusion of the latter with the word *oral*. Tasks require candidates to make a short written response (tick, cross, one word, etc.) or select an appropriate visual response. They may also have to say whether there is any connection between what they hear and what they see; and finally, they must give short verbal answers to questions on the tape. The third element in the test is *Extended Speaking*. Here the candidates must speak for 45-60 seconds. Pictures are normally provided in the candidate's paper as a stimulus for the talk. As can be gathered from this description, visual stimuli are used extensively in the AO.

The other two levels of examination, the AH and AD, have much in common with each other in both content and format. They both examine six areas of competence and are divided into six corresponding sections.

The first section examines *social responses* and is divided into three parts with 20 items in all. In Part 1 the candidate must give appropriate replies to a series of unconnected questions or comments. In Part 2 a situation is described on the tape, and the candidate takes the second part in a conversation on the basis of the information given. In Part 3 the candidate must make a natural comment after listening to a short description of a situation on the tape. In all parts there is a time limit of about 8-10 seconds for responses.

Section 2 in both examinations is devoted to *intelligible speech* and focuses on a candidate's intonation, stress, rhythm, and pronunciation. The task requires

6

the candidate to read a part in a conversation written in the candidate's paper. The other part(s) is recorded on the tape.

Section 3 examines *audial comprehension* (see above). This is done through a variety of tasks requiring candidates to answer questions on spoken texts (interviews, reports, descriptions) by explaining what has happened in a picture, to explain the meaning of words or phrases, to complete sentences started by speakers on the tape, or to mark in the candidates' paper the meaning corresponding most closely to a statement on the tape. This often depends on interpreting intonation or context.

Section 4 requires candidates to produce samples of *sustained speaking*. Stimulus is provided: in AH, a picture story for the candidates to tell after being given the background on tape; in AD, a spoken text (e.g., radio interview) is heard twice, the candidates may make notes, and then retell what they have heard adding comments as they wish.

*Oral accuracy* forms the focus of Section 5. The items are in the form of grammar drills in which the candidates must transform, complete with the correct grammatical form, or provide short answer forms to sentences they hear on the tape.

Section 6 in both examinations gives an opportunity for *free oral expression*. Candidates have 1 minute in AH and 1 1/2 minutes in AD to talk on a topic chosen from a list given to them 20 minutes before the examination. They are not allowed to read from notes.

While AP is clearly different from the other levels in both rationale and content, the distinction between AH and AD is not as clear. The authors write that both AH and AD test the above six skills, but AD does this "to a higher standard." A further difference is that AD tests "the use of English as a medium of abstract and intellectual thought."

After each series of examinations a key is produced for each level. This includes a full tape script and a marking guide, which gives sample answers where possible. For those questions requiring extended speaking, the key includes a list of the criteria used to assess the speech.

Background information on the examinations is provided in two booklets and a brochure. The first booklet, *A Guide for Examination Centres*, gives details of the facilities (language laboratory, tape recorders, etc.) needed to administer the examinations and instructions on how to run a center and deal with administrative aspects of the examinations. The *Guide* is mainly of interest to potential centers. The second booklet, *Rationale, Development and Methods*, provides a brief history of the examinations, their overall aim, an outline of the skills tested at each level, and a brief guide to marking procedures. "Regulations and Outline Syllabuses" covers the dates of examinations, the fee for candidates, a list of centers, and a brief outline of the aim of the examinations and the content at each level. A list of publications (including past papers) is also available. At present the ARELS Examination Trust (AET) does not publish a report on the examinations,

and no statistics on candidate performance are issued.

*Comments*

One of the characteristic features of the ARELS Orals, namely, that they are conducted wholly on tape, gives rise to the difficult question of whether such an interaction can possibly be a natural communication situation. When compared with the inequality of the usual oral interview used for this kind of assessment, the issue appears largely academic. There are several advantages to having a sample of the candidate's performance on tape. It allows borderline cases and random samples to be re-marked, and in this way can foster greater reliability and fairness. The tapes can be sent to a limited number of trained assessors, who can facilitate greater agreement on standards, assuming, of course, that they are consistent in the criteria they use to assess the tapes. This is not easy to do in some parts of the examinations. The difficulty of establishing clear criteria is particularly apparent in the Social English/Responses sections of the papers. The variety of possible responses to the decontextualized statements made in these sections is so wide, taking into consideration the attitudes and personalities of the candidates, that it is difficult to see what criteria might be relevant. This is least problematic in AP where an overall context and role are established for the candidates. This problem of decontextualization emphasizes how difficult it is to test communication skills. Indeed, in Sections 2 (Intelligible Speech) and 5 (Oral Accuracy) of AH and AD, purposeful communication is abandoned altogether. The emphasis is on the skills of verbal articulation and structural manipulation.

No matter which skills are tested, one of the most useful aspects of an examination is the feedback it provides to teachers (and candidates) on what has been taught well and what needs further work. The results of individual candidates, while being of interest to those individuals, are not very helpful in influencing course design. The most useful feedback is a report on overall performance in the examination. Such a report from the AET could make clear to teachers the deficiencies of the candidates (and the teaching) and in this way influence future teaching objectives. In short, it would be one of the best ways for the AET to achieve their stated objective of improving "the focus and quality of language teaching in general." A further element in this campaign would be to provide statistical data showing the tests to be well designed and relatively good measures of the language competence they set out to assess. This sort of information is necessary to assist in the development of the examinations and to give test users confidence in the validity and reliability of the examinations.

A number of issues have been raised here concerning the deficiencies of the ARELS Orals, but it must be remembered that they are also innovative and imaginative examinations offering a focus and a methodology found in no other EFL examinations. This flexibility places them high on the list of measures of the oral and listening skills.

## Reviewer's Notes

The AET has recently established a link with the Oxford Delegacy, which produces examinations of reading and writing with similar communicative aims. Between them, their examinations cover all four English communication skills.

# Australian Second Language Proficiency Ratings

### Reviewed by

**T. J. Quinn and T. F. McNamara**
**University of Melbourne**

### Synopsis

Australian Second Language Proficiency Ratings. ASLPR. Adolescent and adult learners or speakers of a second or foreign language. Specific versions related to ESL, French, Italian, and Japanese are available (with versions in Chinese and Spanish in preparation), but the basic instrument (the version using ESL examples) is applicable to any language. Designed to measure general proficiency in a language learned as a second or foreign language. Learners are rated on a descriptive (criterion-referenced) scale in which the proficiency levels are specified by a number, title, and behavioral description. Each macroskill is rated separately, for example, S:l; L:1 +; R:l; W:l-. Individual administration for S, L, R, but W can be done in group. Interview for S, L, R, and W may vary from 10 to 25 minutes depending on interviewee and skill of interviewer. Administration Manual in preparation. This Manual will include sample reading texts, writing scripts, an introductory paper on the ASLPR, and a copy of the scale. A set of nine videos and accompanying kits has been produced by Film Australia, the Australian Department of Immigration and Ethnic Affairs (DIEA), and the Australian Government Publishing Service (AGPS). Technical report: *Report on the Formal Trialling of the Australian Second Language Proficiency Ratings* (ASLPR) (1984, 136 pp.) published by AGPS and DIEA; information booklet, *Australian Second Language Proficiency Ratings* (1984, 58 pp.), available from AGPS and DIEA through Australian government bookshops, Australian embassies, and Australian trade commissions. Mimeo copy of ASLPR available from authors. Videos available from Film Australia and Australian embassies, trade commissions, and Film Australia out-lets. Manuals, $2.50 (Australian) each; videos, $12.50 (Australian) full set; individual videos available; sample interviews, $65 (Australian) per tape; mimeo copies of ASLPR, free of charge from authors. D. E. Ingram, Brisbane College of Advanced Education, Mt. Gravatt Campus, PO Box 82, Mount Gravatt 4122, Australia, telephone: (07) 343 0611. Elaine Wylie, Department of Education, Brisbane, Qld 4000, Australia. Australian Government Publishing Service and Australian Department of Immigration and Ethnic Affairs, PO Box 25, Belconnen, A.C.T. 2617, Australia, telephone: (062) 64 1111.

### Review

The ASLPR is a structured interview procedure and rating scale designed to provide a measure of language proficiency in the four basic communicative skills. According to the Manual (p.9), it is based on the *absolute proficiency ratings* of the U.S. Foreign Service Institute, otherwise known as the ILR scale (see this volume for review of the ILR). However, the ASLPR differs from the ILR; while the latter is designed for use with well-educated, civil and foreign service personnel, the ASLPR is designed for use with learners whose education and employment is more diverse. The ASLPR scale also permits greater differentiation at the lower end of the scale than does the ILR.

The ASLPR scale has gained wide acceptance in Australia, particularly in the federally funded Adult Migrant Education Program, the dominant area of adult ESL in Australia.

The scale consists essentially of descriptions of language behavior at nine levels ranging from O to native-like proficiency. The nine levels are: 0, 0+, 1-, 1, 1+, 2, 3, 4, and 5. The wider differentiation at the lower levels reflects that most learners in the Adult Migrant Education Program are clustered at the very early stages of proficiency. There is some limited provision for the use of three further levels, 2+, 3+ and 4+, thus allowing the possibility of 12 levels, although there is no description of these last three levels. Each of the four traditional macroskills (speaking, listening, reading, and writing) is described separately, so that a learner's proficiency profile will consist of four components, for example, S1, L1+, R2, W1-. The nine proficiency levels are also given brief descriptive titles, as follows:

0 : zero proficiency
0+ : initial proficiency
1- : elementary proficiency
1 : minimum survival proficiency
1+ : survival proficiency
2 : minimum social proficiency
3 : minimum vocational proficiency
4 : vocational proficiency
5 : native-like proficiency

The ASLPR documentation provides one or more of three kinds of information about each level.

1. A description of the language behavior appropriate to the level. For example, "L2: Minimum social proficiency. Able to understand in routine social situations and limited work situations. Can get the gist of most conversations in everyday social situations though may sometimes misinterpret or need utterances to be repeated."

2. A series of examples of observed behavior or tasks that a learner at a particular level might carry out. These examples are intended to give interviewers some guidance on the sorts of tasks learners can be asked to perform to show their proficiency at each level. For example, "W1+: Survival proficiency. Can write a note to school explaining a child's absence."

3. A series of comments explaining the key features entailed in the transition from one level to the next. For example, "S3: Minimum vocational proficiency. The key factor now emerging is register flexibility." Sometimes, however, the examples of specific tasks (see 2) are very unspecific, and look more like general descriptions of language behavior (see 1). For example, "Frequently interprets questions as statements unless repeated and redundantly marked by sentence structure, Wh-word, strong intonation, or context."

The assignment of a learner to a point on the ASLPR scale is done on the basis of an interview, during which language behavior is elicited in a series of realistic tasks. The resultant behavior is matched to that point on the scale that most nearly describes it. The point of the interview is thus to derive a global impression of the learner's behavior, and to match it with the ASLPR level definition that seems to correspond most closely to the global impression. Therefore, the decision-making rules for assigning a rating to an interviewee represent another difference between the ASLPR and the ILR scales. The ILR scale is noncompensatory; the fact that an examinee is closer to the next higher rating does not mean that the higher rating should be assigned. On the ASLPR scale, on the other hand, the higher rating would be assigned.

According to the *Report on the Formal Trialling of the ASLPR*, reliability and validity of the scale were studied in two data-gathering projects. In the first project, 24 subjects were interviewd for S, L, and R, and these interviews were recorded on video cassettes. They were also given several tasks from which W could be judged. Tapes and writing samples on 16 of the subjects were then rated by 21 Australian and 15 Chinese teachers of ESL, and their ratings were correlated with the official ratings assigned by the test developers. The correlations were all very good, usually above .90. Less impressive correlations were obtained for the same

interviewees with the CELT, and with cloze and dictation exercises.

Interview-based proficiency rating scales like the ASLPR have certain strengths that may make them seem an attractive alternative to formal test instruments. They also have considerable drawbacks. In fact, the strengths and weaknesses of the two approaches might almost be said to be in complementary distribution.

A major weakness of the ASLPR (and other interview-based approaches, such as the ILR Oral Proficiency Interview) is its built-in tendency to become a variable instrument. There is no ASLPR test instrument or item bank (apart from the general guidelines for the conduct of the interview and the sample interview kits), yet ASLPR claims to be a test of the four separate macroskills. It would be more appropriate to call it a scale and a set of procedures. The guidance on the sorts of tasks learners can be asked to perform to show their proficiency at each level is in the form of examples only, with no particular canonical or absolute status.

The rater is, in fact, encouraged to replace one task or exercise that is not deemed appropriate with another that is more appropriate, as long as the latter is of equal complexity. Unfortunately, there is no guidance as to what constitutes equal complexity or equal appropriateness in the behavioral description provided at each point of the scale. Is filling in a deposit form for a bank a task of the same level of complexity (and hence equally appropriate) as filling in a change of address notice at the motor registration bureau? How does one judge? What are the criteria that constitute equivalence of functional, linguistic, or communicative complexity?

The ASLPR provides very specific writing exercises and clear guidelines for scoring them. However, we are told in the trialling study (p. 7) that if the particular task set could not be performed, the supervisor was at liberty to propose another of equivalent complexity. As long as the individual rater is free to substitute any task for the example tasks given, the whole process comes close to being the use of a variable instrument, a possible consequence of which is variable measurements. Although all instruments contain measurement error, it is especially important with the interview-based approach to establish the validity of a rater's interview, and the accuracy and consistency of his or her ratings.

The other serious drawback of an interview-based approach is the influence of interviewing technique on the rating process and its outcome. The ability to relate to a learner and set up a nonthreatening situation where the learner's language proficiency can be explored and analysed in depth must surely require special skills and sensitivities that cannot be assumed to be universally available. It may also be significant that during trial testing of the ASLPR there was no attempt to investigate the effect of the interviewer or interview length on the reliability of ASLPR ratings. Even if one assumes adequate interviewing techniques there is still the problem of interpretation of the scale. Yet, the authors make little of this problem, suggesting that even non-professionals may be able to use it reliably.

What is attractive about rating scales like the ASLPR is the courageous move away from measuring the assumed components of proficiency (lexis, phonology, syntax, etc.) to observation of global performance. Although very different, language assessment has been bedevilled by the dominance of the former, and by the assumption that measuring the former will give an adequate picture of the latter. In this sense, the ASLPR is a welcome antidote to atomistic language tests.

Yet, it must be stressed that a proficiency rating scale is not a test; the reliability and validity of the ASLPR scale are crucially dependent on the stimuli that are used to elicit the learner's behavior in each of the macroskills. It is questionable whether an interview is the appropriate format in which to measure the receptive skills of listening and reading. The validity and reliability data from trials of the reading component, in particular, would seem to support this view. While the ASLPR can provide valuable information about speaking skills and provide a way of referring to the proficiency of learners in broad terms, rating scales shoud be supplemented for most purposes by other kinds of information that can be provided by more rigorous and nonvariable measures.

The extensive use of the ASLPR in the Australian Adult Migrant Education Program will certainly shed welcome light on a most fundamental question: Can an interview-based rating system be adopted on a mass scale without distortion and loss of objectivity? This is a question being asked in other parts of the language teaching world (cf. the current proficiency testing work of ACTFL). The Australian experience will be observed with interest by language testing specialists.

# Basic English Skills Test

### Reviewed by

### Erika Eakin
### San Francisco State University

### Donna Ilyin
### San Francisco Community College District

### Synopsis

Basic English Skills Test. BEST. 1982. Limited English speaking adults. Designed to measure basic functional language skills and competence, determine student progress, provide diagnostic feedback, screen for vocational education. Verbal and written responses are assigned numerical values which are added together for a raw score for each subsection. Core Interview sec-

tion: individual administration; Literacy Skills section: individual or group. Core section: 15 minutes; Literacy Skills section: 45 minutes. Core section, 3 forms (1986, 12 pp.); Literacy Skills section, 3 forms (1986, 16 pp.). Administration Manual (1986, 94 pp.). Technical Manual, part of Administration Manual. $12.50 per Interview section package, including administration/score interpretation booklet, 1 photograph booklet, 20 core section examiner books. $12.50 per Literacy Skills section package, including 1 administration/score interpretation booklet, 20 Literacy Skill section booklets, 20 Literacy scoring sheets ($.63 each or $1.25 for both). Center for Applied Linguistics, 1118 22nd St. N.W., Washington, DC 20037, USA, telephone: (202) 429-9292; and the Psychological Corporation, 555 Academic Court, San Antonio, TX 78204, USA, telephone: (512) 299-1061.

### Test References

Clark, J. L. D., & Grognet, A. G. (1985). Development and validation of a performance-based test of ESL "survival skills." In P. C. Hauptman, R. LeBlanc, & M. B. Wesche (Eds.), *Second language performance testing* (pp. 89-110). Ottawa: University of Ottawa.

### Review

The BEST, a functional language test for very limited English speakers, is unique not only for its innovative approach, but also because it measures reliably and accurately the language skills of low-level students. BEST tests listening comprehension, speaking, reading, and writing, and consists of two sections: a Core section (49 items) and a Literacy Skills section (70 items). The test may be used to provide information on students' language proficiency upon entrance in a language program, to help place students in a language program, and to help in the development of individualized learning activities. It can also be used as an achievement test to measure students' progress or as a screen test for English-medium vocational training courses. The Core section of the test provides the student with live oral stimuli, pictures, and writing on a one-to-one basis. The Literacy Skills section gives students oral as well as written directions. Students respond by speaking, writing, and pointing in the Core section, but only by marking or writing in the Literacy Skills section. Although the test was designed for newly arrived Southeast Asian refugees in adult education programs, it can also be used effectively with students from a wide variety of cultural and linguistic backgrounds who have lived in the U.S. for longer periods of time.

The Core section can take 20 minutes or longer to administer, although the Manual claims 10-15 minutes per examinee. The examiner should be a native speaker who has gone through several hours of training and orientation. Administration of the Core section requires money (two $1 bills and change), picture booklets, scoring booklets and/or answer sheets. The test can be scored manually on each page of the scoring booklet or on an answer sheet. It takes approximately 5 minutes per test to sum the ratings and obtain the total score. There are separate scores for each of the subparts: listening, communication, and fluency, which make up the total score on the Core. In addition, there is a global score for pronunciation and a reading/writing score, which is used to determine if the student is literate enough to procede to the Literacy Skills section. Directions for scoring are clear, but practice and communication between raters are needed to ensure standardization, especially for the communication, pronunciation, and fluency parts.

The Literacy Skills section, administered either individually or on a group basis, presents a variety of reading and writing tasks. Reading tasks range from recognizing dates on the calendar and understanding food and clothing labels, to reading newspaper want ads. Writing tasks include addressing an envelope and writing a rent check. Testing time for the Literacy Skills section is 45 minutes; about 10 minutes per test is required to score. The separate raw scores for the two parts of the Literacy Skills section (reading and writing) are totaled. While scoring directions are clear, practice is needed to ensure standardization for those writing tasks that require ratings (paragraph and composition).

With a few exceptions, the format and presentation of the test are excellent. The directions are clear, and the format is straightforward. The pictures are attractive and culturally unbiased. However, one of the items is confusing: Students use their index finger on a map to follow directions given to them by the examiner. This item can be either hopelessly difficult for students, or so easy that the examiner is unable to speak rapidly enough to challenge students. The linguistic content is as broad as can be expected for a test at this level. The language is natural and situationally appropriate.

The BEST has exceptionally high face validity since the items are based on tasks required for everyday life. The norming sample for the test consisted of 987 students for the Core section and 632 for the Literacy Skills section. The sample consisted of sizable groups of native speakers of Vietnamese, Hmong, Lao, Cambodian, Chinese, Spanish, Polish, Romanian, as well as speakers of other languages. Using a SCALAR analysis program developed at Educational Testing Service, staff at the Center for Applied Linguistics (CAL) found KR-20 reliability for the four separate parts of the Core section range from .73 to .91. On the Literacy Skills section the Reading part showed a reliability of .96, while the Writing part showed a reliability of .89. CAL staff also correlated the scaled scores on Form A (out of print) with instructor's ratings of student language proficiency. Pearson product-moment validity coefficients ranged from .49 to .71 for the four parts of the Core section, and from .51 to .54 for the Literacy Skills section.

The reviewers also found the Core section to be valid. In our field tests it discriminated between various levels of language proficiency. The Core clearly identified different levels for our lower education tract students, which no other test to date has been able to do. The Literacy Skills section of the test, however, was too difficult for our lowest level students and for students with little education, although it did discriminate between the upper-beginning and intermediate levels. Both the Core and the Literacy Skills sections showed moderately high correlations with other placement instruments.

The BEST provides an exciting, integrative approach to assessing language skills and functional life skills. BEST tests content as well as language. However, some of its most impressive strenghts also engender a few weaknesses. Using BEST can be costly, since the Core section must be administered on an individual basis and can take some time to administer and score. If used in lieu of answer sheets, test booklets have to be purchased at $.63 per student. The cost of both administration and scoring time could be cut if there were a single scoring sheet, rather than an entire booklet for each student. We also believe that, especially for the Literacy Skills section, the items should be ordered by difficulty. In this way, students for whom the test is too difficult could take the first part of the test only, and the test could be discontinued if it became too difficult. Many of our test administrators also felt that the Literacy Skills section should include fewer types of tasks with more examples provided per task. Although guidelines for the interpretation of the test scores are presented, the Test Manual should provide more information on how the test can be used for placement and diagnostic needs in larger adult school programs. Charts could also be developed to show specific areas of strength and weakness for each student.

## Reviewers' Notes

We would like to thank the following people who provided information about their experience using the BEST: Terri Goulette, Margaret R. Seufert-Bosco, Bill Fanning, and Thomas F. Sousa.

# Basic Inventory of Natural Language

### Reviewed by

**Gary Hargett**
**University of Washington**

### Synopsis

Basic Inventory of Natural Language. BINL. 1979. Grades K-6; 7-12. Designed to measure oral proficiency in English, with versions available for 32 languages including Spanish, Chinese, Japanese, Portuguese, and

Vietnamese; elementary Forms A and B; secondary, C and D. Pictures are used to elicit natural speech. Spoken sentences are analyzed for fluency, average length of utterance, and level of syntactic complexity. For each grade level scores are classified as non-English speaking (NES), limited-English-speaking (LES), fluent-English-speaking (FES), and proficient-English-speaking (PES). Individually administered. Time varies according to fluency of student, up to 10 minutes. Technical Manual available. $59 per complete kit of any one form and level; kit includes Examiner's Manual (1979, 79 pp.); 400 oral score sheets; class oral language profile card (1977, 1 p.); 20 full-color poster story starters and talk-tiles (1979, 80 picture cards) to elicit speech. Unit costs: $5.35 per 100 oral score sheets, $.20 per class oral language profile card, $36.50 per set of 20 pictures, $12.50 per Instructions Manual. Machine scoring available through publisher at $.80 per score sheet; rapid scoring program diskette available to school districts for $285. Charles H. Herbert, Antonio de Porcel, Renato Cervantes, and Kurt Berg. CHECpoint Systems, Inc., 1520 N. Waterman Ave., San Bernardino, CA 92404, USA, telephone: (714) 888-3296.

## Test References

Guyette, T. W. (1985). Review of basic inventory of natural language. In J. V. Mitchell (Ed.), *The ninth mental measurements yearbook* (pp. 139-40). Lincoln, NE: Buros Institute of Mental Measurements & the University of Nebraska.

Stansfield, C. W. (1978). [Review of basic inventory of natural language]. *The Modern Language Journal, 62,* 64.

## Review

The Basic Inventory of Natural Language (BINL) is a measure of speaking proficiency in English. To the extent that its scores can discriminate among students of greater or lesser proficiency at each grade level and that alternate language forms are equally valid and reliable, it can also be used for placement and to assess language dominance. The central feature of the BINL is its focus on natural language use, without relying on metalinguistic awareness or test-taking skills to provide a measure of language proficiency. In this respect, BINL demonstrates face validity. The high-quality full-color poster photographs can be used to elicit speech on an individual or small group basis. Although only oral production is assessed, separate kits are available for the elementary school levels.

The test describes two methods of scoring the speech samples: count the number of target language words per sentence in the sample (fluency) or calculate a score for linguistic complexity based on a point system (described in the Technical Manual). The latter scoring method can be done on microcomputer programs available through the publisher. It is suggested that a mini-

mum of 10 sentences be elicited. A disadvantage of the BINL may be the lack of clarity in how the performance should be scored and the potential for disagreement among scorers in assigning points. Even with the simpler scoring method (fluency), it is not always clear when one sentence ends and another begins to get a sentence tally.

For each grade level, scores are interpreted to classify examinees as NES, LES, FES, or PES. Unfortunately, it is not clear how the cutoffs for these classifications were determined.

Norms provided in the Technical Manual were obtained from several thousand students ages 4 to 18 in elementary and secondary schools throughout Southern California. If all these students were in bilingual programs as the Manual suggests, the normative data can be said to represent only that population. It is difficult to interpret scores in terms of the proficiency that can be expected of a monolingual native speaker of each language.

While content, predictive, and construct validity are claimed, they were not arrived at through ordinary procedures. Predictive (or criterion-related) validity was set in relation to the San Diego Oral Language ESL Continuum Materials, and the reader is referred to these for more information on the BINL's validity. The actual statistics are not provided. These claims are not made on an empirical basis, but rather on theoretical arguments about the nature of language. Test-retest reliability coefficients are reported for several grade levels. While the coefficients are acceptably high, interrater reliability would have been more interesting, given the potential problems in scoring.

Cultural bias does not seem to be a problem in the BINL. While this issue is not specifically addressed by the publisher, it seems that the reliance on natural speech in a communicative setting, rather than knowledge of certain item types, should be effective in reducing bias.

The publisher attempts to justify the format of the BINL on a variety of theoretical grounds, ranging from contrastive analysis to developmental studies in first language acquisition. But in fact, the test's theoretical basis is never clearly stated.

The greatest appeal of the BINL is its emphasis on natural language use in a communicative setting. Its greatest drawbacks are failure to justify the scoring system either theoretically or empirically, potential disagreements among raters in scoring, and the considerable time required to administer individual or small group oral tests. The normative data are unconvincing, and arguments for validity and reliability are unconventionally presented. In fact, the statistical sections of the Manual and the sections explaining the theoretical background of the test are extremely confusing and difficult to comprehend. The BINL's elicitation technique could be useful to some bilingual programs if the speech samples were evaluated according to locally established criteria, rather than the very complex scoring system the author recommends. However, the BINL might be prohibitively time consuming if large numbers of students must be tested.

# Bilingual Syntax Measure I

*Reviewed by*

**Gary A. Cziko**
**University of Illinois at Urbana-Champaign**

## Synopsis

Bilingual Syntax Measure I. BSM I. 1975. Grades K-2, ages 4-9. Designed to measure oral proficiency in English and/or Spanish grammatical structures and language dominance. Verbal responses scored as correct or incorrect depending on whether child correctly produced targeted grammatical structures; number of questions answered used for classification into Level 1 (no English/Spanish), Level 2 (receptive English/Spanish only); number and type of grammatically correct answers for classification into Level 3 (survival English/Spanish); Level 4 (intermediate English/Spanish); and Level 5 (proficient English/Spanish). Individual administration. 10-15 minutes per language. 2 forms: English (1975, 7 pp.); Spanish version (1975, 15 pp.). Technical Manual I (TMI) (1976, 55 pp.). $123.00 for complete kit, includes box, picture booklet, and Administration Manual in each language; 35 response booklets in each language; and 2 class record sheets. $36.50 per picture booklet, $5.00 per Administration Manual in either language, $32.50 for 35 response booklets in either language, $12.00 for Technical Handbook in English. Marina K. Burt, Heidi C. Dulay, and Eduardo Hernandez-Chavez. Psychological Corporation, 555 Academic Court, San Antonio, TX 78204, USA, telephone: (512) 299-1061 or (800) 228-1752.

## Test References

Bailey, N., Madden, C. & Krashen, S. D. (1974). Is there a natural sequence in adult second language learning? *Language Learning, 24*(2), 235-43.

Dulay, H. C., & Burt, M. K. (1975). A new approach to discovering universal strategies in child second language acquisition. In D. D. Dato (Ed.), *Georgetown University roundtable on languages and linguistics 1975* (pp. 209-33). Washington, DC: Georgetown University.

Bejar, I. I. (1978). [Review of the bilingual syntax measure]. In O. K. Buros (Ed.), *The eighth mental measurements yearbook* (pp. 232-3). Highland Park, NJ: Gryphon.

Graham, C. R. (1978). [Review of the bilingual syntax measure]. In O. K. Buros (Ed.), *The eight mental measurements yearbook* (pp. 234-5). Highland Park, NJ: Gryphon.

Oller, J. W., Jr. (1976). [Review of the bilingual syntax measure]. *Modern Language Journal, 60*(7), 399-400.

Stansfield, C. W. (1976). Testing language dominance. *Bilingual Review, 3*(3), 270-6.

## Review

The Bilingual Syntax Measure I (BSM) is well known throughout the United States as the first extensively used test designed to measure the English and Spanish oral language proficiency of bilingual children in elementary schools. The BSM is a short, oral test that includes 25 questions in each language based on seven colorful cartoon drawings. The examiner writes each response in the response booklet and scores them as either *correct* or *incorrect*.

The BSM has gained a reputation as a well-designed test based on both theoretical reasoning and empirical research. Presented in an attractive format, the materials for test takers are clear, and the directions and scoring procedures for test administrators are straightforward. However, the requirements of language proficiency testing go beyond these considerations, and it is in the areas of demonstrated reliability and validity where the BSM does not fare nearly so well. Accordingly, this review will focus on these aspects of the BSM, based on information provided in the test's Technical Handbook (implied when only page or table references are given), as well as on studies conducted by independent researchers (for which author references are given).

### Reliability

The Technical Handbook provides information on both the test-retest and interscorer reliability of the test. Test-retest data obtained from 154 children showed that almost a quarter of these children were placed into a different proficiency level using the Spanish version; approximately one third were reclassified by the English version across two administrations of the test spaced 2 weeks apart (Table 35). However, since a number of consistent classifications are expected by chance, the Kappa coefficient (the appropriateness of which has been questioned by Rosansky, 1979) was used to estimate the proportion of consistent test-retest classifications after chance agreements have been excluded. While the highest Kappa values obtained for the total sample on the Spanish and English tests, .62 and .64, respectively, (Table 36) are well above chance, their values nonetheless appear quite low for a test designed to be useful in making educational decisions for individual children. While it is argued that the low reliability of the test is due to variability in the acquisition of syntactic structures (p. 45), Oller (1976) points out that this argument makes sense only if "the low reliabilities, in fact, reflect real changes in the child's speech" (p. 400). As discussed below, this has not been demonstrated in studies of the test's validity. Similarly moderate reliabilities are reported for the language dominance classifications for 139 children tested twice with both the English and Spanish test versions (Table 39).

Interscorer reliability between two independent raters showed 83.8% and 80.1% agreement among the top three levels of the English and Spanish versions, respectively (Tables 42 and 43). However, since these raters were given the same written responses to judge, possible error due to inaccuracy in writing down responses was not examined. Using a tape recorder to collect the children's responses would undoubtedly help eliminate this source of possible error, but its use is not mentioned in the administration instructions.

In addition, no information is provided concerning the internal consistency of the test as typically computed using the Kuder-Richardson formulas for Cronbach's alpha or the homogeneity of the test as assessed using scalogram analysis or Loevinger's.

## Validity

Construct validity is addressed by discussing research that shows an orderly acquisition of the syntactic structures of a language by both first and second language learners, and by demonstrating that the child's ability to produce these structures can be tapped in assessing language proficiency. However, both Porter (1975) and Rosansky (1979) have questioned the specific order of syntactic constructions used in the test stating that the hierarchy of structures described in the Technical Handbook may well be an artifact of the test itself and consequently not a valid continuum for assessing language proficiency. Krashen (1978), however, has argued that the hierarchy is not an artifact of the test.

Some evidence of the test's construct validity is provided by the field testing which demonstrated that older English-speaking children performed better than younger children on the English version of the test (p. 32). However, older children can be expected to perform better than younger children on any measure of language, cognitive, or physical ability, and, therefore, these findings fail to supply clear evidence for the construct validity of the BSM as a measure of language proficiency. Stronger evidence for construct validity lies in the fact that the length of residence of Spanish-speaking children in the United States was positively related to performance on the English version (Tables 16, 17 & 18).

Ulibarri, Spencer, and Rivas (1971) investigated the concurrent and predictive validity of the BSM using other measures of language proficiency and tests of academic achievement in reading and mathematics. Only 275 to 47% of the major classifications of BSM agreed with those of the BINL and LAS (providing Spearman rank order correlations of .24 to .76). No

significant correlations (.16 to .26) were found between the BSM and reading or mathematics achievement. Gillmore and Dickerson (1979) also found low correlations (-.03 to .15) between scores on the BSM English version and tests of academic achievement. While these independent studies may suffer from some methodological weaknesses (e.g., pooling data from a number of different achievement tests and using the BSM for Grade 3 and 5 students), they do not support the criterion-related validity of the test. One must remember, however, that language proficiency plays only a limited role in academic achievement and other factors, such as aptitude and motivation, are probably more directly related to this criterion.

Recent theoretical formulations of models of communicative competence (e.g., Canale, 1983) reflect a growing acceptance of the importance of discourse, strategic and sociolinguistic competence. In fact, Swain (1983) found that native English-speaking children who were noticeably weak in certain areas of French grammar were nevertheless very successful academically in a program where most instruction had been given in French. On the other hand, Cummins' (1982) work suggests that children who are able to perform well in a context-embedded communicative situation like that provided by the BSM may nevertheless be unsuccessful in using the language for academic purposes. Thus, it appears that even if the BSM could be shown to be an accurate measure of a child's communicative competence, the type of competence it appears to measure may not be sufficient for success in school. Consequently, academic placement decisions based solely on the BSM would appear to be at risk.

## Other Considerations

In addition to the limitations in reliability and validity noted above, the BSM suffers from other weaknesses. These include (a) the unavailability of alternate forms, (b) its inappropriateness for assessing competence in nonstandard dialects of English (p. 30), and (c) reasons to doubt the comparability of the English and Spanish versions of the test (see Merino & Spencer, 1983). Also, its administration may take longer than the 10-15 minutes per child reported in the Administrator's Manual.

## Conclusion

While the BSM may well have been the best measure of its kind when first introduced, it is clear that recent research and theory on language acquisition and testing have cast doubt on its validity. Accordingly, this should be taken into account by those who use it for educational placement decisions. The BSM may continue to be of use in language acquisition research as a method of eliciting the production of specific syntactic structures in English and Spanish by young children. However, the test user must be cautioned that the acquisition sequence elicited may be an artifact of the test.

## Reviewer's References

Cummins, J. (1982). The role of primary language development in promoting educational success for language minority students. In *Schooling and language minority students: A theoretical framework*. Los Angeles: California State University, Evaluation Dissemination and Assessment Center.

Gillmore, G., & Dickerson, A. (1979). *The relationship between instruments used for identifying children of limited English-speaking ability in Texas*. Arlington, VA: Educational Resources Information Center. (ERIC Document Reproduction Service No. ED 191907).

Krashen, S. D. (1978). Is the natural order an artifact of the Bilingual Syntax Measure? *Language Learning, 28*(1), 187-191.

McCollum, P. A., & Day, E. C. (1981). Quasi-integrative approaches. In J. G. Erickson & D. R. Omark (Eds.), *Communication assessment of the bilingual bicultural child* (pp. 163-177). Baltimore: University Park.

Merino, B. J., & Spencer, M. (1982). The comparability of English and Spanish versions of oral language proficiency instruments. *NABE Journal, 7*(2), 1-21.

Oller, J. W., Jr. (1976). Review of the measurement of bilingualism. *The Modern Language Journal, 60*, 399-400.

Oller, J. W., Jr. (1975). *Language tests at school*. London: Longman.

Porter, J. (1975). *A cross-sectional study of morpheme acquisition in first language learners*. Unpublished manuscript, Harvard University, Cambridge, MA.

Rosansky, E. J. (1979). [A review of the bilingual syntax measure]. In B. Spolsky (Ed.), *Some major tests* (pp. 116-135). Advances in Language Testing Series: 1. Arlington, VA: Center for Applied Linguistics.

Swain, M. (1983). *Communcative competence: Some roles for comprehensible input and comprehensible output in its development*. Paper presented at the Second Language Research Forum, University of Southern California, Los Angeles.

Ulibarri, D. M., Spencer, M. L., & Rivas, G. A. (1981). Language proficiency and academic achievement: A study of language proficiency tests and their relationship to school ratings as predictors of academic achievement. *NABE Journal, 5*(3), 47-80.

# Bilingual Syntax Measure II

*Reviewed By*

**Zoe Ann Hayes-Brown**
**Kahuku High and Elementary School**
**Kahuku, Hawaii**

## Synopsis

Bilingual Syntax Measure II. BSM II. 1978. Grades 3-12. Oral production test of linguistic proficiency. Designed to identify student control of grammatical structures in English and Spanish. Individually administered. 10-15 minutes per student per language. Items (22 English, 21 Spanish) scored and categorized into proficiency levels. Levels 1-4 indicate limited proficiency. Level 5 indicates either limited or proficient skills, depending upon specific school district norms or policies. Level 6 is highest and denotes proficiency. Two versions: English (1978, 8 pp.); Spanish (1978, 8 pp.). Administration Manuals: English (1978, 11 pp.); Spanish (1978, 11 pp.). Technical Manual II (1980, 32 pp.). $132.00 for complete kit, including box, picture booklet, Administration Manual in each language, Technical Manual, 35 response booklets in each language, 2 class record booklets, and 1 expanding envelope. $36.50 per picture booklet, $5.00 per Administration Manual in either language, $39.00 for 35 response booklets in either language, $12.00 for Technical Manual in English. Marina K. Burt, Heidi C. Dulay, Eduardo Hernandez-Chavez and Elizabeth Taleporos. Psychological Corporation, 555 Academic Court, San Antonio, TX 78204, USA, telephone: (512) 299-1061 or (800) 228-1752.

## Review

The Bilingual Syntax Measure II (BSM II) is an oral production test of linguistic proficiency that stimulates real conversation, through a structured interview, to provide a more direct measure of syntactic proficiency than is currently available in standardized form. The instrument identifies student control of grammatical structures in English or Spanish using a colorful picture booklet as stimulus. Student and examiner engage in dialogue about a story depicted by the test's cartoon characters; students are asked questions that refer to one or more of the pictures. Items are scored directly following test administration and are categorized into proficiency levels.

BSM II, the upward extension of BSM I, provides proficiency data for students in Grades 3 through 12, with suggested use in a variety of situations (Technical Manual II [TM II], p. 3). The BSM II English levels (NEP, LEP, FEP/fluent English proficient) are used to determine which non-English language background students need bilingual education, English as a second language, or other special language services, such as speech therapy. As an indicator of skill in English and Spanish, the test provides comparative proficiency scores and levels. BSM II can also be an effective tool for language acquisition research. The strong theoretical foundation that led to its development provides an instrument for investigation of the creative construction hypothesis as well as the hierarchial order of syntax acquisition, as measured by the test.

*Validity*

At first glance one might expect that tests of language proficiency used to make placement decisions should predict those students who can and cannot achieve in regular classrooms. Typically, however, oral language proficiency is only moderately related to achievement (Ulibarri, Spencer & Rivas, 1981; Hayes, 1981, 1984; Gillmore & Dickerson, 1979; DeAvila, Cervantes & Duncan, 1978). This is not surprising since other factors, particularly academic aptitude, have a more pervasive influence on academic achievement. Ulibarri et al. (1981) found that the correlation of Bilingual Syntax Measure I NEP/LEP/FEP categories with achievement in math and reading ranged from .15 to .22. Hayes (1981) found simple correlation of BSM II levels with math, reading, and language achievement test scores ranging from .14 to .34.

The BSM II levels may not adequately sample content from those language situations and skills which indicate effective functioning in English. Measuring only syntax, the test does not assess students' skills in vocabulary, pronunciation, or functional use. English skills necessary for effective functioning in school might include these skills as well as more academic English. Here Cummins' (1981) distinction between Basic Interpersonal Communication Skills (BICS) and Cognitive/Academic Language Proficiency (CALP) may be relevant. Perhaps BSM II samples English items which measure BICS rather than CALP. Simpler communication skills may be quite different from those cognitive language skills needed for achievement in school. The BSM II has limited content validity, either as an overall language proficiency test or as an instrument for assessing cognitive/academic language.

Although adequate construct validity of BSM II is offered by the test's authors (TM I, pp. 30-33; TM II, p. 8), other more educationally relevant validation is not provided. Lacking sufficient content and criterion validity, the BSM II should not be used as the sole source of data in educational decision-making.

*Reliability*

BSM II provides evidence of internal consistency and test-retest reliabilities for English and Spanish. Test-retest reliability is described in terms of percent of agreement in proficiency level classifications. While there was 68% agreement in English level classification of 85 students tested on two separate occasions, for 32% of the students there was disagreement in level

assignment (TM II, p. 28). This high percentage of disagreement on two test occasions within the same month indicates a need for further investigation of the test's reliability. What factors influence this change in test scores?

High internal consistency coefficients, .90 for English, .82 for Spanish (TM II, p. 27), indicate homogeneity of test items. It is not the items, therefore, that influence error of measurement. This type of reliability does not show the influence of outside factors on scores. For example, BSM II may be susceptible to the influence of both testers and scorers. If the test depends "on the development of rapport between examiner and student," as suggested by Merino and Spencer (1983), intertester reliability should be reported. This information is not provided by the test's authors. Moreover, scoring the BSM II may not be as straightforward as suggested by Graham (1978). Because "there is an element of subjectivity in deciding whether a specific response is or is not grammatical" (TM I, p. 44), interscorer reliabilities are needed. Although interscorer reliabilities are provided for the BSM I (TM I, p. 44), they are absent from the BSM II.

The effects of both testers and scorers on BSM II scores were investigated by Hayes (1981). Using analysis of variance to determine effects of test order and tester, she found strong main effects of testers (significant at the .001 level) in both English and Spanish. The test appears to be sensitive to differences in test administrators. To investigate interscorer reliability of the BSM II she chose a random subsample of 40 students. Response booklets were scored by both test administrators and independent scorers. Intraclass correlations indicated that, for comparisons of groups of students, interscorer reliabilities were acceptable. However, she found low English reliabilities for total scores (.69) and levels (.65), due to a restricted range of students' English skills.

In conclusion, internal consistency and test-retest reliabilities provide a limited picture of the consistency of BSM II to measure oral language proficiency. Because of possible susceptibility of the test to testers and scorers, it should be used with caution as a tool in making individual decisions for program placement.

*Scoring Procedures*

BSM II items have been categorized into hierarchical clusters, using the *ordering theoretic method* (Bart & Krus, 1973), which considers response patterns to pairs of items. Items are placed in a hierarchy based upon this method, and cutoff levels are determined. Because there are "no strict empirical guidelines" for the selection of items or cutoff levels (TM II, p. 21), the authors set their own criteria for item inclusion. Cutoff levels, however, have not been theoretically or empirically justified.

While items in Cluster 5/6 are, for the most part, more difficult than items in Cluster 3/4, the designation of Level 3 versus Level 4 or Level 5 versus Level 6 is not determined by passing progressively more difficult items. Rather, these levels are determined by the number of items correctly answered within each cluster, although the item difficulties ($p$ values) vary considerably within each cluster. This may be an important concern when the differences between Level 5 and Level 6 or between Level 4 and Level 5 indicates eligibility for funding and special services.

Another problem with BSM II level classifications is their susceptibility to misuse. As indicated in the Technical Manual (TM II, p. 22), either Level 5 or Level 6 can be used to designate proficiency in English. This choice is left up to the user, who may decide on one or the other based upon their school district English norms or on a number of other factors. For example, if limited funds are available for English language services, a district could choose Level 5 to indicate FEP. If, on the other hand, a district could provide language services until they are no longer needed, Level 6 might be used. This possible use of the FEP levels is also examined by Hayes (1981). A sample of 183 third grade bilingual students were administered the BSM II. If Level 6 were used as the cutoff for proficiency in English, 95% of this sample would be classified as needing a special program; if Level 5 were used, 22% would be thus classified. The difference between using Level 5 or Level 6 could mean that over 70% of these students could be classified differently.

Lack of valid criteria for establishing cutoff levels directly affects the reliability of BSM II level classifications. Studies comparing the BSM (I and II) with other language proficiency tests do not indicate substantial agreement in classifying students. The agreement in classifications when several pairs of oral language tests were compared ranges from 14% (Cervantes & Nakano, 1979) to 78% (Gillmore & Dickerson, 1979). What appears to be fluent English proficiency on one test may appear as limited proficiency on another, and vice versa.

Given the problems with the validity and reliability of BSM II levels, test total scores might provide a better indicator of proficiency. Ulibarri et al. (1981) found high correlations among language tests when total scores, rather than proficiency levels, were used in analysis. Hayes (1981) correlated BSM II levels with BSM II total scores, other measures of oral language proficiency and achievement. All correlations of BSM II English total scores with every other variable exceeded that of the BSM II English levels with the same variables. These consistently lower correlations suggest that the BSM II levels are less reliable than the total scores. A certain amount of precision has been lost in collapsing these total scores to a 6-point scale. Users are advised to disregard the established levels of BSM II and to use the test's total scores with cutoff levels determined by prediction of grade level achievement in their place.

*Summary and Recommendations*

The BSM II provides a colorful, pictorial stimulus to elicit conversational data which can help language researchers validate various hypotheses about the acquisition of syntax. It is an improvement on the BSM I because of its extension to older students. The format and layout are of exceptional quality with easy to follow examiner instructions.

These favorable characteristics must be considered along with the test's technical weaknesses. Low reliability, due to test length and susceptibility to effects of testers and scorers as well as questionable validity due to restricted content, limit the test's credibility. Moreover, the test's language proficiency levels have not been validated and do not reliably classify students. These results suggest caution in the use of BSM II.

For researchers and clinicians, the BSM II may be a useful tool. For others, particularly teachers and school district administrators, its use is only recommended if these guidelines are followed:

1. Multiple measures: Use the BSM II in conjunction with other indicators of language proficiency.

2. Individual decisions: For students not yet proficient in English, using the test results for diagnosis or placement is not advised. Do not try to distinguish among students very similar in language ability.

3. Scorers: Try to have more than one person score the same student's response booklet or have one scorer score all students.

4. Total scores versus levels: Disregard established BSM II proficiency levels. Rather, use the test's total scores with district specific grade level predicted cut-off scores for NEP/LEP/FEP decisions.

### Reviewer's References

Bart, W. B., & Krus, D. J. (1973). An ordering-theoretic method to determine hierarchies among items. *Educational and Psychological Measurement, 33*, 291-300.

Burt, M. K., Dulay, H. C., & Hernandez-Chavez, E. (1976). *Technical handbook: Bilingual syntax measure.* New York: Harcourt Brace Jovanovich.

Burt, M. K., & Taleporos, E. (1980). *Technical handbook: Bilingual syntax measure II.* New York: Harcourt Brace Jovanovich.

Cervantes, R. & Nakano, P. (1979). *Oral language tests: The language assessment scales and bilingual syntax measure.* Unpublished paper, Sacramento, CA.

DeAvila, E., Cervantes, R. A., & Duncan, S. E. (1978, May). *Bilingual program exit criteria.* Paper submitted to the Office of Program Evaluation and Research, California State Department of Education.

Graham, C. R. (1978). [Review of bilingual syntax measure I]. In O. K. Buros (Ed.), *The eighth mental measurements yearbook* (pp. 234-5). New Brunswick, NJ: Gryphon Press.

Gillmore, G., & Dickerson, A. (1979). *The relationship between instruments used for identifying children of limited English speaking ability in Texas.* Houston: Region IV Bilingual Education Service Center.

Hayes, Z. A. (1981). *"Limited" language proficiency: A problem in the definition and measurement of bilingualism.* Unpublished doctoral dissertation, Stanford University, Palo Alto, CA.

Hayes, Z. A. (1984). Linguistic and communicative assessment of bilingual children. In C. Rivera (Ed.), Placement procedures in bilingual education: Education and policy issues (pp. 40-105). Clevedon, Avon: Multilingual Matters.

Merino, B. J. & Spencer, M. (1983). The comparability of English and Spanish versions of oral language proficiency instruments. *NABE Journal,* 7(2), 1-31.

Rosansky, E. J. (1979). [A review of the Bilingual Syntax Measure]. In B. Spolsky (Ed.), *Some major tests: Vol. 1. Advances in language testing series* (pp. 116-35). Arlington, VA: Center for Applied Linguistics.

Ulibarri, D. M., Spencer, M. L., & Rivas, G. A. (1981). Language proficiency and achievement: A study of language proficiency tests and their relationship to school ratings as predictors of academic achievement. *NABE Journal,* 5(3), 47-80.

# Bilingual Vocational Oral Proficiency Test

### Reviewed by

### Dorothy S. Messerschmitt
### University of San Francisco

### Synopsis

Bilingual Vocational Oral Proficiency Test. BVOPT. 1981. Adults entering or already in adult education and vocational programs. Designed to measure receptive (listening) and productive (speaking) skills through four subtests which require either verbal responses or physical actions from the examinees. Verbal and physical responses are individually scored on 2-point or 3-point scales. Individual administration. 20 minutes. Two forms: A for pretest and B for posttest. Administrator's Manual (1981, 70 pp.). $49.95 for kit, containing Administrator's Manual, 19 full-color posters, 30 scoring sheets with recording space for both forms. Administrator's Manual (includes technical information), $12.95; color posters, $30.00; scoring sheets (pack of 60), $24.95. Originally developed with U.S. government funding granted to Resource Development Institute, Inc., Austin. Mary Galvan. Melon Peninsula, Inc., 111 Leslie Street, Dallas, TX 75207, USA, telephone: (800) 527-7830; in Texas, (214) 748-0564.

### Review

The aim of the Bilingual Vocational Oral Proficiency Test (BVOPT) is to assess the low-level adult student's functional language skills for bilingual vocational training classes. BVOPT attempts to examine the student's ability to understand and respond to work-related instructions, warnings, and precautions. The test's language comes from samples of the actual language of instruction in vocational education. The BVOPT is not a test of literacy, nor was the BVOPT designed for work environment classes (on site vocational ESL or pre-employment ESL) or "survival English" assessment.

The BVOPT is an integrative test examining overall language skill rather than discrete grammatical points. The only exception to this is the subpart, Imperatives. The reason for the emphasis on this particular grammatical point is undoubtedly due to its frequency of use in the work place. Although the focus is not on discrete points of grammar, the linguistic structures represented in the test items are listed.

The authors claim the test is criterion-referenced, stating that each item is referenced to a set of communicative criteria that are explicitly stated in the Administrator's Manual. One of its purposes as stated in the Manual is to "screen people for enrollment in a bilingual vocational training program" (p. 2). However, cut-off scores for entry and graduation are not indicated; individual programs are directed to establish these norms internally. Instructors who have used the test, therefore, find it inappropriate when the goal of their testing procedures is to place students in the correct section of a multilevel ESL program. The Manual briefly interprets scores, indicating three levels of beginning language proficiency. The other stated purpose of the test is to "determine the gain in English proficiency achieved during the training period." The two forms of the test make it applicable for demonstrating language growth over time. This feature of the test can be important for those programs that must undergo periodic evaluations for funding purposes.

The subparts of the test are (a) a question and answer section, (b) an open-ended interview section, (c) an elicited imitation section, and (d) an imperative (aural comprehension) section. Raw scores are converted to adjusted scores as the different subparts are not equally weighted.

In the question and answer subpart the examiner asks a series of increasingly difficult questions which are scored immediately as either *appropriate* or *inappropriate*. The purpose of the open-ended interview is to obtain a 4 to 5 minute sample of the examinee's speech. Ratings are made after the entire subpart is completed. Three levels are identified, and within each an additional three. Both of these subparts utilize color posters.

The elicited imitation subpart asks the student to repeat sentences of increasing length and grammatical difficulty. Responses are rated as either *retains meaning* or *meaning lost*. It is not immediately clear how much of the task is memory and how much is language. Informal checking by the reviewer with both native and high-level nonnative speakers in a class on second language testing did indicate a clear difference in success on this section, thus supporting the validity of this item type. In using such a task, the authors made use of some recent research (Natalicio, 1976) on the utility of sentence repetition as a language proficiency assessment technique. It would be useful for the authors to have cited this research since on the face of it, such items appear to test memory.

The listening comprehension (Imperatives) section of the test asks the student to manipulate plastic objects, that is, cups, plates, and a box (not supplied by publisher), in response to specific commands. Actions are rated as either *correct response, incorrect response,* or *no response*. This is a very practical way to check a student's aural comprehension without involving the reading skill.

Finally, it is important to note that the instructions for the test must be given in the student's native language. The purpose is to reduce tension and frustration on the part of the student. Thus, the examiner must be bilingual in the student's language or have a tape made for use during the testing session. This may be an administrative difficulty for some programs. The scoring procedures are extremely clear, and the color posters are excellent.

In summary, the BVOPT is a useful test designed for low-level adult students in vocational training programs. It is not the optimum test to use for placement into multilevel programs, as it lacks placement information. If literacy is not a concern, the two forms of the BVOPT offer a good integrative test for determining growth in language over time.

## Reviewer's References

Natalicio, D. D. (1976, April). *Sentence repetition as a language assessment technique: Some issues and applications*. Paper presented at the 60th annual meeting of the American Educational Research Association, San Francisco. (ERIC Document Reproduction Service, ED 123-261.)

# Cambridge First Certificate in English

*Reviewed by*

**Liz Hamp-Lyons**
**The University of Michigan**

## Synopsis

Cambridge First Certificate in English. FCE. 1984. Intermediate level students, usually ages 14 plus. Designed to represent a general standard of competence in English at an intermediate level and as an effective basis for further study, with "widespread recognition in commerce and industry, both in Britain and overseas, and in individual university faculties, polytechnics and other institutions." Five compulsory papers: Reading Comprehension, 1 hour, multiple-choice, 40 marks; Composition, 1 1/2 hours, subjective, 40 marks; Use of English, 2 hours, open-completion/ transformation and directed writing, 40 marks; Listening Comprehension, approximately 30 minutes, various objective, T/F, labeling, and reordering, 20 marks; Interview, approximately 20 minutes, subjective, 40 marks. Total time, approximately 5 1/2 hours. Individual. No choice of form. No administrative manual publicly available, no technical manual publicly available. See Regulations for 1984, General Information Sheet, and Cambridge Examinations in English, Changes of Regulations in 1984, published 1982 (contains specimen paper and discussion notes). Practice material available as Cambridge First Certificate Examination Practice series (Cambridge University Press) and similar from other U.K. publishers. Test administered centrally from UCLES. Fee per candidate £19.35, plus a local fee. Test dates for 1984, June 18 and 19, December 10 and 11. University of Cambridge Local Examinations Syndicate (UCLES), Syndicate Buildings. 1 Hills Road, Cambridge CB1 2EU, England, telephone: (44)-223 61111.

## Review

The Cambridge First Certificate in English was taken by 75,284 candidates in 1983 of whom 73% received passing certificates (latest available figures). FCE is centrally administered, and decisions of UCLES concerning results are final. The certificate the candidates receives shows an aggregate of A, B, or C (passing), D or E (failing). British universities do not usually accept FCE as proof of language competence, although it may be accepted by individual departments; it is accepted by some polytechnics, many colleges of further education and of technology, and outside Britain it is commonly required for jobs in banking and tourism.

The new version of FCE claims to place more emphasis on authentic material and situations, interaction, and the oral-aural skills than the previous version used from 1975-83. The most significant changes come in

Papers 4 and 5; Paper 2 has changed slightly. Each paper is briefly described and commented on below.

*Paper 1, Reading Comprehension,* contains 40 multiple-choice items. The purpose of this paper is to test usage based on grammatical and semantic correctness and contextual appropriacy. The item types are not very different from those in the earlier version. Each item is pretested and is included for its ability to discriminate: A discrimination index of at least 0.25 and a facility value between 0.25 and 0.80 are required. The average discrimination is 0.34, and the average facility is 0.69.

*Paper 2, Composition,* offers a choice of questions, two of which must be answered. Letters and descriptive, narrative, and discursive topics are included. Questions on prescribed texts have been introduced as an alternative to free composition. The two compositions are marked impressionistically by one marker within a moderation system, taking into account quality of language, range and appropriateness of vocabulary and syntax, correctness of grammar, punctuation and spelling, and relevance and organization of the composition. Sample compositions at the five overall certificate grades are available in the UCLES report; however, their usefulness as criteria is severely marred because they are presented as examples of the five aggregated certificate grades rather than the standards set for the composition paper itself. This assumes that candidates necessarily perform at the same level on every paper, which is not the case. No reliability data are available. The direct testing of writing presents serious problems of reliability, and for this reason many large-scale testing bodies eschew it. While UCLES deserves the credit for increasing the validity of their test by including a Composition paper, it is regrettable that levels of inter- and intramarker reliability are not reported. Official information on the scoring criteria for the subjectively assessed Composition paper is minimal, despite the fact that this paper has remained substantially unchanged for 10 years and the criteria should by now be well established and amenable to precise description for the benefit of teacher.

*Paper 3, Use of English,* retains the form of the 1975-1983 version of the test. This paper has two sections, the first of which tests usage primarily through modified cloze and sentence transformation, plus such question types as word formation, text construction from given elements, construction of question forms, changes from reported to direct speech or vice versa, and vocabulary or structure selection. The second section is a restricted composition task, an exercise in information retrieval within what is intended to be an authentic context. In the *Change of Syllabus in 1984* handbook, the reader is referred to another UCLES publication, *Report of the Work of Candidates in the Examinations of June and December 1975* for details of candidates' performance on Paper 3, in which a frequency count of correct responses for a random sample of 50 candidates on the 20 item modified cloze is given. A general report on Paper 3 issued in 1978 provides

similar information for 200 candidates and examines the discrimination and facility of the questions set.

*Paper 4, Listening Comprehension,* now uses recorded material instead of texts spoken by the examiner and replaces a multiple-choice test with a variety of objective and semi-objective items. No information on the pretest performance of the items is available.

*Paper 5, Interview,* involves discussion of photograph, reading aloud, and a situational task such as participation in a simulation with the examiner. Sample recordings of interviews are available. Again, no pretest data is available, and no indication is given of how interviewer reliability and question validity are monitored.

This test is very influential within Britain, Europe, Latin America, and elsewhere. It is heartening to see the syndicate's attempts to bring it in line with pedagogic developments, particularly in communicative teaching/learning. What is of serious concern to test consumers, that is, teachers of the many FCE preparation courses, and the testees themselves, is the lack of hard information about the test. Although there are many commercial textbooks claiming to be complete preparations for the FCE there is only one official specimen paper, although the practice series by Cambridge University Press may be considered of official status. Information on text types, item types, and item selection available from UCLES is very limited, and what exists is rather vague. Similar to the Composition paper, little information is available on scoring criteria for the Interview paper. This lack of information poses a problem to the teacher, as many have little idea of what is expected of their student in face-to-face interaction with an interviewer.

While the five papers have been constructed to test active and receptive skills in the written and spoken language in a comprehensive and balanced way, marks on all the tests are aggregated and reported only as one of five very broad categories. Since much shorter standardized tests with documented reliability information are available, arguments in favor of FCE presumably rest on content and construct validity. However, such arguments are greatly weakened because information about which communicative or other tasks the testee could perform is lost in the reporting of only one broad grade. It has been suggested by UCLES (personal communication) that such information is only of "academic interest," but the use made of another UCLES-administered test, the ELTS, (see review in this volume) has shown that this is not the case. Further, the failure to report essential statistical data, even in occasional reports with limited circulation, means that no one wishing to use the test or test results knows what the grades mean. The fact that most score consumers are unaware of the need to treat test scores with caution does not mean that detailed information is of academic interest; rather, it means there is a long way to go before tests and their scores are treated with the responsibility that their nature and function require.

# Certificate of Proficiency in English

*Reviewed by*

## Alan Davies
## University of Edinburgh

### Synopsis

Certificate of Proficiency in English. CPE. Foreign teachers of English and others. Designed as language qualification for foreign teachers of English to indicate an advanced level of competence; recognized for matriculation by universities in Britain and many other English speaking countries, with corresponding recognition by many professional bodies. In a number of countries it is a qualification for teaching English at various levels. Reading Comprehension (Paper 1), multiple-choice items; Composition (Paper 2), impression marking; Use of English (Paper 3), semi-objective and impression marking; Listening Comprehension (Paper 4), multiple-choice; Oral Interview (Paper 5), impression marking on 2 x 5 pt. scales; optional papers in Translation and Literature, both impression marking. Group administered. Paper 1, 1 hour; Paper 2, 2 hours; Paper 3, 2 hours; Paper 4, approximately 30 minutes; Paper 5, approximately 20 minutes; total, 5 hours 50 minutes. New form for each test administration in June and December. Papers 1-4, 24 pages. No administration or technical manual publicly available. *Survey of Examination Centres* (1981, 16 pp.); *Annual Survey* (1983, 11 pp.). £23.25 per examinee, £10 per CPE Practice Tests and Practice Tests 2 (Cambridge University Press, 1982). Joint Committee of University of Cambridge Local Examinations Syndicate (UCLES) and British Council. UCLES, Syndicate Building, 1 Hills Road, Cambridge CB1 2EU, England, telephone: 0223-61111.

### Review

#### Background

The University of Cambridge Local Examinations Syndicate (UCLES) is responsible for some of the best known EFL examinations. These Cambridge *Examinations in English* have been offered at several levels for many years and are used in over 60 countries. They are accepted as widely understood proficiency measures, as accreditation for teacher registration, and as equivalences of various kinds, such as a language qualification for entry to universities.

The Cambridge Examinations in English exist at four levels: the Diploma of English Studies (DES); the Certificate of Proficiency in English (CPE); the First Certificate in English (FCE), formerly known as the Lower Certificate in English; and the most recent Preliminary Certificate in English. These examinations have an established history which gives users confidence in their validity and interpretation. They are seen as interlocking so that after success on FCE a candidate may hope to move up to CPE. Over the years there have been about three FCE matriculations for every one CPE matriculation.

The CPE began in 1913 "to meet the special needs of foreign teachers of English" (UCLES, 1982, p. 1). The British Council became formally involved with UCLES in 1941. For some years literature was a compulsory paper. In 1966 a major change to a semiobjective mode of testing resulted in a purely language examination, and literature became an option. Research programs led to a new syllabus in 1975, and to a modification and streamlining of that syllabus in 1984 (see UCLES, 1984).

UCLES claims that over time CPE Development has been directed and informed by teachers and educational ideas. Thus "the rate of increase in main examination entries has clearly shown the relevance to current teaching aims and techniques of this plan of examination, with its emphasis on active and realistic skills and its association of English with international communication rather than British culture" (UCLES, 1982, p. 2). Indeed the number of annual CPE entries has increased from about 500 in the 1930's to 20,000 in 1984.

Very modest research is done in modifying and streamlining the syllabus. Examination centers within and outside of the United Kingdom are consulted, and their advice considered. In 1981, the UCLES published a report on the conduct of their EFL examinations after the introduction of the new syllabus in 1975. The report refers to widespread approval of the examinations within and outside of the U.K. and points to two urgent needs: (a) The examinations should reflect their international function, the varying backgrounds and needs of candidates, and (b) they should take into account modern teaching methods and views of the nature of language performance. Thus, it can be said that the UCLES recognizes the importance of keeping in step with the ESL teaching profession and changes in the examinee population.

The report concludes that the two needs would be met by "increasing the emphasis on functional aspects particularly in respect of the weight and character of the oral testing, and by aiming the examinations, while preserving their recognized level, less at candidates of markedly literary or academic background" (UCLES, 1984, p. 3). There is merit in this observation. Although Literature is no longer a compulsory test, the literary emphasis is still maintained in the texts examples for the Reading Comprehension paper (see UCLES, 1982).

The report also draws attention to comments from examination centers on (a) a proposal for the use of recorded listening material; (b) the need to streamline the syllabus; and (c) the need for a more detailed specification of levels of performance, and the standard and intention of different parts of the examination.

The published reports and statements give a favorable impression of an EFL examination system which is valued, widely used, and maintains its relevance to changing needs and ideas. The Cambridge examinations not only appear to be attractive, they are.

## Current test

CPE provides wide coverage, containing five compulsory written and oral tests. The new, shortened version seeks to provide a suitable assessment for communicative approaches to teaching, particularly with respect to the oral element.

All papers are scaled, as part of an interpaper control system to give an overall mark weighing (40 each in Papers 1, 2, and 3; 20 in Paper 4; 40 in Paper 5) of 2/3 written and 1/3 oral/aural.

The total test time for CPE is 5 hours 50 minutes, which is a very generous amount of time for a language test. However, in part it is due to the CPE's ample coverage of content and skills.

The emphasis throughout is on practical general purpose English. This is understandable since the tests are aimed at students of English who may become teachers of English, and not at EAP or ESP students. In spite of this focus, the Cambridge examinations test the code language, rather than the use of the language or pragmatics. (Note the comment in the same 1984 specifications on the need felt by teachers to move toward a more communicative approach.) UCLES is a conservative testing body, and the Cambridge examinations reflect this conservatism, which commendably does not move too fast for most of its consumers. There is caution (even in the 1980s!) about using recordings. Clearly UCLES is aware of the practical problems in some parts of the world of using any mechanical aids.

However, there are three serious demerits about CPE, in particular, and the Cambridge examinations, in general. In spite of the more than 70 years testing experience (probably as long as any institution in the EFL field), there is little evidence of research carried out on test procedures and item types or analyses of the data accumulated. UCLES carried out research for internal use, but this is not published. So much data over so many years surely merit analyses that would be of considerable interest in language teaching and language testing circles.

Statistical information is available in the form of annual reports on entries and overall results, but it would be of interest to know what relation parts of the examination bear to other parts. The influence of the CPE is such that for many people it is synonymous with English. It would be useful to learn something about its construct validity, or about any other kind of validity and reliability.

We have praised the conservatism of the test. Nonetheless, in 70 years UCLES could and should have given more encouragement to innovation in language testing in the areas of communicative language, diagnostics, ESP, oral and written language. If UCLES cannot lead, which examining body can?

## Reviewer's References

University of Cambridge Local Examinations Syndicate. (1981). *Examinations in English as a foreign language.* Cambridge: Author.

University of Cambridge Local Examinations Syndicate. (1982). *Cambridge examinations in English: Changes of syllabus in 1984.* Cambridge: Author.

# University of Cambridge Local Examinations Syndicate: Preliminary English Test

*Reviewed By*

**Keith Morrow**
**Bell Educational Trust**
**Norwich**

## Synopsis

University of Cambridge Local Examinations Syndicate: Preliminary English Test. (UCLES) PET. Adult elementary level (350 hours) students of English as a foreign language. Designed to provide a marker of achievement in the early stages of learning. No information publicly available about scoring method. Question formats include: selection of vocabulary items from choice of options in connected passage or discrete sentences, filling in blanks, connected passage or discrete sentences, short directed writing exercises, oral/aural component with selection of items on basis of recorded input, question and answer, and mini role playing. Group administration, except for individual oral test. 122-minutes, including 7-minute oral test. Bank of test versions, from which selection is made for each session of the examination (March, May, July-August, November). Administration Manual: *Preliminary English Test-Information for Centres and Candidates* (1980, 20 pp.). No technical manual available. Cost per candidate £10. Administration Manual, £.25. Offered by arrangement with the Secretary, University of Cambridge Local Examinations Syndicate, Syndicate Buildings, 1 Hills Road, Cambridge CB1 2EU, England, telephone: (0223) 61111.

## Review

The official specification and description of these examinations is vague. As always with examinations from this source, it is necessary to infer the rationale and the approach adopted from sample papers. No explicit specification of the content is provided beyond very general statements in the information booklet.

The examination is in three sections: Written (40 marks), Listening (15 marks), and Speaking (25 marks). Results are reported as overall *pass* or *fail*. However, it is not clear whether candidates must pass all three sections or if compensation is permitted. Furthermore, no public information is available indicating the marking criteria made public, nor the pass marks for any section.

PET's stated purpose is "to test written and spoken communicative competence in relation to listening and reading ability, up to a level represented by about 350 study hours from beginner level." In the absence of an explicit statement of target competence, we are left to guess what any individual will have achieved in 350 hours.

In addition, UCLES's terminology is very loose. Page 1 of the *Information for Centres*, states, "Preliminary English Test is a test of achievement." In the absence of a specification of test content this use of "achievement" is idiosyncratic. On Page 9 specimen questions from the Written section are described and exemplified. A gap-filling exercise is presented as a dialogue which the candidates must complete. The rubric describes the context: "Situation: in a public place (e.g., station or airport). Notions: asking for help; giving instructions." A charitable description of this use of the term "notion" would be "idiosyncratic."

The Written section contains four parts, ranging from more discrete to more integrated skills tested. The first is a vocabulary/reading test that would fit well into the analysis of elements/skills presented by Lado (1961), requiring the candidate to select the best of five one-word options to complete a blank in a sentence. The second tests structure and usage, but in a discrete-point format. The third and fourth parts involve free writing with minimal specification of context and content.

All of the questions raise serious doubts in this reviewer's mind about their communicative validity. If linguistic competence is to be measured, then it might appear that discrete items such as those in Section 1 are adequate. If we accept that communicative competence subsumes linguistic competence, and that the latter is a necessary part of the former, such a test might appear to have validity if it included sections where the sociolinguistic aspects of language use were measured. Parts 3 and 4 of this section do not seem to offer such a test for at least two reasons:

> 1. The contextual, situational, role and purpose parameters that define appropriacy of language use are not made explicit. What is to be produced is a piece of writing quite divorced from any real focus.

> 2. The questions are essentially tests of imagination, rather than of use that is indicative of real-life communicative abilities.

The Written section tests performance rather than competence. This distinction may seem academic, but it is unfortunate that no information is given about the marking criteria for the free writing parts, since only from these could one judge whether the test focuses on communication or on language form. It is essential to know whether a piece of writing is to be evaluated as an attempt at communication or in terms of what it reveals of the candidate's underlying linguistic abilities, irrespective of its communicative effect.

The Listening test is less ambiguous in terms of competence/performance. The candidate listens to ten brief, discrete, uncontextualised utterances, and for each one must choose the best of four suggested rejoinders. The relation between this and real language use is tenuous, although it is arguable that these utterances are a necessary part of knowing how to communicate in a foreign language.

## Conclusion

A test at the lower-intermediate level from an internationally recognized testing body is potentially of great value. This exam is likely to become widely used despite its deficiencies. It should be made more rigorous in terms of the way it follows its objectives, and more explicit in terms of the information it makes available.

### Reviewer's References

Lado, R. (1961). *Language testing*. New York: McGraw-Hill.

# Comprehensive English Language Test

*Reviewed by*

**Rebecca Oxford**
**Center for Applied Linguistics**
**Washington, DC**

### Synopsis

Comprehensive English Language Test. CELT. 1986. High school, college, and adult learners of ESL/EFL at the intermediate and advanced levels. Designed to measure English language proficiency of nonnative speakers of English; useful for placement and assessment of progress in an ESL/EFL course. Scoring is based on the percentage of items answered correctly, with incorrect responses and omitted responses counted as incorrect. Punched scoring key (template) performed manually. Group administered. Approximate testing time: 2 1/4 hours. Forms A and B (1986, 30 pp. each); Examiner's Instructions and Technical Manual (1986,

27 pp.). One booklet contains both instructions and Technical Manual. Test book sets, 10 books per set, $20.00; Examiner's kit, $6.95; cassettes, $6.95; answer sheets: package of 100, $10.00. David P. Harris and Leslie A. Palmer. McGraw- Hill Book Company, 1221 Avenue of the Americas, New York, NY 10020, USA, telephone: (212) 512-4327.

## Review

Harris and Palmer have done a very creditable job developing the CELT as a test of English language proficiency for high school, college, and adult learners of English as a second or foreign language, particularly at the intermediate and advanced levels. Until 1986, the CELT had only one form, but the 1986 edition of the test included a second and parallel form. Anyone who has dealt with large scale testing knows the advantage of having more than one form to ensure test security, and for pretesting and posttesting. The two forms (A and B) appear to be parallel and interchangeable, with only minor differences in mean scores between the forms when used with three groups of university ESL students. Perfect parallelism between the two forms would be possible through statistical equating of the norms, but the existing differences between the forms in terms of student performance may not merit the effort of such an adjustment.

The CELT contains three sections: Listening, Structure, and Vocabulary. The Listening section has three parts, with a total of 50 items. Administered by a cassette recording, the total time for the section is 40 minutes. Part I involves answering 20 four-option multiple-choice questions: 15 are *wh*-questions (beginning with interrogatives, such as *what*), and 5 are *yes/no* questions (beginning with verbs, such as *would*). Part II consists of 20 short statements on cassette, each followed by four paraphrased responses. Part III is comprised of 10 dialogues between a male and a female; each dialogue is followed by a comprehension question by a third speaker with four response options. All response options for the three parts of the Listening section are printed in the test booklet; all questions (Part I), statements (Part II), and dialogues (Part III) are on cassette. Care appears to have been taken to restrict the reading difficulty of the response options. While there is no average reliability coefficient reported for the Listening section across the six reference groups cited by the authors, the reliabilities all fall into an acceptable range (.82 - .94, depending on the reference group). These reliabilities are the standard Kuder-Richardson (KR-20) coefficients, which show the degree of consistency of measurement within a test or subtest.

The Structure section contains 75 problems to be answered in 45 minutes. Each item consists of a brief printed dialogue in which one or more words are omitted from the last sentence. The student completes the sentence by selecting from among the four alternatives appearing beneath the dialogue. Only one of the four

completions reflects standard English usage. All items in the Structure section assess points found to present problems to foreign learners of English. Choice of verbs and verb forms is the most frequent type of structural problem represented, with 44% of the items in this section devoted to verb difficulties. There is no overall reliability coefficient given for the Structure section across all six reference groups, but the reliabilites (KR-20) range from .88 to .96 for the six groups.

The Vocabulary section is comprised of two parts with a total of 75 items to be answered within 35 minutes. Part I consists of 35 sentences from which one word has been omitted, followed by sets of four words. For each problem the student selects the one alternative that logically completes the sentence. Part II consists of 40 short definitions followed by sets of four words. The student selects the one word which matches each definition from among the alternatives. Vocabulary words in this section were selected to represent the vocabulary that students might encounter in general college courses. The Technical Manual shows the percentage of test words in the Vocabulary section found in the ord-frequency counts provided by the Thorndike-Lorge (1944) list. According to these counts, the vocabulary words in this section do not appear among the most frequently used 3,000 words in English. Although the Thorndike-Lorge list is outdated, it does serve to show that the vocabulary in this section is not found in the most frequent word categories. This finding is a good one, because the CELT is not intended for beginning English learners but is geared to intermediate and advanced English learners who are not native speakers. As the other two sections of the CELT, the Vocabulary section does not have an overall reliability coefficient across the six reference groups. KR-20 reliabilities for this section range from .88 to .97 for the six groups.

Although the reliabilities are good for each of the sections, it would be helpful to see an overall reliability for the whole test. The Technical Manual states that the KR-20 reliability for one of the reference discriminated between the groups. However, the test authors should be applauded for making a move toward discriminant validity, although they did not label it as such.

The authors demonstrated that the CELT can be sensitive to students' progress in an ESL course, at least for one sample of students. One study of 75 students in a university ESL institute showed substantial differences between pretest and posttest CELT scores, with a 15-week intensive English program intervening. A T-test between the means would have been useful to indicate whether the difference was statistically significant. Replication of this study with other groups would also be helpful. Certainly the results of the reported study are an interesting demonstration of one type of validity.

The Technical Manual for the CELT claims that the three sections—Listening, Structure, and Vocabulary— measure "somewhat different aspects of language competence." Emphasis should be placed on the "somewhat," since intercorrelations among the sections are fairly high (.51 - .71 for one group and .45 - .66 for another group). The meaningfulness of this result needs to be further explored but does not add to or detract from the overall usefulness of the test.

One problem with the CELT is the tentativeness of the norms provided in the Technical Manual. According to the authors, "the small size of some of the samples prevents us from treating [the norms] as anything but rough estimates." Although some of the six reference groups appear to have many characteristics in common, the authors refrain from combining any of these groups to produce an adequate norming sample. Instead, the authors provide separate norms for each of the six groups, the largest of which contains 200 adult nonnative speakers of English who took only Form B of the CELT. The authors encourage users to develop their own local norms. However, many users want to see how their students perform in relation to larger norm groups, representing the whole population. Furthermore, many users are psychometrically untrained and do not know how to generate local norms. In the absence of solid norming data, these users will likely avoid creating local norms and will simply pick a set of norms developed from one of the six reference groups shown in the Technical Manual. If an inappropriate norm group is chosen from the Technical Manual, interpretation of the results will be dubious.

Therefore, several recommendations are warranted regarding norming. First, the authors could either combine some of the existing reference group data to create more adequate norms or gather new data on larger norming groups. This would allow psychometrically untrained users to have readily available, valid score interpretation via norms. Second, some narrative descriptions could be attached to various percentile score ranges, once solid norms are available. Third, standard scores (T-scores, Z-scores, or normal curve equivalents) could be provided along with percentiles. Standard scores, unlike percentiles, can legitimately be averaged across individuals and across the three sections of the test.

In sum, the authors have created a test that is reliable, valid, and useful for nonnative speakers of English. The test appears to measure English language proficiency in a way that is easy to administer and score. More work on norming would make the test more useful. This matter deserves attention before the next edition of the CELT is published.

## Reviewer's References

Thorndike, E. L., & Lorge, I. (1944). *The teacher's word book of 30,000 words*. New York: Teachers College.

# Delta Oral Placement Test
*Reviewed by*

**James Dean Brown**
**University of Hawaii at Manoa**

## Synopsis

Delta Oral Placement Test. DOPT. 1982. Low-level adult ESL. Designed to measure listening comprehension and oral control of lexis (Section I), morphology (Section II), and syntax (Section III). Verbal responses are scored as *0, 1,* or *2* by comparing them to suggested responses and scoring criteria. The three level sections (10 questions each) are scored separately, and students are placed into the first level wherein they score 13 or less out of the 20 possible points. Individually administered. 5 minutes. One form (1982, 61 pp.); Manual includes administration and technical information (1982, 11 pp.). $32.95 per test package, including Manual, flip-card test booklet (30 questions, 30 corresponding pictures and suggested possible responses), and 50 score sheets (student data forms on one side and scoring forms on reverse). $20.85 per test booklet. $7.65 per Manual. $5.50 per set of 50 score sheets. 7% extra for postage and handling. Sandra Berkley and Gary W. Moore. Delta Systems, Inc., 215 N. Arlington Heights Road, Arlington Heights, IL 60004, USA, telephone: (312) 551-9595.

## Review

The Delta Oral Placement Test (DOPT) is designed to measure listening comprehension and oral control of lexis (Section I), morphology (Section II), and syntax (Section III). It is targeted for the "low-level adult ESL program" that is, a program that comes before vocational English, General Education Development (GED) or pre-university ESL instruction. The test is based on an analysis of the vocabulary and structure found in *English as a Second Language: A New Approach for the 21st Century* (Iwataki, 1975). These materials were developed for adult Asian students by the Los Angeles Unified School District with funding from the U.S. Office of Education.

The DOPT is a 5-minute interview procedure. An examiner (native or near-native) asks each question while showing an accompanying picture to the student. The student's response is compared to example answers and scored *0* (no response or incorrect), *1*, (partially correct) or *2* (totally correct). The examiner circles *0, 1,* or *2* for the appropriate question on the score sheet and adds up these numbers at the end of each section. In order to avoid an uncomfortable experience, a student who scores 13 or less out of 20 the interview is stopped without continuing to the subsequent sections. There are 30 questions for students who complete the entire test: 10 for each of the three sections.

The test package includes a flip-card test booklet, 50 score sheets, and a Manual. The package is very well formatted, and the flip-card booklet is convenient to use. The score sheets are highly functional and include a section on the reverse side for student data (e.g., country of origin, primary language, etc.). The Test Manual is also well organized and easy to follow. However, the details of the Test Manual and flip-card booklet present some problems.

The Manual discusses the need for training examiners and suggests methods for doing so, but there are no provisions in the materials themselves for such training other than a brief section entitled "Instructions for the Examiners." More complete instructions for a training session along with a training tape (with examples of actual interviews and resultant scoring sheets) would be very helpful, especially if scores are to be compared across examiners, levels, or programs.

Similarly, more information should be provided detailing what constitutes a 0, 1 or 2 response. While general guidelines are given in the Manual and a few example answers are provided in the flip-card booklet, each decision must be made quickly, leaving a great deal to the examiner's spontaneous judgment. This situation could be remedied by providing more example answers for each score.

Experience with the test suggests that some of the illustrations may be confusing. For instance in one drawing, lightening emanates from a woman's head to represent a headache, while in another drawing lightening comes from telephone to symbolize ringing. Are these representations universal?

There are also several considerations that arise with respect to the theoretical basis of the test. The very labels applied to sections—Lexis, Morphology, and Syntax—indicate a structuralist orientation, which is not necessarily bad. But, posing a hierarchy of difficulty from Lexis to Morphology to Syntax (students are stopped in any section where they score 13 or less out of 20) may be a problem. Is there any reason in theory or practice to believe that such a hierarchy exists?

Furthermore, complete sentence responses (cued by stimulus words at the bottom of illustrations) are required in nearly two-thirds of the questions. If students give a one word response, they are asked to restart and produce a complete sentence. One word authentic answers are counted incorrect. Combined with the observation that all discourse in the test is limited to the two utterance level, one wonders if the authors are aware that language teaching is changing to include the communicative aspect of language learning. Accommodating these ideas would require major revisions. One useful approach might be to eliminate the Morphology section (which accounts for 3.5% of the variance), move the Syntax section forward, include a Communicative section, and have all students proceed through the entire test.

Having the students take the whole test might solve some of the statistical problems that seem to have occurred. Based on a sample of 446 students, descriptive statistics indicate how problems arose. The mean and standard deviation, which are not reported here, are common indicators of the central tendency of the scores and of how students' scores are dispersed around the mean. Calculating backward from the reliability estimate and standard error of measurement, as well as the item means, we discover a whole test mean of approximately 24.93 and a standard deviation of about 15.36. In a 60-point test, this seems to indicate a positive skew in the distribution, which has probably affected the reliability and validity results in unpredictable ways. Other statistical problems are apparent in the reported results, but the length of this review, as well as the basic flaw of a skewed distribution precludes further criticism here.

In sum, the potential user should carefully consider both the merits and drawbacks of the DOPT before adopting it. It is well formatted, quick, and easy to use. However, the information provided for training examiners is minimal, items may be confusing due to the cultural assumptions made in some of the illustrations, and the theoretical underpinnings (structural) may not be appropriate for today's programs. Finally, fundamental problems with the statistics make it difficult to interpret the reliability and validity claims made for the test.

## Reviewer's References

Iwataki, S. (1975). *English as a second language: A new approach for the 21st century.* San Juan Capistrano, CA: Modulearn, Inc.

# English Language Battery

*Reviewed by*

**J. Charles Alderson**
**University of Lancaster**

## Synopsis

English Language Battery. ELBA. Intermediate to advanced ESL learners who are candidates for study at tertiary level. Used to identify students who have sufficient command of English to pursue studies in institutions of higher education where the language instruction is English. Multiple-choice. Group administered. 75 minutes. One form only (1967, Part 1, 8 pp.; Part 2, 11 pp.). Test Manual (1967, 19 pp.). Test kit contains Administration and Technical Manual, tape for Part 1, scoring key, interpretative guide, Parts 1 and 2 of test. £1 per test booklet. Elisabeth Ingram. Institute for Applied Language Studies, University of Edinburgh, 21 Hill Place, Edinburgh EH8 9DP, Scotland, telephone: 031-667- 1011.

## Review

The English Language Battery (ELBA) was written in the mid-1960s by a well-known psycholinguist and language tester, Elisabeth Ingram, at a time when scientific approaches to the assessment of linguistic proficiency were in their infancy in the U.K. ELBA is still one of the few British proficiency tests whose properties are reasonably well established and on which published statistics are available. A Test Manual, available in mimeo only, contains details of the internal and external validity of the test, together with information about its reliability. Two mimeoed research reports (Ingram, 1970; Howatt & Davies, 1979) are also available, giving details of the predictive validity of the test. In addition, an extensive study of the relationship among the ELBA, the cloze and dictation test, as well as an investigation of the factorial validity of the test, is available in Alderson (1978).

In the first section of Part 1, Sound Recognition (100 items), the test taker hears one word read aloud and identifies which word was read from a group of three printed words. This is essentially a phoneme discrimination task. In the Intonation section (10 items), the candidate reads and hears a sentence, and decides what the speaker means from a set of choices: *issues a command, repeats an utterance in disbelief, requests information*. In the Stress section (10 items), the candidate reads and hears a sentence, and indicates the sentence tonic beneath the appropriate syllable. In the final section of Part 1, Listening Comprehension (30 items), the test taker hears a question or the beginning of a conversational exchange, and decides which of four written alternatives is the most suitable for completion or response.

The first section of Part 2, Grammar (50 items), contains incomplete sentences to be completed with the most grammatical alternative. The second section, Vocabulary (50 items), presents single words or phrases whose nearest synonym must be chosen from four alternatives. The final section, Reading Comprehension (20 items), consists of four short (6 to 10 line) passages with several comprehension questions on each.

The reported reliability for the entire test is entirely satisfactory: .97. The reliability of Part 1 is reported at .93 and of Part 2 at .96. Section reliabilities are inevitably lower, but satisfactory (ranging from .77 to .93), except for Intonation which gives only .64. Since this section is only 10 items and partial scores are not reported, this is not of concern. Item facilities and discriminations are also reported, and are satisfactory, except for the Sound Recognition section, where a mean item discrimination index of only .19 is reported. This is probably due to the redundancy of many items for any linguistic subset of the test population, which was linguistically heterogeneous.

Internal validity coefficients are reported in the Manual and largely confirmed, although at somewhat lower levels, in Alderson (1978). These show the closest subtest relationships to exist among Listening, Grammar and Vocabulary; lower coefficients are found for the other Listening sections and Reading Comprehension. A factor analysis in Alderson (1978) shows that one main factor, *loading*, especially on Listening Comprehension, Grammar and Vocabulary, can be clearly identified. Occasionally a second and third factor emerge which relate Intonation, Stress, and Reading Comprehension, however one chooses to identify these factors or explain the interrelationships (Alderson refers to a "core proficiency" factor and "higher order," possibly "metalingual" factors). These results suggest that the identification by the author of two parts, Listening and Reading, is not supported by the data. This would cast some doubt on the value of reporting two part scores, as is sometimes done.

The external and particularly predictive validity of proficiency tests is problematic, and the ELBA is no exception. A variety of correlations and contingency tables is reported, taken from a range of different sample groups, and the results vary considerably. Correlations with teachers' ratings range from .61 to .84. The correlation with the English Proficiency Test Battery, (versions A, B, C, D), commonly known as the Davies test, is reported at .68 for a small sample. Concurrent validity appears to be moderately satisfactory.

Contingency tables of ELBA scores against the first available subject outcome (grade) for a range of different groups of students are reported in the Manual and two subsequent papers (Ingram, 1970; Howatt & Davies, 1979). The results are complex but suggest support for a cut-off score of 50% as indicating need for remedial language tuition. The conclusions are rightfully cautious and cannot be interpreted as establishing a pass/fail cut-off. Experience in English (rather than Scottish) institutions suggests that many students can survive English-medium studies, although only with great effort and with ELBA scores below 40%. The two biggest problems in such studies are truncated samples of the population (only those actually admitted to U.K. study took the test) and the small number of students actually failing their academic courses. Other obvious problems relate less to this test than to the general problem of the use of language proficiency tests for admission decisions: The extent to which it can be shown that language is a significantly contributory factor in academic success.

Perhaps the greatest problem the test faces is that it was produced more than 20 years ago, when language theory was quite different. Neither the Manual nor subsequent reports offer a theoretical justification for the test's content, but it is clearly not intended to simulate the conditions under which the language will be used in study situations. The reasons for selecting particular grammatical structures, specific lexical items, and particular decontextualized mono- and bisyllabic words for aural discrimination remain unknown. Similarly, the selection of short texts on a limited number of topics and questions testing unspecified, largely inferential reading skills remain unjustified, as do the particular combination of sentential comprehension tasks in the Listening section.

ELBA belongs to the test theory, if not applied linguistic theory, that favors discrete-point, analytic, and largely atomistic approaches to language. As this approach is no longer current, the face validity of the test is in question. Insofar as the test exerts a washback effect on the syllabus, it is likely to be an undesirable one. The test does not claim to be diagnositc, and its value as a placement instrument is minimal. Nevertheless, it remains to be demonstrated that tests with greater face, content, and construct validity (TEEP or ELTS tests) are superior instruments for identifying students who will experience serious language difficulties in ESL/EFL instruction.

These comments notwithstanding, Ingram is to be congratulated for attempting to measure the test's validity, as well as its reliability. This reviewer would welcome similar attempts for other U.K. proficiency tests.

### Reviewer's References

Alderson, J. C. (1978). *A study of the cloze procedure with native and nonnative speakers of English.* Unpublished doctoral dissertation, University of Edinburgh, Scotland.

Howatt, A. P. R., & Davies, A. (1979). *ELBA testing 1973-1977: Interim report on analysis of results.* Edinburgh: University of Edinburgh, Institute for Applied Language Studies.

Ingram, E. (1970). *Short report on the testing of English proficiency of first-year students at Edinburgh University, whose native tongue is not English.* Unpublished manuscript, University of Edinburgh, Department of Linguistics.

# English Language Skills Assessment

*Reviewed by*

**Chau Tran**
**North York Board of Education**
**Ontario**

### Synopsis

English Language Skills Assessment in a Reading Context. ELSA. 1980. Students in upper elementary, high school and adult education programs. Designed to measure reading ability; primarily a placement test but can be used to measure achievement or gains. Multiple-choice cloze format; reusable test copies and separate answer sheets. Three levels of difficulty: beginning (B), intermediate (I), and advanced (A). Two forms at the Beginning and Intermediate levels, one using a conversation format (C) and the other a narrative format (N). At the Advanced level, forms AN using a narrative format and AL using a letter format. Test scores are converted into *ELSA levels* of proficiency within each general ability category: Levels 100-300 for the Beginning tests, 300-500 for the Intermediate tests, and 500-800 for the Advanced tests. Group administration. Six tests of 25 items each. 25 to 30 minutes. ELSA test sheets (1980, 1 p.). Technical Manual (1981, 33 pp.) includes directions for administering. $9.00 per package of 25 tests, 50 answer sheets, and 1 answer key for each test form. $4.00 per Technical Manual. Donna Ilyin, Cecelia Doherty, Lauri Fried Lee, Lynn Levy, and Phillip Carlton. Harper & Row Publishers, Keystone Industrial Park, Scranton, PA 18512, USA, telephone: (800) 242-7737 or (800) 343-1240.

### Review

English Language Skills Assessment adopts an integrative approach to testing. Instead of using an agglomeration of isolated, nonrelated vocabulary and grammar items which often plague ESL tests, each test in the ELSA series is comprised of a reading passage constructed to reflect the structural syllabus of a particular ESL level of proficiency.[1] Achieving this goal and lending a natural and realistic tone to the test passages is not an easy task. ELSA's authors have succeeded nonetheless.

Although the tests were originally designed for and field tested with ESL students in adult education programs, the authors claim that the tests can also be used with upper elementary and high school ESL students. However, we feel that ELSA is not suitable for upper elementary students. The situations and language in the test passages are oriented to adults and therefore may not appeal to these students. Furthermore, ESL programs for elementary school children are generally oriented to theme and activity rather than structure, as programs for adults tend to be.

However, ELSA has potential as a placement or achievement test in high school ESL programs, particularly programs in which reading ability plays an important factor. Tran conducted a study in which ELSA tests were administered to beginning (N = 42), intermediate (N = 50), and advanced (N = 75) ESL students in two high schools in North York, Ontario. Teacher ratings of student reading ability and student background data were also obtained.

Preliminary analyses of the data showed some interesting results. The correlation coefficients between teacher ratings of reading ability and ELSA scores vary from .48 to .67, all signifcant and moderately high. The mean scores and standard deviations for ELSA-BN (beginning narrative format), IN (intermediate narrative), and AV (advanced narrative) based on the high school population are quite similar to those reported by ELSA's authors, who obtained their ratings mainly from students in adult education programs. The reliability coefficients of the tests are .80 or above (KR-20 or KR-21 depending on form). Empirical validity studies were also carried out.

Test statistics reported for the five ELSA tests (see Synopsis) in the 1980 version are based on samples of adult students enrolled in ESL programs in San Francisco Community College Centers. These samples vary in size from 158 to 672, with most samples involving more than 400 subjects. Men and women are fairly equally represented in the sample, the largest number of students falling in the 21-34 age group. About 75% of the students have secondary or postsecondary education.

Norms are not available, but test scores can be easily converted into percentages and into ELSA levels of proficiency ranging from 100 to 800, a unique feature of the test series. (The information is made readily available on the hole-punched answer keys.) For each of these levels, a brief description of the related ESL structural syllabus (as designed for adult ESL programs in the San Francisco area) is given to facilitate placement. However, unless the test users' ESL program is organized along the same lines as the San Francisco program, the syllabus description are of little help. Perhaps the most useful function for the ELSA levels is to provide further differentiation within each of the three general levels of ability—beginning, intermediate, and advanced.

The authors claim that it is "a criterion-referenced series of reading tests that measure the student's understanding of meaning in a context, as well as the student's grammatical ability" (Technical Manual, p. 1). However, they provide no information concerning the specific reading skills and grammatical structures covered in each test to fully justify this claim.[2]

The development of ELSA was originally prompted by the need to have an economical instrument that could substitute for a lengthy battery of tests and at the same time provide a measurement of global proficiency. ELSA test scores were correlated with those obtained from the same group of students on other published tests: Comprehensive English Language Test for Speakers of English as a Second Language (CELT), the Listening Comprehension Picture Test (LCPT), the Michigan Test of English Language Proficiency (MTELP), Structure Tests-English Language (STEL), and the Test of English as a Foreign Language (TOEFL). With the exception of the listening tests (LCPT and CELT-LISTENING) the correlations obtained were high, ranging from .73 to .84. In view of these results, ELSA's authors determined that the tests should be used to measure reading and grammar rather than global proficiency.

ELSA is easy to administer. Administration procedures are clearly explained on the front of each test booklet as well as in the Technical Manual. Manual scoring with a hole-punched answer key only takes a few seconds. Scores can be easily converted into levels of proficiency for within-group comparison or placement purpose. Conversion tables are handily presented on the answer keys. In addition to its primary use as a placement instrument, ELSA is also usable as a pre- and posttest to measure gains in language skills.

The Technical Manual is very readable. Information about the background and development of the tests, validity studies, and suggested uses are clearly presented. In sum, ELSA is a valuable instrument for the busy practitioner.

### Footnotes

[1]The syllabi of the ESL program in adult education at the San Francisco Community College Centers were used.

[2]Printed information about the San Francisco Community College program can be obtained by writing to the Teachers' Resource Center, 31 Gough Street, San Francisco, CA 94102. A pamphlet, *Concerned about Testing*, which relates all the Ilyin tests and several others to the San Francisco program, is available from the test publisher.

# English Language Testing Service

*Reviewed by*

**Cyril J. Weir**
**University of Reading**

### Synopsis

English Language Testing Service. ELTS. Nonnative speakers of English enrolling in further education in the U.K. Designed to determine if a student's ability in English will meet the demands of a course of study in Great Britain. Reading and Listening subtests G1, M1, and G2: four option multiple-choice formats, raw scores on each translated into proficiency bands on a scale of 1-9. Writing M2: two pieces of extended writing assessed by a single rater in relation to a proficiency band on a scale of 1-9. Oral M3: interview assessed by a single rater in relation to a proficiency band on a scale of 1-9. Individual administration for M3 interview; group for all other subtests. General Subtests: Reading Comprehension, G1, 40 minutes; Listening Comprehension, G2, 30 minutes. Modular subtests: Specialist Modules (Reading Comprehension, M1), 55 minutes; Writing, M2, 40 minutes; Interview, M3, 10 minutes; 175 minutes total. Two operational versions of G1, G2, M2, M3; one of M1. Administrator's Manual not publicly available. No technical manual. English Language Testing Service, An Introduction (9 pp.); User Handbook (9 pp.); First Report (February 1982, 5 pp.) and Second Annual Report, (November 1982, 5 pp.). Secure test. Copies not publicly available, but some sample test material in User Handbook and Introduction. Central fee, £15 (1985), plus local fee. English Language and Literature Division, The British Council, 10 Spring Gardens, London, SW1A 2BN, England, and University of Cambridge Local Examinations Syndicate (ELTS), 1 Hills Road, Cambridge, CB1 2EU, England, telephone: 0223-61111.

## Review

As described in the handbook, *English Language Testing Service, An Introduction*, ELTS consists of two sections:

> 1. A General (G) section which tests reading and listening skills, and is intended to test general ability in the use of English.

> 2. A Modular (M) section which tests language study skills used in reading, writing, listening, and speaking, and is related to a specific subject area.

The specific subject areas for the Modular section are Life Sciences, Medicine, Physical Sciences, Social Studies, and Technology. There is also a General Academic module for candidates whose area of study is not covered by one of the other modules. The General section is taken irrespective of subject area, but the Modular section reflects the professional field of the applicant.

ELTS is designed to allow the examinee to take either the whole test or selected subtests depending on variables, such as language background, and length and type of intended course. There are five ELTS testing patterns.

*Pattern A:* All five subtests. The basic pattern for academic courses in the U.K., providing comprehensive information for making decisions about placement and language tuition.

*Pattern B:* Subtests M1, M2 and M3. The pattern for applicants for academic courses who have used English to a major extent in their education and/or occupation.

*Pattern C:* Non-Academic Training Module. Special subtests: Listening, M1; Reading and Writing, M2; Interview, M3. The pattern for candidates whose training will be of a practical/technical nature and largely workshop-based. This test uses different materials from the other ELTS patterns.

*Pattern D:* Subtest, G1, plus a written statement of educational and language background. Intended as a screening device for use by the British Council.

*Pattern E:* Subtests, G1, M2, and M3; General Academic. The pattern for short stay (3 months or less); professional visitors who need to show some evidence of language ability.

The test results appear on a report form which shows the pattern of subtests taken, the module and version taken, and the date of the entry. A profile band (level of ability) is reported for each of the subtests together with an overall band score. Each band is defined by a description of the linguistic features characterizing it.

The bands range from 9 (expert user) to 1 (nonuser).

The levels achieved are interpreted in relation to four basic types of course study: linguistically exacting academic study, such as law; to linguistically less exacting training courses. Minimum levels of acceptability for these courses in terms of overall band scores are stated. However, it is understood that individual institutions are in the best position to interpret how the candidates' perceived ability in English, as revealed by the test, relates to the language demands of courses of study or training.

In reporting proficiency test results, there may be a problem of trying to serve different users. Administrators in the receiving institutions normally wish to know only whether the evidence supports admission or counsels against it, that is, they want a single overall score with a clearly defined cutoff point. Those providing remedial language tuition usually require a more comprehensive profile. ELTS has sought to satisfy both the demand for an overall score and the demand for the details of performance on the individual subtests (G1, G2, M1, M2, M3). However, it may be difficult to relate these specific achieved band scores to target language behavior in the academic context, given that such behavior is still not adequately defined.

### Construction

ELTS is an English for specific purposes (ESP) test in orientation. The language realizations tested arise out of the individual communicative needs of specific users in different courses.

The ELTS specifications, developed under the guidance of Carroll (1978), are based on the Munby (1978) model. Munby's approach to needs analysis has been shown elsewhere to be problematic (see Davies, 1981; Wilkins, 1980; Weir, 1983). It is difficult to sample effectively from such a theoretical model for test purposes. Carroll's specifications for the test categories lack data-based evidence.

Further problems arise at the test realization stage. Due to the provision of specific subject tests in the Modular section, it is sometimes difficult to match students to tests. For example, should a postgraduate student in urban and regional studies, whose course includes law, economics, and technology, take the Social Science, the General Academic, or the Technology module of the ELTS battery.

Also, there is some doubt about the comparability of these specific modules, even though the tests are secure and the same versions are reused. As no research on the parallelism of the forms seems to be conducted prior to operational use, there is a possibility that a candidate might achieve a higher band on one form than another. If new versions are to be prepared periodically, the problems of construction are likely to be greater, and the parallelism of the texts more difficult to ensure.

Any test used to assess proficiency in English for academic purposes (EAP) must be highly sensitive to text selection, in light of evidence that science and engineering students as a group are disadvantaged when faced with texts from the social sciences and humanities (Weir, 1983; Alderson & Urquhart, 1985). However, while there may be a need for some degree of specificity, it could be at a broader level than the six areas selected by ELTS.

Despite the test's communicative orientation, the formats employed in the General sections (G1 and G2) appear surprisingly similar to those employed in the previous, more traditional test employed by the British Council (see Davies, 1965). While items now test enabling skills extrapolated from the Munby framework, it is open to doubt how much they can be generalized, given the limited empirical basis for the test specifications. Furthermore, all the skills that are specified do not appear uniformly in every text selected.

There is the further problem in the selection of neutral texts for tests of general proficiency. For the General section taken by all candidates, the identification of satisfactory general texts is problematic. If the aim of the test is to assess communicative competence in relation to specific needs, the question arises as to whether specific subject reading texts should also be provided in the General section.

Given the communication paradigm within which the test purports to operate, the use of multiple-choice formats throughout G1, G2, and M1 is questionable. If the test is designed to reflect what students do in their actual studies, then this discrete-point approach would negate the communicative paradigm, notwithstanding the relationship between direct and indirect forms of testing.

However, in contrast to most other tests designated for similar purposes, efforts have been made to include realistic tests of written and spoken production in the battery (M2, M3). Markers are comprehensively trained in actual examples of typical gradings at various levels in these skills. However, there are problems in the band scales employed. These omit certain crucial aspects of communicative language performance, for example, the differing cultural conventions obtained in different national groups. The scales also confuse task dimensions of target level activity with evaluation criteria. Furthermore, the scales tend to assume that the language features employed as level descriptions in a band co-occur to the same degree in each candidate: As candidates gain in fluency, growth is accompanied by a similar improvement in linguistic accuracy.

## Reliability/Validity

In terms of face validity ELTS is superior to almost all existing standardized tests designed for similar purposes. In terms of construct and content validity it is open to the specific criticisms outlined above. No external validation studies prior to the launching of the test are reported.

The only test statistics available can be found in the ELTS First Report, February 1982. These consist of various descriptive statistics relating to some early pilot modules. Means, standard deviations, and KR-20 reliability indices for the G1, G2, and M1 modules are listed. No figures are supplied for the written and spoken production parts of the test.

No reliability indices are supplied for any of the actual test components. There appears to have been little attempt to validate externally the tests prior to their public introduction in 1980; if there was, the results have not yet been made public. However, external validation studies are currently under way, and hopefully the results will be available soon.

## Conclusion

Despite the reservations expressed regarding the specification of communicative demands on which the test is based, this test is nevertheless a distinct improvement on those hitherto available. Most tests of this type lack any attempt at a priori validation. ELTS recognizes the necessity of attempting to specify the communicative purposes for which students will need English before a test is constructed. The commitment to profiling ability in various skill areas represents a positive departure from the single grades currently accepted as evidence of language proficiency for further study in the U.K. ELTS's worldwide availability through British Council enhances its usefulness.

British Council and UCLES are planning go undertake an extensive revision of the ELTS during 1987-89. This revision will take account of the finding of the validation study completed in June 1986 by the University of Edinburgh.

## Reviewer's References

Alderson, J. C., & Urquhart, A. H. (1983). The effect of students' academic discipline on their performance on ESP reading tests: A pilot study. *Language Testing, 2*(2), 192-204.

Carroll, B. J. (1978). *An English language testing service: Specifications*. London: British Council.

Davies, A. (1965). *Proficiency in English as a second language*. Unpublished doctoral dissertation, University of Birmingham, England.

Davies, A. (1981). [A review of communicative syllabus design]. *TESOL Quarterly, 15*(3), 332-6.

Munby, J. (1978). *Communicative syllabus design*. Cambridge: Cambridge University.

Seaton, I. (1983). The English language testing service (ELTS): Two issues in the design of the new "non-academic module." In A. Hughes & D. Porter (Eds.), *Current developments in language testing* (pp. 129-40). London: Academic Press.

Weir, C. J. (1983). *Identifying the language problem of overseas students in tertiary education in the United Kingdom*. Unpublished doctoral dissertation, University of London.

Wilkins, D. (1980). [Review of communicative syllabus design]. *British Journal of Educational Studies*, 28.

# English Proficiency Test Battery

*Reviewed by*

**Arthur Hughes**
**University of Reading**

### Synopsis

English Proficiency Test Battery (Form D). EPTB, also known as the Davies Test. Nonnative speakers of English applying to British higher education institutions, normally universities. Designed to determine whether a candidate has sufficient ability in English to follow university level courses successfully in Great Britain. Scores on listening, grammar (multiple-choice), and rational deletion cloze (exact word) converted to assign candidate to one of the following three levels: sufficient English; requires 4-12 weeks intensive tuition in English in Great Britain prior to academic course; or requires minimum of 6-months full-time preliminary tuition. Supplementary test components (reading speed, essay, interview) used to distinguish between first two levels in borderline cases to determine length of preliminary tuition necessary for a candidate assigned to the second level. 75-minutes with additional 15-minutes for supplementary components. One form current (1977, 26 pp.). Scoring instructions with some technical details (1977, 14 pp.). £25. Alan Davies and Charles Alderson. Institute for Applied Language Studies, University of Edinburgh, 21 Hill Place, Edinburgh EH8 9DP, Scotland, telephone: 031-667-1011, extensions 4592 and 4596.

### Review

The EPTB was commissioned by the British Council and administered to as many as 5,000 students a year over a period of approximately 15 years beginning in 1964. It was replaced by the various versions of English Language Testing Service (ELTS).

By comparison with some recent British tests the EPTB may be considered outmoded; however, this is not sufficient reason to dismiss it as unsatisfactory. This review will judge it by the accepted criteria for language tests: reliability, validity, and practicality. Discussion will concentrate on Form D, as Davies (1984, pp. 58-9) regards the Listening components of earlier forms to be inferior.

### Reliability

Davies (1984, p. 60) reports the following Kuder-Richardson 21 reliability estimates based on 189 overseas students in the U.K.: Listening Comprehension .79; Modified Cloze .91; Grammar .82; Reading Speed .92. It would be interesting to know the reliability estimate for all parts of the basic test when combined (*short version*), as well as the standard error of measurement, preferably based on the full range of candidates taking the test in their own countries. This information could then be related to the scores used to assign candidates to levels.

Although one or two sentence descriptors are provided to assist in grading oral ability and the essay (Scale A-E), the essay and the interview may well have been unreliable since they were often administered and scored by nonprofessionals. It is probably fortunate that the purpose of these is to provide only "supplementary" information.

### Content Validity

Unlike ELTS, the EPTB does not have different versions for candidates from different academic disciplines. The test reflects the view that "what is required in terms of English language by all overseas students is a minimum proficiency" (Davies, 1984, p. 57). It claims to concentrate on listening and reading comprehension. The listening tasks involve interpretation of sentence stress (25 items), recognition of appropriate responses in discourse (25 items), and identification of written notes correctly summarizing points made in an interview (17 items). The reading tasks are a single modified cloze passage (containing 50 syntactic deletions with the first letter supplied) and a multiple-choice grammar test (50 items). Noticeably absent are reading comprehension passages and a vocabulary section, which were dropped from the original trial version due to length constraints. In addition, performance on the tasks that the student will be engaged in at a university are not directly measured; however, this is by no means uncommon. Nonetheless, it may have had an unhealthy backwash effect. The minimum score indicating *sufficient English* rose from 36 to 44 over 10 years. Presumably through preparation for the test, candidates were able to score higher than their predecessors with the same level of English. The lack of reliable measures of writing and speaking ability indicates that this test provides less diagnostic information than one that has them.

### Criterion-Related Validity

Proof for a test of this kind is in criterion-related validation. Form A (1964) scores on the basic test correlated with students' university grades or examination results at .46 and correlated with teachers' or tutors' estimates of students' English proficiency at .45. Taking into account the reduced range of students reaching the required score for proceeding to tertiary education in Britain (75% of candidates), the various nonlinguistic factors contributing to academic success, and the fact that some tutors gave their judgments much later than the time of the test, these validity coefficients are respectable. Unfortunately the later forms of the test (including D) were not validated in this way; they were simply correlated with Form A, and in the case of Form D not directly. Form C correlated with Form A at .78, while Form D (in which the structure of the Listening component had been changed for the first time) correlated with Form C at .71. This leaves us wondering how scores on Form D correlate with those on Form A and, more important, with student performance at a university.

## Practicality

Administration of the basic test is as easy as any other test that involves the use of tape recordings. The objective scoring is more difficult than expected, since answers are recorded in the question booklet, not on an answer sheet. Interpretation is straightforward.

## Conclusion

The EPTB appears to have functioned well over many years for the purpose for which it was designed, despite the lack of proper validation of later forms. The superiority, in terms of criterion-related validity, of its longer, more expensive, and less practical successor has yet to be demonstrated.

### Reviewer's Reference

Davies, A. (1984). Validating three tests of English language proficiency. *Language Testing*, 1, 50-69.

# Royal Society of Arts: Examinations in the Communicative Use of English as a Foreign Language

*Reviewed by*

**Peter Hargreaves**
**The British Council**
**London**

### Synopsis

Royal Society of Arts: Examinations in the Communica-

tive Use of English as a Foreign Language. RSA CUEL. 1981. Adult nonnative speakers primarily in Great Britain, but also ESL/EFL speakers outside of Great Britain at basic, intermediate, advanced levels. Designed to measure ability to perform tasks in English at the different levels in four independent modes: Reading, Listening, Writing, and Oral Interaction. Reading and Listening: multiple-choice, true/false, and single word/phrase fill in; Writing and Oral Interaction, open-ended responses matched to perform specifications for each level, pass marks determined by criterion targets. Oral Interaction administered part individually, part paired; other modes group administered. Reading: 1 hour, plus 10 minutes reading time at all three levels. Listening: 25-30 minutes at all three levels. Writing: Basic, 1 hour; Intermediate, 1 and 1/2 hours; Advanced, 2 hours; all with 10 minutes reading time. Oral Interaction: approximately 15 minutes (three parts each of 5 minutes) at all three levels. New versions for each of two administrations yearly (June and November), possibility exists for (a) administration at alternative times, (b) specially designed versions, (c) RSA certification of locally devised variations. Syllabus and detailed specifications (1985, 20 pp.) £1.20, with annual insert. Assessment on and Certification for Non-Standard Schemes (a-c above, 1983, 12 pp.); Reports on Examinations (most recent on May 1983, 27 pp.). General Instructions for Local Secretaries, etc. (Autumn 1983, 4 pp.); Rationale in report commissioned by RSA "Techniques of Evaluation for a Notional Syllabus" (Morrow, 1977, 58 pp.); Reports on Examinations (1982, 14 pp.; 1983, 27 pp.). Past papers available 1981, 1982, 1983; price 40 pence per mode at each level. Audio cassettes, £2.25 for each level. Examinations available to accepted centers only, for example, recognized language schools in Great Britain, British Council Centers outside of Great Britain and so forth. Basic, £5.85; £5.75 (U.K.), £6.65 (outside of Great Britain): variable local fee for administration outside of Great Britain. Various authors commissioned by RSA moderators headed by Chief Examiner, Keith Morrow. Royal Society of Arts, John Adam Street, Adelphi, London, WC2N 6E2, England, telephone: 09 930 5155.

### Review

The RSA CUEFL examinations have been developed as a direct response to moves to make language teaching more communicative. The choice of "communicative" and "use" in the title are a deliberate attempt to reflect the examination's commitment to testing the use (as opposed to usage) of English—through listening, speaking, reading or writing—in order to complete tasks which typically do not have a linguistic goal. The detailed specifications and description of formats from the different modes (Reading, etc.) which are contained in the Syllabus and Detailed Specifications draw extensively on the ideas in the report referred to in the synopsis (Morrow, 1977). The report discusses the main elements of communication (authenticity of input, roles of initiator and respondent, etc.) and how these can be translated into communicative testing, both discrete and integrative. The present CUEFL examinations can be seen as a practical realization of the theoretical framework embodied in the report.

To the question, "Is this a real English text being used for a relevant purpose?" (posed by the Information pamphlet as one of the criteria of authenticity), the answer is by and large affirmative. The spoken texts for the Listening tests are authentic recordings or adaptations at the Basic, Intermediate, and Advanced levels. The difference in level is determined by the complexity of the tasks. The Listening topics are presented as radio programs, including announcements, advertisements, extracts of interviews, and lectures. The source texts for the Reading tests are reproduced as near as possible in their original form and include complete copies of self-contained extracts of the (BBC) Radio Times, tourist brochures, and magazines. Monolingual or bilingual dictionaries are allowed. Material for the Writing tests often takes the form of extracts from advertisements, surveys, and informational brochures.

The examples of source texts indicate a distinct bias towards content relevant to the use of English in Great Britain, what the information pamphlet calls "in-Britain English." Yet the RSA is conscious of the user outside of Britain who has no likelihood of contact with Britain. In the Oral Interaction Test, alternative tests have been introduced with tasks more suited to in-country uses of English. More radically, centers outside of Britain have the option of designing versions suited to local needs for certification by the RSA (see synopsis). To date no examples of these local variations have been produced.

The information pamphlet poses the question "Is this the sort of task which a real person in real life might want to do?" as a criterion of task authenticity. Varying according to the test and items, the answer is generally affirmative with reference to the integrative tasks which characterize the Writing and Oral Interaction tests. Admittedly, the candidate has to role play, but the roles are usually authentic. Neither integrative nor discrete tasks depend solely on the skill being assessed. "There is no intention that the test of the various skills . . . should be entirely 'pure'" (Report on May 1983 Examinations). A certain level of reading competence is assumed in the Listening, Writing and Oral Interaction tests at all levels even though its communicative importance is played down.

In the discrete task most typical of the Listening and Reading tests, we have the strongest reservations about authenticity. Some of the reservations relate to items which depend on familiarity with communicative events, particularly with text types which the test taker is required to identify. For example, Intermediate Listening: "Do you think you have been listening to part of a(n) (a) discussion (b) lecture (c) anecdote (d) commentary?". While students may need to recognize these differences implicitly in order to interpret the message, they rarely need to identify them explicitly in real life.

Other examples of discrete tasks are suspect both on the grounds of authenticity and test practicality. In one (Advanced) Listening test, the test taker is asked to listen to an interview (taking notes if necessary), listen to two people making statements about the interview, and at the same time, respond by indicating *agree* or *disagree*. The test item examines the candidate's ability "to evaluate content in terms of subsequently given information" (Syllabus and Detailed Specifications, p. 10). The intention is laudable, but the result is a task where complexity appears to have been achieved only at the expense of authenticity.

Some of the problems in item format and design are the inevitable consequence of the RSA CUEFL being an examination rather than a test, according to Davies' (1982) characterization of these terms. With two completely new versions, each with four modes at the three different levels, pretesting and statistical validation cannot be as rigorous as with tests which have longer-running versions. The RSA CUEFL is, however, no worse in this respect than rival EFL examinations in Great Britain.

As far as marking and assessment are concerned, the criterion-referenced (assesses the test taker's performance against a target performance) CUEFL is less straightforward than traditional, norm-referenced tests in setting pass/fail scores. A pass in a particular test is related to the criterion, "the score at which a candidate has achieved the target performance specified for the level question" (Examiners Report, May 1983, p. 8). In practice, this works out at about two-thirds of the marks available. Since the tests are "intended to measure whether or not the candidates can do certain things in English" (Syllabus and Detailed Specifications, p. 4), there is a problem in deciding whether a candidate needs to reach criterion in each of the subtests/tasks/questions that make up a test or whether deficiencies in one task can be compensated for by overachievement in others.

Aside from the difficulty of standardization of tests from year to year (see Examiner's Report for May 1983, p. 10), there are problems which derive from having separate examinations for the three different levels, each with its own criterion pass mark. The implication is that it is possible to perform tasks in English basically, intermediately, and advanced. Although the specifications for the different levels are cumulative, assessment at each level is not related to other levels. Failure to achieve criterion at one level says nothing about performance at another.

The separate examinations for each level in each mode enables candidates "to choose different combinations of levels and areas to meet their own requirements or abilities" (Syllabus and Detailed Specifications, p. 5). This allows a flexible profile assessment of different candidates (see Table 1).

Marking integrative tasks, chiefly associated with the Writing and Oral Interaction tests, is largely subjective. Considerable care has been taken by the RSA to standardize subjective marking procedures. All oral

|  | Read | Write | Listen | Oral |
|---|---|---|---|---|
| Advanced |  |  | x | x |
| Intermediate | x |  | y |  |
| Basic | y | x |  | y |

x — candidate 1
y — candidate 2

assessors are trained, and there are regular briefings and workshops to improve intermarker reliability for the writing tests. Assessors meet for a "marking weekend" and as a result a high degree of standardization has been achieved (see Examiner's Report, May 1983, p. 9).

In sum, the RSA CUEFL is a welcome addition to the array of nonspecific EFL examinations available to adult learners. CUEFL represents a systematic attempt to apply the principles of communicative (General English) language learning to the rigorous domain of language testing. If there are flaws in the construction of individual tests, there is also clear evidence (from Examiner's Report) that the RSA is making continual efforts to improve the design and operation of the instrument. In addition, much effort has gone into specifying the operations, text types, and degrees of skill required at each level in the focus modes tested. The benefits of these efforts accrue to the candidates, those preparing them, and, indeed, all professionals who recognize the merits of a communicative approach and the positive backwash effect of such examinations.

## Reviewer's References

Davies, A. (1982). Criteria for evaluation of tests of English as a foreign language. *Views on Language and Language Teaching*, 8(1), 7-16.

# General Tests of English Language Proficiency

*Reviewed by*

**Harold S. Madsen**
**Brigham Young University**

### Synopsis

General Tests of English Language Proficiency. G-TELP. 1985. All levels of classroom-trained ESL/EFL learners. Designed to measure proficiency in task performance in listening, reading, and speaking, as well as competence in grammar and vocabulary. Grammar, Listening, Reading and Vocabulary are multiple-choice subtests scored with an answer key; the optional Speaking test is recorded and scored by two professional native-speaker raters, who evaluate appropriateness of response, grammar, vocabulary, pronunciation, and fluency. The Core tests of Grammar, Listening, Reading and Vocabulary can be group administered in a traditional classroom setting. The Speaking test can be group administered in a language laboratory. Beginning level Core test, 90 minutes: Grammar, 20 minutes; Listening, 25 minutes; Reading, 45 minutes. Intermediate level Core test, 110 minutes: Grammar, 20 minutes; Listening, 40 minutes; Reading, 50 minutes. Advanced level Core test, 105 minutes: Listening, 30 minutes; Reading, 75 minutes. Speaking test, 35 minutes. Three forms of Beginning and Intermediate level Core tests; one form of the Advanced level Core test, and one form of the Speaking test. There are 70 items on the Beginning level Core test (16 grammar, 22 listening, 32 reading); 85 items on the Intermediate level test (15 grammar, 22 listening, 40 reading); and 90 on the Advanced level test (27 listening, 63 reading). Administration Manual (1985, 26 pp.). Technical Manual in preparation. Information Bulletin (1986, 28 pp.). Sample test bulletin (1986, 49 pp.). Tests are administered by agents for TENEC International, and answer sheets are returned to TENEC for scoring. Core test, $25; Speaking test, $25. In the U.S.: TENEC International, 4665 Lampson Avenue, Los Alamitos, CA 90720-5199, telephone: (714) 891-6308. In Japan: c/o Time T.I. Communication Co., Time & Life Bldg., 2-3-6, Otemachi, Chiyoda-ku, Tokyo 100.

### Review

General Tests of English Language Proficiency (G-TELP) is a multilevel, general purpose battery, which meets assessment needs not addressed by other ESL tests in the U.S.: (a) utilizes task-focused items; (b) incorporates detailed diagnostic score reporting; and (c) facilitates evaluation at varying ability levels.

### Advantages

While contemporary tests incorporate a variety of language tasks, performance on G-TELP's criterion-referenced tasks is reported individually and enables users to identify areas of strengths and weakness on language tasks: a student's relative proficiency in listening to and understanding announcements, or reading and understanding personal letters. Diagnostic reporting includes not only an indication of general ability level but also a subscore for broad language subskills (listening, reading, vocabulary, and grammar). In addition, a criterion score on task performance and a breakdown of each student's performance in grammatical categories, such as pronouns and present perfect tense, are indicated. Another helpful diagnostic feature is a reporting of performance on literal, inferential, and lexical questions.

In facilitating evaluation at varying ability levels, G-TELP resembles some British tests such as the Cambridge, RSA, and Oxford EFL exams. Generally, ESL/EFL tests in the U.S. are targeted to a specific level: the BEST for beginners or the TOEFL for more advanced university-bound students. Exceptions include the IRL, FSIL, or ACTFL ETS-ILR interview, all of which include extensive examiner training; or BSM I and BSM II, which focuses on grammar and the IOI, which focuses on speaking. G-TELP provides parallel tests at three levels of ability. The G-TELP sample tests can assist with decisions about the appropriate level. Also, students can be matched with performance criteria for the three levels.

Commendable are the realistic situations, the ample context in the grammar section, and the good variety of speakers utilized in the Listening section. Moreover, the proportion of vocabulary to reading comprehension questions is appropriate. The criterion-referenced descriptions of tasks and skills are both unique and potentially helpful to teachers and students.

## Limitations and Special Considerations

While G-TELP score reports provide detailed diagnostic information, they are not designed to provide a single score equatable across all levels or equatable with other ESL tests such as the CELT, Michigan, or TOEFL. In contrast with the well-known ILR or FSI rating system, the highest level is a *1*, next highest *2*, and so forth. Moreover, while score reports of language skills, tasks, and structures are straightforward and readily interpretable, others would probably need clarification for most student or teacher users, such as the Mastery Score Conversion Chart and the Profile B ratio scores on question/information type. Additional clarification would be useful in assisting students and teachers to determine which Core level to select when taking G-TELP.

Research references would be useful to assure users that the tasks utilized on the exam are representative of communicative listening tasks in general. The draft history of G-TELP alludes to a needs analysis in Japan, which apparently relates to task selection.

A debatable practice on the Listening test is the initial focus on the questions: On Levels 2 and 3, students not only see the questions but hear them read aloud prior to listening to the taped test passage. Students are informed that they can take notes during a tape—a logical procedure during a lecture, but less appropriate for other listening situations tested. Nevertheless, this procedure does help prepare students for the somewhat detailed questions that they encounter on the test. The most surprising omission is writing. While the Michigan battery incorporates an essay and the TOEFL is initiating an essay (3 out of 12 administrations per year), G-TELP does not presently include a Writing section.

Like most other U.S. and British exams, there is some national bias. Contexts are generally American. Most speakers in the listening subtest are from the United States. And furthermore, as with any commercial exam scored by a central agency, users must wait for results to be processed by the home office. Since the core test is entirely objective, the wait is likely minimal.

Finally, test users will welcome the publication of forthcoming information on G-TELP validation.

### Summary

Despite its minor limitations, notably the absence of a direct test of writing, G-TELP is strongly recommended. For those needing a writing sample, a local essay could be administered and scored. G-TELP's criterion-referenced task orientation coupled with its detailed diagnostic reporting of proficiency on tasks, question types, and language subskills fills a need not met by other commerical ESL/EFL tests.

# Henderson-Moriarty ESL Placement Test

*Reviewed by*

**Neil J. Anderson**
**Center for Applied Linguistics**
**Manila**

**Synopsis**

The Henderson-Moriarty ESL/Placement Test. HELP. 1982. Adult. ESL placement test for Southeast Asian refugee adults in a nonacademic program. Students who have (a) no reading or writing skills in any language, (b) minimal reading and writing skills in native language, or (c) reading and writing skills in a non-Roman alphabet. Three sections: Section 1, background information and native language literacy assessment; Section 2, oral English; Section 3, reading comprehension. Section 1 scored for fluency in native language, Section 2 and 3 scored for communication. Individual administration (Sections 1 and 2) and group (Section 3). 20-25 minutes. Examiner's Guide (1982, 30 pp.). No technical manual. $13.95 per individual kit. Examiner's Guide contains stimulus pictures, sample answer sheet, sample learner identification form, sample circle the word sheet, intake form, appointment card, alphabet chips, answer sheets, native language literacy assessment cards. Cindy Henderson and Pia Moriarty. Alemany Press, 2501 Industrial Parkway West, Hayward, CA 94545, USA, telephone: (415) 887-7070.

## Review

The HELP Test is an ESL placement test for Southeast Asian refugee adults in a nonacademic program. HELP addresses the special needs of literacy learners. Created when there were very few available assessment tools for preliterate students, the HELP Test is designed to meet the need of ESL professionals to identify and group refugee students into special classes that can meet their needs. The test gets at more than simple reading and writing skills in English; it looks at the recognition, preproduction, and production of English listening, speaking, reading, and writing skills. The test attempts to provide a successful test taking experience for students with different skills, since not all responses require a written or oral response.

### Test Description

*Part I, Intake Information and First Language Assessment.* A bilingual intake worker gathers biographical information on each student. It is important to have the correct spelling of the student's name to be used later in the test. The student's language, literacy background, and occupation are recorded, as well as other information needed by the program.

A native language literacy assessment is made during this portion of the test. Each student is asked to read aloud a short paragraph in their native language. Cantonese, Khmer, Lao and Vietnamese are the languages assessed and scored for fluency of reading.

The test assesses and categorizes student literacy skills as:

1. No reading or writing skills in any language.

2. Minimal reading and writing skills in the native language.

3. Reading and writing skills in a non-Roman alphabet language.

Scoring is indicated with one of three marks: a vertical line for a correct response, a horizontal line for an incorrect response, and a circle for an omitted test item. The intake worker notes whether the student reads the native language script right side up, identifies the language, and reads the passage with ease or difficulty. Examiners are encouraged to record any anecdotal information that may be of value for diagnostic purposes. The student's ESL background is also assessed in Part 1.

*Part II, Oral English Assessment.* The student's oral, reading, and manipulative skills are evaluated. This section is administered individually to each student. An answer sheet is provided for the tester to score student responses. The questions are ordered from easy to difficult. The examiner may skip questions that are circled on the answer sheet if the student is unable to respond to the initial question in the group. Alterna-

tive cues are given for the examiner's use if the original cue is not understood. The alternative cues facilitate the use of HELP as a posttest if the program desires.

This section assesses social language, recognition of the Roman alphabet, recognition of numbers, telling of time, identification of vocabulary items through the use of picture cues, use of U.S. currency, word copying skills, and sight word recognition. In addition, one item assesses the student's ability to make eye contact, a difficult yet important point of evaluation for the target test groups. The scoring for Part II is identical to that of Part I. The focus of this section is on communication not grammatical accuracy.

*Part III, Written English Assessment.* Administered in a group setting, Part III assesses the student's ability to fill out a basic form requesting name, address, sex, marital status, and so forth. Scoring is identical to Parts I and II.

### Guidelines for Use of Test Results

The handbook recommends that both the oral and writing scores be tallied separately, not combined into a total score. Placement cut-off scores are given, but test users are encouraged to establish cut-off points appropriate for use in their own ESL program. The separate oral and writing scores can then be used by program administrators to group students together with similar oral and literacy scores. This has the advantage of grouping students with high oral abilities but low literacy skills in a class and students with low oral and low literacy skills in another class. There could also be groups with high oral and high literacy skills, or low oral and high literacy skills, although the latter is an unlikely combination with this population.

### Technical Information

No technical information is provided except that this is a criterion-referenced test based on teaching experience with the target population. The Manual indicates that technical assistance was provided by two consultants, Donna Ilyin and Lynn Savage. No data is given on test reliability or validity. The oral assessment questions are given in a progressively more difficult sequence, yet nowhere are we told what data was used to develop the sequence.

### Conclusions

Although the Manual indicates that the HELP can be used as an achievement test to evaluate program effectiveness, the reviewer feels that it would be of limited use for this purpose because there are so few items that assess a given skill area. The Manual also suggests the use of the test as a diagnostic tool. Because there are so few items that deal with a given area, diagnostic results should not relied upon heavily. A practical criticism suggests that the print size for the native language literacy section should be enlarged.

Southeast Asian refugee students often have vision problems and therefore require a larger size print.

This test was prepared at a time when the influx of preliterate refugees from Southeast Asia was quite heavy, and there were few assessment tools available to effectively deal with this type of learner. Although Henderson and Moriarty filled a need of many adult education ESL programs, no data from institutions using the test has yet been incorported into the manual. Such data would provide more information about the low level ESL refugee student, a group that continues to be neglected by educators.

# Idea Oral Language Proficiency Test

*Reviewed by*

**Pamela McCollum**
**University of Texas at Austin**

## Synopsis

Idea Oral Language Proficiency Test. IPT. 1979 and 1982. Grades K-6. Designed to measure oral proficiency in English or Spanish. Verbal responses are scored either *correct* or *incorrect* as the student progresses through five or six parts (A/B through F) of the test. The total correct is converted into one of seven proficiency levels that can be changed to a LAU category, NES/LES/FES (non-English speaking/limited English speaking/fluent English speaking), for bilingual program classification. Individual administration. 14-minutes average administration time. English version: two forms, A and B (1979, 1982, 4 pp. each). Spanish version: one form (1980, 5 pp.). Administration Manual: English, Forms A and B (1979, 1982 19 pp.); Spanish, (1980, 19 pp.). Technical Manual: English version, Forms A & B (1979, 1982, 35 pp. plus appendices); Spanish version (1980, 28 pp.). $87.00 per test kit containing a book of test pictures, 50 pupil test booklets or 50 diagnostic score cards (desired form must be stipulated), an Examiner's Manual, a Technical Manual, 50 test level summaries, and 10 class or group lists. Cost per individual item: $29.00 per Form A or Form B test pictures, $19.00 per 50 Form A or Form B pupil test booklets, $19.00 per 50 diagnostic score cards, $12.00 per Examiner's Manual, $20.00 per Technical Manual, $6.00 per 50 test level summaries, $3.00 per 10 class lists. 5% extra for shipping and handling (8% extra east of the Mississippi River), 10% extra for UPS, 15% extra for foreign surface, 2nd day UPS or First Class, 20% extra for Next Day Air. Wanda S. Ballard, Phyllis L. Tighe and Enrique F. Dalton. Ballard & Tighe, Inc., 480 Atlas Street, Brea, CA 92621, USA, telephone: (714) 990-4332. Outside CA (800) 321-4332.

## Review

The Idea Oral Language Proficiency Test-1 (IPT) is part of the IDEA program which consists of the Idea Oral Language Proficiency Test in Spanish and English and two instructional programs, the IDEA Oral language Management Program of Development English Activities and the Carousel of Ideas, an ESL program. The IPT-I is used widely in the public schools to assess the language proficiency of students who speak languages other than English prior to program placement. The authors state, "This test assists in the classification of a student as being NES, LES, FES and, upon the student's completion of a special intervention program emphasizing English oral language development, in the reclassification of that student into the mainstream educational program" (IPT Examiner's Manual, p. 3). The results of the IPT testing can be used to place students into an appropriate instructional level in the IDEA Oral Language Management Program of Developmental English Activities, which develops oral skills as a preparation for reading. The IPT-I was originally designed for Grades K-8 but is presently recommended by the publisher for use with Grades K-6. The new IPT-II for students in Grades 7-11 is available in English. A Spanish version will be available in January 1987.

### Test Format

The English version of the IPT-I has two forms which consist of 83 items that measure proficiency in the areas of vocabulary, syntax, comprehension, and verbal expression. Thirty-five of the test items call for responses to questions about line drawings. The remainder of the items consist of the following types: discriminating between minimal pairs, responding to commands, retelling a short story, describing an object, and identifying the main idea from a passage that is read to the student. The Spanish version of the test has one form that also consists of 83 items.

The IPT divides language proficiency into seven developmental levels. The content knowledge and language skills that students are to possess at each level are specified and generally correspond to the material in the IDEA Oral Language Management Program Levels. While the authors cite an impressive list of research studies supporting the inclusion of many items in the test, the placement of certain items within proficiency levels and across skill levels does not seem logical. One wonders when examining the test if items across a skill area always reflect a progression from less to more complex in terms of the type of tasks which students are asked to perform. However, statistical evidence provided indicates that mean scores across each skill area progress from less to more complex tasks, as evidenced by fewer and fewer students supplying correct answers.

The language used in some of the IPT test items might be made more direct. At times, the direction or cues designed to elicit language seem too difficult for the level of language proficiency being tested. For example, a child at Level C proficiency might be able to respond with the desired response, "I have a table and chair," but be unable to understand the five sentence prompts designed to elicit it.

## Scoring

IPT-I scoring is discrete-point. Responses are scored for appropriateness and completeness, that is, with the exception of items requiring single lexical items, answers must be in complete sentences. Verbal responses are scored as either *correct* or *incorrect* as one moves through Levels A/B to F. The IPT-I begins with Level B, but a student answering less than 50% of the Level B items correct is placed at Level A. Throughout the test, if one fails to answer at least 80% of the items at a given level correctly, testing is discontinued, and that level score is assigned. Two additional placement designations, A and M, are included. The former indicates that one failed to respond to 7 or more of the 12 items in Level B; such students are placed at Level A. Level M, the mastery level, indicates that one responded correctly to 80% or more of the Level F test items. Such students can be fully mainstreamed and do not require placement in one of the IDEA English language programs.

A score conversion table is provided to derive the corresponding NES/LES/FES classifications from the IPT level scores in order to place, reclassify, or exit students from bilingual programs. The IPT-I score and its NES/LES/FES equivalent are on a sliding scale that corresponds to the student's grade level. There are five grade level designations (kindergarten, initial identification and reclassification, first grade, second grade and grades three through six) to which the seven IPT score levels are related. Thus, the student must score higher on the IPT as he or she increases in grade level in order to receive a classification of LES or FES.

## Validity and Reliability

The IPT Technical Manual presents the results of the 1979 and 1981 field testing on which the norms are based. Two additional studies, the correlational study between IPT-I Results and Reading/Language Assessment and the IPT Kindergarten Fall Field Study, are referred to but must be requested from the publishers. The original 1979 field testing was carried out on a fairly large sample (2,061) of children identified as NES/LES/FES students in Grades K-8 in rural, urban, and suburban schools in California. The 1981 testing was done at the request of the California Department of Education to determine the degree of correlation between Form A and Form B of the IPT-I and to norm the test on a monolingual English speaking population. At that time the IPT-I was changed from a K-8 to K-6

measure. In 1983 the IPT-II was developed for Grades 7 through 12. No rationale for this change in grade level designation is given in the Technical Manual.

The Technical Manual is replete with statistics on the reliability and validity of the IPT-I as a measure of language proficiency. Close examination of the construct, content, and criterion-related validity studies (see McCollum, 1983), however, raises some questions about the theoretical underpinnings of the IPT-I. The construct validity section, which should present the authors' conceptualization of the construct of oral language proficiency, supplies generalities and facts about language, language acquisition, and linguistic performance, instead of providing a definition or model of the construct the test purports to measure. A criterion-related validity study correlating the scores on the IPT-I with the NES/LES/FES classifications based on scores on the California State approved language proficiency tests found high positive correlations between the IPT and other California approved tests. This is surprising, as Ulibarri, Spencer, and Rivas (1981) found that four of the tests used to establish criterion validity for the IPT-I produced highly disparate classifications when administered to the same population.

The reliability of the IPT appears to be excellent. Using different formulas the Manual reports an internal consistency reliability of .99 for each form. Given the fact that oral language tests have traditionally suffered from a lack of reliability, a .99 is unexpected.

## Summary

The authors of the IPT attempted to fill a void by producing an oral language proficiency instrument whose results can be used to place students into appropriate LAU categories and the accompanying English language development programs. There appear to be some shortcomings in validity, while the reported reliability is extremely high for an oral language test. Although teachers and administrators are anxious for a diagnostic/prescriptive, self-contained package, the IPT (as most oral language proficiency tests) should be used only in conjunction with other evidence of language proficiency, when placing or reclassifying nonnative English speaking children in bilingual programs. It may, however, be used to accurately place students in the IDEA Oral Language Management Program of developmental activities.

## Reviewer's References

McCollum, P. A. (1983). The Idea oral language proficiency test: A critical review. In S. S. Seidner (Ed.), *Issues of language assessment. Volume II: Language assessment and curriculum planning* (pp. 85-93). Chicago: Illinois State Board of Education.

Ulibarri, D. M., Spencer, M. L., & Rivas, G. A. (1981). Language proficiency and academic achievement: Relationship to school ratings as predictors of academic achievement. *NABE Journal, 5*(3), 47-80.

# Idea Proficiency Test II

*Reviewed by*

**Charlene Rivera**
*and*
**Annette M. Zehler**
**Development Associates, Inc.**
**Arlington, Virginia**

## Synopsis

Idea Proficiency Test II. 1983. IPT II. Grades 7-12. Designed to measure oral language proficiency in English (and Spanish through field test version). Pointing, naming, completing sentences, and responding verbally are scored for accurate comprehension and correct production of grammatical forms, within six levels of difficulty. The score is the highest level successfully completed. Level A, non-English proficient (NEP); Levels B through E, limited-English proficiency (LEP); Level F, fluent English proficiency (FEP). Individual administration. 15 minutes. Two forms, Form A (1983, 12 pp.) and Form B (1983, 12 pp.). Technical Manual (1983, 78 pp.), Examiner's Manual (1983, 20 pp.). $87 per examiners kit (no cost listed for Spanish version), including Technical Manual, Examiner's Manual, test picture booklet, 50 test level summaries, 10 class lists, and 50 test booklets or 50 diagnostic score cards. $19 for 50 test booklets or 50 diagnostic score cards. $29 per picture booklet. $20 per Technical Manual. $12 per Examiner's Manual. $6 for 50 level summaries. $2 for 10 group lists. 10% or minimum $3 for postage and handling. Enrique F. Dalton and Beverly A. Amori. Ballard & Tighe, Inc., 480 Atlas Street, Brea, CA 92621, USA, telephone: (714) 990-IDEA or (800) 321-IDEA, outside CA.

## Review

The IPT II is designed to test oral English language proficiency of nonnative English speakers in Grades 7-12 through an individually administered discrete-point assessment of oral language skills, focusing on vocabulary, syntax, noun and verb morphology, and sentence and story comprehension. The two alternate forms are designed to distinguish among six levels of proficiency (A,B,C,D,E,F) and three categories of proficiency (non-English proficiency, limited-English proficiency, and fluent English proficiency). In addition to distinguishing among levels of oral proficiency, the test is described as a diagnostic instrument, which will provide information to guide instruction.

### Test Administration

The administration of the test is divided into six levels and takes from about 3 to 25 minutes, depending on the student's English oral language proficiency. If the student cannot respond beyond giving his or her name, the test is not continued. While administering each level of the test it is necessary to keep in mind the number of incorrect responses made. These determine whether the testing should be continued to the next level, or whether the student should be scored at the level just completed. It is essential that the administrator carefully read the Examiner's Manual and become very familiar with the testing materials, since the testing booklet assumes a fully informed test administrator.

Although the administration instructions provided in the Examiner's Manual are clear, they are brief and not organized as effectively as possible. It would be helpful if the instructions began with a clear, concise statement of basic information on the test. New information to include would be a definition of oral language proficiency, the age range appropriate to the test, a suggestion of who should do the testing, a specific range of testing time (not only the average time), and some description of how best to physically organize the materials within the testing situation. An effective organization of the Instruction section would lead the administrator from basic information about the test, to overview of test format, to setting up the testing situation, and finally to specific administration instructions. Item-by-item instructions incorporating guidance for effective presentation as well as trouble-shooting information would be extremely useful, particularly since items vary in types of directions needed. For example, some items require special stress or intonation patterns to obtain the appropriate response, others require more secondary prompting or require instructions regarding "appropriate" responses.

### Format of Materials

The testing materials are designed for very convenient use, with a stand-up picture booklet and an easy-to-mark test booklet. The illustrations provided in the picure booklet are effective and clear, with only a few exceptions (e.g., in Form A, Item 62, the depiction of Easter was not clear to the reviewers or to the student tested). However, some improvements would greatly help the test administrator. The test booklet should include a brief statement of administration instructions, including sample comments for the beginning of a session. The booklet should include an explanation of the format, for example, the italicized statements are back-up prompts for use when the initial prompt does not elicit the desired response. In addition, directions for items involving special administration guidelines, as well as for items involving potential scoring difficulties, should be built into the booklet. In its present form, the test booklet relies on the test administrator's recall of the Examiner's Manual or on the test administrator's best judgment. Finally, with regard to the picture booklet, a single item per page format would be preferable to the present multi-item format.

## Scoring

Once a student has responded to an item, it is immediately checked as *correct* or *incorrect* in the test booklet. The procedure for scoring the test overall is very simple and is completed with the end of the test session: The highest level completed is the score received. An advantage to this procedure is that the administrator is not required beyond the actual testing time. The instructions provided for determining correct versus incorrect responses are limited and are given, for the most part, in general terms. More specific item-by-item instructions should be provided, along with some discussion designed to trouble shoot difficulties in scoring. The lack of item specific discussion leaves the test administrator with scoring questions.

## Test Content

The test authors have not provided any discussion or definition of oral language proficiency to guide the test administrator. The best indication of what the test assesses is gained by looking at the individual items presented and at the analyses of these items. In the IPT II, nearly a quarter of the items require naming of objects. For some of these items, the goal is to examine cultural and scientific knowledge, as well as linguistic skills. For example, students are asked to name four pictured holidays and the seasons in which they occur, to identify which three of six pictured underwater creatures need air, and to read a graph and identify specific dollar amounts. However valid and admirable the goal of assessing academic language skills in a test of oral language ability, academic communicative skills include vocabulary knowledge requiring much more in the way of linguistic skills. Such skills are not concerned with the correctness of the information conveyed as much as with the ability to communicate about more abstract, context-reduced ideas.

Many of the test items assess control of particular grammatical forms, although in some cases control of a form (e.g., regular plural) is assessed through only a single item. For several items the attempt to elicit a specific grammatical form results in unnatural discourse. In these items, there is the danger that an incorrect response is due to item construction rather than to lack of control of the form being assessed. As an example, one set refers to an illustration of a woman at the cashier's counter in a grocery store handing the cashier money. The first question prompt is "What is she doing?" The very likely response, "She is paying the cashier/

paying for the food," leads to a decided strangeness in the next two prompts. In these, the concept of payment is repeated and segmented into a giving and receiving of cash: "What does he (the cashier) want?" "What will she do?" Further awkwardness is introduced by the fact that the last of these prompts uses the future tense and expects the future tense in reply, while the illustration and the verb tense of the two prior prompts indicate ongoing action.

There are three items that assess control of English phonology. Since the test administrator pronounces the target words, there is no standardization of the items and no way of knowing whether variation in performance is due to differences in presentation or differences in student proficiency. An audiotape should be created for the items 55-57, or the items could be deleted.

## Technical Manual

To interpret the test items, the authors have attempted to categorize them in a number of ways. The Technical Manual presents an analysis in which each item is categorized in terms of Bloom's (1956) taxonomy of cognitive skills and of the distinction between Basic Interpersonal Communicative Skills (BICS) and Cognitive Academic Language Proficiency (CALP) described by Cummins (1980). A third column in the item analysis lists skills classifications based on the test authors' taxonomy. These analyses are uniformly presented without any definition of the terms or of the criteria used in categorizing the items. Test administrators are likely to be particularly confused by the authors' system of explications of skills tested. Some of the terms and skill definitions provided are general, others are more specific to the item, and not all are linguistic in nature (e.g., "justifies," "infers and identifies moods," "combines money units"). Since this classification system has been developed for the IPT II, the test administrator has no references to which to turn for explanation.

A Test Level Summary sheet is provided with the set of test materials. This sheet will not clarify the item analyses and may cause some confusion since the skills listed are not always congruent with the item analyses. It will be important to a test administrator's understanding of the test—and critical for any use of the test as a diagnostic instrument—to have a discussion and justification of the item analyses and of the relationships among them included in the Technical Manual. The Technical Manual provides much data on the validity and reliability of the test. The data are not presented, however, within the context of sufficient descriptive and explanatory text regarding the tests and analyses carried out. The analyses presented in the Manual describe data for 306 monolingual English students and only 153 language minority students; it would have been preferable to involve a larger population of language minority students in the testing and analyses.

*Summary*

The IPT II provides an individually administered assessment of oral language proficiency tested as knowledge of discrete grammatical skills. In describing the test and analyzing the item content, the authors make reference to processes of language acquisition and classification of cognitive skills, but do not explain these or their reflection in the test items. No definition of oral language proficiency is offered which might clarify the approach taken. While the test is described as a diagnostic instrument, specific guidance for its use in this way is not provided, and the lack of clarity in the item analyses makes it difficult to fully justify its use as a diagnostic tool. The strength of the test is that it makes it possible to distinguish between NEP, LEP, and FEP levels of English proficiency and that it does so within a format that is easily implemented.

### Reviewer's References

Bloom, B. (Ed.). (1956.) *Taxonomy of educational objectives: The classification of educational goals. Handbook I: Cognitive domain.* New York: David McKay.

Cummins, J. (1980). The cross-lingual dimensions of language proficiency: Implications for bilingual education and the optimal age issue. *TESOL Quarterly, 14*(2), 175-87.

# Ilyin Oral Interview

*Reviewed by*

**Roseanne Duenas Gonzalez**
**University of Arizona**

### Synopsis

Ilyin Oral Interview. IOI. Adults and students in Grades 5-12 of beginning and intermediate levels. Designed to assess oral proficiency in English in a controlled picture sequence situation and to provide diagnostic information on individual performance. Verbal responses are scored on a 0-2 scale, with one point for appropriateness of the response and one point for structural and grammatical accuracy. If incorrect information is rendered, no points for accuracy are awarded. Total possible points are 100. The total score corresponds to five ESL program levels of the San Francisco Community College District: ESL 100 (0-24), ESL 200 (25-30), ESL 300 (40-59), ESL 400 (60-74), and ESL 500/600 (75-100). Individual administration. 5-30 minutes. Two alternate forms labelled BILL and TOM (1976, 47 pp.). Test booklet includes a Technical and Administration Manual (1976, pp. 1-19). $27.45 per kit including Test Book manual and scoring pads of 50 sheets; $.11 per scoring pad, $21.95 per illustrated Test Book Manual, $5.50 per scoring pads of 50. Donna Ilyin. Newbury House, Harper & Row, Keystone Industrial Park, Scranton, PA 18512, USA, telephone: (800) 242-7737.

### Test References

Guyette, T. W. (1985). [Review of Ilyin oral interview]. In J. V. Mitchell, Jr. (Ed.), *The ninth mental measurement yearbook* (pp. 677-8). Lincoln, NE: Buros Institute of Mental Measurements & the University of Nebraska.

Day, E. C. (1981). Assessing communicative competence: Integrative assessment of second language learners. In J. G. Erickson & D. R. Omark (Eds.), *Communication assessment of the bilingual bicultural child* (pp. 179-97). Baltimore: University Park.

### Review

The Ilyin Oral Interview (IOI) ocupies a significant place in the development of direct assessments of oral communication in a controlled setting. It represents an attempt toward the assessment of natural speech, eliminating some of the difficulties in administration and scoring that are generally associated with informal interview assessments. Despite some shortcomings, the IOI is prototypical of the long line of controlled interview oral proficiency instruments that have followed. The primary contribution of this instrument is its focus on measuring the communicative value of examinee responses.

### Test Construction

One of the strengths of the IOI is its format consisting of a series of pictures sequentially arranged to elicit responses to 50 items (or 30 items in the abbreviated version of the test) pertaining to scenes depicting the daily activities of a young man. The Interview procedure comprises two forms that are labeled BILL and TOM respectively. The TOM Form accommodates weekday administrations (except Mondays); the BILL Form can be given on any day except Fridays (to keep the referents of "yesterday" and "tommorrow" consistent with weekdays or weekends). Divided into past, present, and future categories and various times of the day or the evening, the pictures act as stimuli for the elicitation of questions by both examiner and examinee. Two alternative forms of the test facilitate pre- and posttesting and allow for alternation of forms for test security purposes.

Like other oral production picture-based examinations, the IOI attempts to engage examinees in quasi-realistic activities for the purpose of eliciting natural speech. Responding to questions within contextual frameworks, students are tested on their ability to join various elements in the depicted scenes in an appropriate manner that corresponds with the extralinguistic context. As Oller (1979, p. 316) suggests, a sequence of pictures constitutes the basis for posing a wide range of meaningful questions. They also allow the examiner to proceed from eliciting simple to more complex responses while including the testing of different types of structures and a wide range of complexities of information. However, the IOI does not exploit the picture stimuli to the fullest extent possible. Instead, questions are posed in chronological order focusing on the activities of the fictitious person on a particular day moving from present to past or future respectively. Examinees are not challenged to tell a story based on the pictures or provide missing information in a story related by the examiner. As Oller suggests, creative examiners can expand testing strategies to create a more communicatively oriented tool.

### Test Administration Procedures

One of the most significant features of the IOI is its ease of administration. Taping and other complex analyses of responses are not required since scoring is completed as responses are elicited. The combination of the Administrative and Technical Test Manual with the test booklet allows for quick reference, thereby encouraging uniform and proper administration and scoring procedures. The IOI Manual also provides guidance concerning the selection of examinees and examiners. Administration procedures recommend an examiner who is an educated speaker of English, can conduct the interview in a friendly and conversational manner, and can recognize appropriate informational and structurally correct responses. However, test users have concluded that raters should be trained along more carefully selected guidelines than recommended in the Manual to prevent any interrater agreement problems that have been noted (Spurling, Richards, McGraw, & Setian, 1980, p. 50).

### Test Scoring Procedures

Scoring responses is neither time consuming nor complicated for an ESL professional. Responses are manually recorded and scored only when appropriate information has been communicated. Scoring is facilitated by delimiting the range of possible appropriate responses through the picture content. Based on a 3-point scale, scores range from 0-2, which corresponds to inappropriate or unintelligible information, appropriate or intelligible information with one or more grammatical errors, and appropriate and intelligible information with entire grammatical accuracy. The scoring is dependent on the meaningfulness of the responses; structural accuracy is subordinate to content accuracy. Despite the emphasis on communication, the Examination Manual explicitly calls for complete sentence structures. Phrasal units are not acceptable, and the examinee is asked to answer in a complete sentence in order to receive a score. In fact, the examiner is instructed in the Manual to show "a long span with index fingers," in order to indicate that a longer answer is required. This may tend to elicit artifical language that is not representative of a student's communicative competence. The scoring procedure does not encourage the creative use of language and may even discriminate against sophisticated language users.

### Users of the Ilyin Oral Interview

The IOI is useful for a variety of purposes and settings. Although the primary use of the IOI is to guide the placement of students in beginning and intermediate ESL classes, the Test Manual describes additional uses, such as screening for job placement, monitoring student achievement by means of pre- and posttesting procedures, and providing diagnostic information for teacher use. A significant feature of the IOI is that it discriminates particularly well at the beginning to intermediate level, a characteristic many oral proficiency instruments do not possess.

### Test Norms, Test Reliability, and Validity

According to the IOI Manual, placement levels and norms "should be used only as tentative until test users can see their own norms and guidelines for their particular programs" (Ilyin, 1976, p. M2). Though the information provided by the Manual correlating the scores to course levels used in San Francisco Community College District are helpful, more specific information defining the functional proficiency of these courses can be found in the Newbury House publication, *Concerned about Testing*. As indicated in the Manual, reliability scores in the experimental and first edition of the IOI were high, and small scale correlation studies between the IOI and other assessment measures indicated some relationship. Other test users reported that additional empirical studies have bourne out the IOI as a reliable and valid oral proficiency instrument. An external validity study conducted by Engelskirchen, Cottrell, and Oller (1981, pp. 83-93) concluded that the IOI shows substantial validity. Their interrater reliability study also yielded a satisfactory outcome which was upheld by Spurling et al. (1980, pp. 45-50). In the Engelskirchen study, reliability and validity criteria were tested in terms of agreement among native speakers rendering the IOI "a dependable measure of oral proficiency" (p. 83). The IOI Manual does not report the methodology and results of early or more current reliability and validity studies in adequate detail.

### Conclusions

An easy-to-administer placement instrument for beginning to intermediate ESL students, the IOI has served its purpose well. Forging the way for other communicative oral production measures, its major contribution has been to encourage the widespread use of oral production testing as an important component in language proficiency assessment. As Engleskirchen et al. (1981) observe, the IOI has filled the gap in the need for reliable and valid oral production instruments. The instrument continues to have merit, but it would benefit from a modification in its administration and scoring procedures that would reflect a more communicative perspective. The more natural the language sample elicited, the greater the possibility of assessing the examinee's true competency.

## Reviewer's References

Newbury House. *Concerned about testing.* Rowley, MA: Author.

Engelskirchen, A., Cottrell, E., & Oller, J. W., Jr. (1981). A study of the reliability and validity of the Ilyin oral interview. In A. S. Palmer, P. J. M. Groot, & G. A. Trosper (Eds.), *The construct validation of tests of communicative competence* (pp. 83-93). Washington, DC: Teachers of English to Speakers of Other Languages.

Gonzales, R. D. (1977). The design and validation of an evaluative procedure to diagnose the English aural-oral competency of a Spanish speaking person in the justice system. Unpublished doctoral dissertation, University of Arizona, Tuscon.

Ilyin, D. (1976). *The Ilyin oral interview.* Rowley, MA: Newbury.

Ilyin, D. (1982). Placement: Where and how? *Cross Currents, 9,* 67-80.

Oller, J. W., Jr. (1979). *Language tests at school.* London: Longman.

Spurling, S., Richards, E., McGraw, G., & Setian, R. (1980). The English language placement test and the oral ability of ELU arts students. *Language Centre Journal, 4*(1), 48-55.

# Interagency Language Roundtable Oral Proficiency Interview

*Reviewed by*

**Pardee Lowe, Jr.**
**US Government Interagency Language Roundtable**
**Rosslyn, Virginia**

## Synopsis

Interagency Language Roundtable (ILR) Oral (Proficiency) Interview. Formerly referred to as the Foreign Service Institute Oral Proficiency Interview (FSIOPI), sometimes called the OI (oral interview) or LPI (Language Proficiency Interview). Adolescents and educated adults. Designed to measure oral language skills in any language. Oral responses scored holistically against the ILR proficiency scale. The American Council on the Teaching of Foreign Languages/Educational Testing Service (ACTFL/ETS) Proficiency Guidelines are a derivative scale. Individual administration: requiring one (academic) or two (government) trained interviewers plus examinee. Time depends on examinee's level: 10-40 minutes, higher levels and problem cases require longer. Number of parallel forms infinite, depending on administrator's ability. Tester training required. Administration Manual: ETS Oral Proficiency Testing Manual (1982, 207 pp.), available only with ACTFL/ETS training. Technical Manual: *The ILR Handbook on Oral Interview Testing* (1983, 410 pp.), available only with ILR training. Cost of training by ACTFL or ETS depends on length and type. Familiarization is 1 hour to 2 days, full training is 3 to 5 days with subsequent interviews taped and conducted by the trainees and critiqued by the workshop leader(s). U.S. Government Interagency Language Roundtable, Box 9212, Rosslyn, VA 22209, USA. Publishers/trainers: ACTFL, 579 Broadway, Hastings-on-Hudson, NY 10076, USA, telephone: (914) 478-2011. ETS, Princeton, NJ 08541, USA, telephone: (609) 734-1487.

## Test References

Clark, J. L. D. (Ed.). (1978). *Direct testing of speaking proficiency: Theory and application.* Princeton, NJ: Educational Testing Service.

Frith, J. R. (Ed.). (1980). *Measuring spoken language proficiency.* Washington, DC: Georgetown University.

Higgs, T. V. (Ed.). (1984). *Teaching for proficiency, the organizing principle.* Lincolnwood, IL: National Textbook Company.

Lowe, P., & Liskin-Gasparro, J. E. (1982). *Testing speaking proficiency: The oral interview.* Washington, DC: Center for Applied Linguistics.

Lowe, P. (1985). The ILR proficiency scale as a synthesizing research principle: The view from the mountain. In C. J. James (Ed.), *Foreign language proficiency in the classroom and beyond* (pp. 9-53). Lincolnwood, IL: National Textbook Company.

## Review

The Oral (Proficiency) Interview is a direct test of language speaking ability. The test format varies by interviewer and, to a lesser extent, by agency. The basic intention of the OPI is to elicit from the examinee the richest possible sample of language in the shortest period of time. In a 10 to 40-minute period, a trained interviewer determines the extent to which an examinee's second language skills approximate those of an educated native speaker. Normally, the speech sample is tape recorded for later verification. Although interviews in academia may have only one administrator, all

| ILR Scale | ACTFL/ETS Scale |
|---|---|
| 5 | Superior |
| 4+ 4 | |
| 3+ 3 | |
| 2+ | Advanced Plus |
| 2 | Advanced |
| 1+ | Intermediate — High |
| 1 | Intermediate — Middle |
| | Intermediate — Low |
| 0+ | Novice — Middle |
| | Novice — Low |
| | 0 |

*Figure 1.* Relationship between the ILR scale and the ACTFL/ETS scale.

government interviews receive two ratings. Whenever a disagreement arises, a third rater is involved. The examinee's proficiency in general language is rated on a scale from 0 (no ability to communicate effectively in the language) to 5 (functioning as an educated native speaker). The scale includes +'s at Levels 0 through 4, for performance that substantially surpasses the requirements for a given level but fail to sustain perfor-

mance at the next higher level, thus furnishing an 11-point scale. The ACTFL/ETS scale, derived from the ILR scale, provides three distinctions each at the ILR 0-0+ and 1-1+ levels. Although more sensitive than the ILR scale at the lower levels of proficiency, the ACTFL/ETS scale places all ILR levels above three under an omnibus designation, *superior*. The ACTFL/ETS scale has a 9-point range (see Figure 1). The following comments apply to both scales.

The OPI is divided into four phases: Warm-up, Level Check, Probes, and Wind-down. The Warm-up introduces the interviewee to the OPI procedure, places the interviewee into the language, and provides the interviewer with a preliminary indication of level. The Level Check ascertains the accuracy of the preliminary indication and determines the breadth and depth of the interviewee's vocabulary, structure, and so forth, at the level in question. The third phase, Probes, confirms the highest level at which the interviewee can perform by seeking evidence of breakdown in structure, vocabulary, sociolinguistics, culture, and so forth. The final phase, Wind-down, provides a feeling of accomplishment by returning the interviewee from the rigors of the Probes to the comfortable level where he or she performed best earlier in the interview. In the hands of skilled interviewers, the four phases are encompassed within the framework of a relaxed, natural conversation.

Central to the OPI is the elicitation of performance requiring ACTFL/ETS/ILR (AEI for short) functions (see Figure 2), sometimes called "AEI task universals" to distinguish them from "functions and notions." The lower the level, the more lenient the accuracy requirements; the higher, the more stringent. By Level 3 (ACTFL/ETS Superior) in an interview of 20 minutes or longer only sporadic errors in basic structures are admissible. Using the preliminary determination of the student's level obtained in the Warm-up, the interviewer proceeds through the phases, formulating questions accordingly and focussing on performance on the AEI task universals indicative of the levels in question. A possible Level 1 interviewee would be asked to answer simple questions, to ask such questions in turn, and to roleplay Level 1 situations. Sustained performance on these tasks would suggest that the interviewee operates at a Level 1. Probing would establish whether the interviewee could perform at a higher level by concentrating on Level 2 tasks: operating in past and future time, joining sentences in limited discourse to describe and narrate, and handling situations with built-in complications. If the interviewee fails to accomplish these tasks or attempts them without the sustained and consistent performance outlined in the Level 2 definition, the Probes receive a rating of Level 2.

Content proves the most variable of the trisections' aspects. At the lowest levels, ILR 0/0+ (ACTFL/ETS Novice Low, Mid, and High), the content reflects achievement. At Level 1 and higher the content becomes more varied, and the interviewee must possess suitable breadth for the level in question. The ILR definitions stress survival areas, for example, purchasing a plane ticket or asking for directions, but numerous other areas could be and have been tested. In effect, interviewes operate with what they have, and testers seek content only when the interviewee is not forthcoming. To rate at a given level the test taker must perform suitable functions with requisite accuracy and sufficient control to prove sustained and consistent proficiency at the level in question. Training reveals the wide variety in acceptable content that is difficult to describe concisely here. It is the interplay of function, content, and accuracy that ultimately determines the final rating.

The ILR scale is developmental in nature. At the summit the scale refers to the proficiency of an educated native speaker (ENS). This does not imply that all natives are at Level 5. ENS status is normally acquired through long-term familiarization (from infancy to university graduate school) with varying kinds of language and social groups over a wide number of concrete and abstract subject areas. Although most individuals at Level 5 possess a diploma, ENS status is proven by the examinee's ability to use the language. ILR experience shows that the majority of native speakers of English probably fall at Level 3. In ILR experience, the number of nonnative Level 5's is miniscule. Due to the scale's developmental nature, it is impossible for a 10-year-old to obtain Level 5, as a child that age lacks the required higher level vocabulary and the ability to handle highly abstract concepts and ideas. The interview has focused on adults, although high school students have been tested; experiments using the ACTFL/

| Level | Functions | Content | Accuracy |
|---|---|---|---|
| ILR Speaking Level | Task accomplished, attitudes expressed, tone conveyed. | Topics, subject areas, activities, and jobs addressed. | Acceptability, quality, and accuracy of message conveyed. |
| 5 | Functions equivalent to an Educated Native Speaker (ENS). | All subjects. | Performance equivalent to Educated Native Speaker. |
| 4 | Able to tailor language to fit audience, counsel, persuade, negotiate, represent a point of view, and interpret for dignitaries. | All topic normally pertinent to professional needs. | Nearly equivalent to ENS. Speech is extensive, precise, appropriate to every occasion with only occasional errors. |
| 3 | Can converse in formal and informal situations, resolve problem situations, deal with unfamiliar topics, provide explanations, describe in detail, support opinions, and hypothesize. | Practical, social, professional, and abstract topics, particular interests, and special fields of competence. | Errors virtually never interfere with understanding and rarely disturb the ENS. Only sporadic errors in basic structures. |
| 2 | Able to fully participate in casual conversations; can express facts; give instructions; describe, report on, and provide narration about current, past, and future activities. | Concrete topics such as own background, family, and interests, work, travel, and current events. | Understandable to NS *not* used to dealing with foreigners; sometimes miscommunicates. |
| 1 | Can create with the language; ask and answer questions, participate in short conversations. | Everyday survival topics and courtesy requirements. | Intelligible to an NS used to dealing with foreigners. |
| 0 | No functional ability. | None. | Unintelligible. |

*Figure 2.* Functional Trisection of Oral Proficiency Levels

ETS scale with younger speakers are underway.

The interview is a sophisticated, integrative testing procedure, permitting the checking of vocabulary, grammar, pronunciation, fluency, and culture. These are reflected through the normal linguistic components of language as well as through subtleties of meaning expressed through nuances, register, and attitude. The test is not an *instrument* because the procedure is neither fixed in print nor invariable. The procedure varies with the ability of the examinee and the skill of the interviewer(s), which represents both a strength and a weakness.

## Training

Training interviewers is language-specific: The pattern of errors characterizing a language that relies on word order differs from that of inflected languages. Thus, interviewer training often involves the discussion of typical errors or inadequacies in the learner's second language. The high incidence of colloquial speakers in ESL compared to the more common classroom-trained speakers in foreign languages (French, etc.) also strengthens the case for language-specific training.

To officially administer the procedure, interviewers must be certified, and recertified after a lapse of 2 years. Training in government lasts 2 weeks; training in academia usually 4 1/2 days with subsequent interviews taped and conducted by the trainee and critiqued by the workshop leaders. Certification for testing in the academic setting is available through ACTFL.

## Stability of the Standard

Interviewers maintain the standard by frequently administering tests. If too few tests are administered or all examinees comprise only in a limited range of proficiency levels, an interviewer's grasp of the standards may drift. Both retraining and a set of calibrated standard tapes should be available to combat this problem.

## Uses

This testing procedure is best employed as an end-of-course measure in order to demonstrate to administrators, teachers, and students the functional ability the student has attained. The procedure may serve as a part of a placement battery when a prospective student possesses extensive oral skills, possibly from intensive language training, language houses, study or living abroad. The OPI should not be used frequently in class. Peace Corps interviews conducted at 2-week intervals revealed no progress on the ILR scale in intensive language courses lasting 6 hours a day (C. Wilds, 1980, personal communication). Moreover, the OPI procedure, even in the ACTFL/ETS version, does not discriminate finely at the lower end. A number of other tests are better suited to discrete-point measurement, which is more useful at this level. One such oral test is the Ilyin Oral Interview.

## Reliability, Validity, Practicality

In interview testing the critical psychometric considerations of reliability and validity manifest themselves as interrater reliability and content validity. Unlike other types of foreign language test procedures, such as the cloze, there are few studies of the reliability and validity of the OPI. The major data are experimental; the procedure has proved accurate for assigning government employees to positions requiring specific ILR levels. The most accessible government study (Adams, 1978) demonstrates the OPI's high degree of interrater reliability—the ability of two different trained interviewers to assign the same rating to a performance sample—citing Pearson product moment corelations of .87 and higher.

The content validity of the interview depends, among other things, on the question types used at each level. Different levels require different question types, topics, and functions (Lowe, 1981). In U.S. government OPI programs, validity and reliability are maintained by monitoring interviews and ratings and by periodic refresher training.

Studies conducted outside the U.S. government context have also addressed reliability and validity issues. Shohamy (1983) found that choice of task could affect the content validity of oral interviews similar to the ILR. Bachman and Palmer (1981) investigated the OPI's construct validity and the traits of both speaking and reading through the classic multitrait-multimethod matrix, supplemented by Campbell-Fiske criteria for convergent and discriminant validity and also by confirmatory factor analysis. They found evidence for the convergent and discriminant validity of their version of the oral interview procedure and strong support for the distinctness of speaking and reading as traits, thus rejecting the unitary trait hypothesis of language proficiency in favor of partially divisible language competence.

As studies of oral interview procedures proliferate, a cautionary note is, perhaps, in order. A classification of such procedures might prove necessary with accompanying studies investigating the psychometric properties of a given oral interview procedure. Currently, three categories of OPI suffice: (a) ILR oral interviews in the strictest sense; (b) ILR-like interviews approximating, but not strictly following the ILR practice (in which group one might place Shohamy and Bachman and Palmer); and (c) non-ILR-like oral interview procedures, such as the Ilyin Oral Interview.

In its strictest form, the OPI possesses a high degree of face validity because it requires examinees to use spoken language. Unlike recorded or paper-and-pencil tests, the OPI requires both a highly trained test administrator and rater, rendering its frequent official administration costly and impractical. On the other hand, no other procedure, to our knowledge, assesses an equally wide range of speaking abilities with suitable high face validity. Whether one wants to know if a speaker can survive for a day or two as a tourist, live and work in the country, or discuss abstract topics, the

OPI is a suitable assessment procedure.

## Conclusion

This discussion of the OPI has addressed the interrelationship of the ILR scale to the ACTFL/ETS scale, the OPI procedure and its use, the necessity of training, the stability of standards, and the reliability, validity, and practicality of the procedure. It remains to be stressed that with properly trained interviewers, the OPI's greatest utility probably lies in exit and placement testing. Its ultimate utility may lie beyond testing per se in its effect on curriculum. In this case, teaching for the test—teaching for general function foreign language ability—is not to be discouraged.

## Reviewer's References

Adams, M. L. (1978). Measuring foreign language speaking proficiency: A study of agreement among raters. In J. L. D. Clark (Ed.), *Direct testing of speaking proficiency: Theory and application* (pp. 129-49). Princeton, NJ: Educational Testing Service.

Bachman, L. F., & Palmer, A. S. (1981). The construct validation of the FSI oral interview. *Language Learning, 31*(1), 67-86.

Higgs, T. V., & Clifford, R.T. (1982). The push toward communication. In T. V. Higgs (Ed.), *Curriculum, competence, and the foreign language teacher* (pp. 57-79). Skokie, IL: National Textbook Company.

Lowe, P., Jr. (1978). Third rating of FSI interviews. In J. L. D. Clark (Ed.), *Direct testing of speaking proficiency: Theory and application* (pp.159-69). Princeton, NJ: Educational Testing Service.

Lowe, P., Jr. (1981). Structure of the oral interview and content validity. In A. S. Palmer, P. J. M. Groot, & G. A. Trosper (Eds.), *The construct validation of tests of communicative competence* (pp. 71-80). Washington, DC: TESOL.

Shohamy, E. (1983). The stability of oral proficiency assessment in the oral interview testing procedures. *Language Learning, 33*(4), 527-40.

# John/Fred Test

*Reviewed by*

**Linda Smith Kharde**
**Center for Applied Linguistics**
**Washington, DC**

## Synopsis

The John Test: A Test of Oral Proficiency for ESL Placement. 1975. Adult. Designed as an oral placement test for adults in nonacademic ESL programs. Test contains three parts: Comprehension Questions; Connected Discourse; and Asking Questions. Verbal responses in Parts I and III scored as follows: 0 = no response; 1 = response indicated understanding of the question but contains one or more errors; 2 = response is completely correct. One point is subtracted for each requested repetition. Verbal responses in Part II are rated separately for fluency, structure, pronunciation, and vocabulary. Individual. 10-15 minutes. Two forms: The John Test (1975) and The Fred Test (1983); two pages of picture cues and one page answer sheet per form; a short form of The John Test is also included. Administration manuals: The John Test (1975, 4 pp.); The John Test and The Fred Test (1983, 9 pp.). Technical information about form equivalence and a table of standard scores is included in the Administration Manual (1983). $5.00 per examiner's kit for each form, including Manual, 2 picture booklets, 20 answer sheets, 1 answer sheet on ditto master, and 1 shortened version (John only). The John Test is not copyrighted; additional copies may be duplicated without reordering or permission. The Fred Test is copyrighted, but the publisher does not require permission for duplication for program use. Ray Kesper, Linda Ann Kunz, O. T. Leyds, and Robert Viscount at Regional Opportunity Centers, CUNY, for The John Test; Jean Bodman and Jack Richmond for the Shortened Version of The John Test; and Linda Ann Kunz, et al., for The Fred Test, Language Innovations, Inc. (LINC), 2112 Broadway, Room 515, New York, NY 10023, USA, telephone: (212) 873-9476, Tues. and Fri. 1-5 p.m.

## Review of The John Test

The John Test and The Fred Test are alternate forms of a placement test developed specifically for use in ESL programs for nonacademic adult students in the U.S. and Canada. The forms test listening and speaking skills through a series of seven pictures, which show a day in the life of John (or Fred). The test can be used with adults from any ethnic group and with nonliterates.

Designed as a quick placement tool, the test makes level distinctions that are adequate for most adult programs, that is, it can place students into five or six levels ranging from beginning to high intermediate. It contains natural, everyday language, including common verbs and simple past tense in a generally familiar, although somewhat overly urban context.

The test is fairly easy to administer and takes 10 to 15 minutes to administer. A "Shortened Version" of The John Test is also available; although several users have reported that it is less reliable than the longer forms.

Administration and scoring instructions are summarized on the first page of the Test Manual; this provides an overview for first-time test users and a succinct review for experienced testers who have not recently administered the test. It is also a necessary reference during test administration, since the oral cues are on this page. Until these oral cues have been memorized, the tester must refer between the Manual and the answer sheet. Visual highlighting of the oral cues in the Manual would minimize this problem.

Individual test items are scored during the test. Only a few minutes are required after the test for the examiner to tally the points earned and to note some general comments about the examinee. If all three parts are given, the total score (range = 1-100) can be converted to a standard score based on a mean of 50 and a standard deviation of 10 by referring to a table in the Test Manual. Thus, minor differences in the difficulty of the two forms have been adjusted statistically, albeit based on the results of a study involving a small sample.

The Manual also contains a short section on interpreting scores in which programs are advised to set their own norms for placement, depending on the characteristics of their students, program goals, and the level of each course.

## Comments on Individual Parts of the Test

In Part I, Comprehension Questions, listening and speaking skills are tested together. Credit is given (1 point) for responses that are comprehensible, but not grammatically accurate. An additional point is awarded for responses that are accurate, that is, as a native speaker would respond. This innovative distinction is particularly appropriate in a test designed for use with nonacademic adults, for whom the ability to convey a message, without respect to grammatical accuracy, is often the paramount need. Another aspect of the scoring in this section (and in Part III) is that one point is subtracted each time the examinee requests a repetition. This practice may be too severe, particularly in a test for lower level students.

The illustrations are a crucial element: The examinee must understand them in order to understand the test as a whole, as well as individual items. A certain amount of ambiguity, sex-role stereotyping, and cultural bias is unavoidable in the pictures for almost any test; this test is no exception. For example, it may be difficult for an examinee to answer the question, "What is the bus driver doing?", because it is not clear from the picture that John is putting money in the fare box. The pictures are readily compehended, however, and should not pose serious problems for examinees.

In Part II, "Connected Discourse", the student is asked to retell the story, that is, to describe John's (or Fred's) day in the past tense. Because the examinee is familiar with the pictures and the overall context from Part I, it is usually possible to elicit some narrative, depending on the examinee's level. Scoring of Part II is subjective, relying on the tester's judgment to determine a score on four scales: fluency, structure, pronunciation, and vocabulary. Guidelines for each scale are provided in the Test Manual. In these guidelines, the highest score on the scale is described as "equal to a native speaker"; however, elsewhere in the Test Manual, "comparison with other students being tested at the time" is suggested. These instructions are contradictory. Nonetheless, individual programs can determine local guidelines for the scales so that raters will score reliably. Once this has been accomplished, this part of the test can provide useful information for student placement.

In the third and final part of the test, "Asking Questions," the examinee is instructed to ask questions based on an oral cue, for example, "Ask me how old he is." Although the task in this part of the test is worthwhile, this item type is confusing for the examinee and does not resemble natural communication. In addition, examinees with prior (classroom) experience with this elicitation technique will have an advantage over others who have never been exposed to it. It is the practice in many programs to omit this part of the test.

Tester-training can be done in 1-2 hour session which includes practice in administering tests and scoring; this is particularly important for Part II. Some useful training suggestions are included in the Manual. Testers should preferably be trained ESL teachers and native speakers of English, in order to make scoring judgements about performance on the language scales in Part II and about native speaker-like responses in Parts I and II.

The Manual does not provide recommendations about tester qualifications or interrater reliability figures. Nonetheless, a number of adult programs currently using the test have reported that, with periodic inhouse training and discussion, raters generally provide comparable ratings on all parts of the test.

It is interesting to note that all of the test users interviewed have modified or adapted the test. For example, one program colored John's hair yellow to help the examinee locate John in each picture. Since the test is not copyrighted, there is no reason not to revise the test as necessary, with the understanding that this reduces their ability to compare test results with those of other test users. The publisher does not appear to be concerned about loss of income through the duplication of materials without permission. It is commendable that the sole motivation in producing the test was to meet the need for a test of this nature, at a time when there were no commercially available tests designed specifically for use in adult-level programs. There are tentative plans to revise the test to incorporate some of the changes that have been suggested by test users. If this were done, revision of the Test Manual to contain notes for individual items would clarify existing scoring ambiguities.

The John and Fred Tests are short, easy to administer and score, and have been used effectively to place students into adult-level programs in which oral/aural skills are emphasized. The test is adequate to serve the purposes of program placement, but its validity as an adult-level general proficiency test is limited, because the full range of survival competencies is not covered. Use of this test should be carefully weighted by programs in which pre- and posttesting with a statistically reliable and valid proficiency test is required for program evaluation purposes.

# Language Assessment Battery

*Reviewed by*

**Gerald E. DeMauro**
**Educational Testing Service**
**Princeton, New Jersey**

### Synopsis

Language Assessment Battery. LAB-82. Limited-English-proficient, nonnative English-speaking students. Grades K-12. Designed to measure English and Spanish proficiency for program placement and program evaluation. Verbal and written responses scored as correct or incorrect according to key. Total correct for each section and total test referred to English proficient or limited-English-proficient norms (English version) or Spanish-proficient norms (Spanish version). Speaking section (Grades 3-12) and Listening/Speaking section (Grades K-2), individually administered. Reading/Writing section (Grades 1-2) and the Beginning Reading section for spring of kindergarten or fall of Grade 1, group administered. Two forms in each of two languages (English and Spanish): Examiner's Manuals (1982, 32 pp. at Level I, 24 pp. at Levels II, III, IV). No published technical manual; technical data and content specifications available on request. $5.00 per specimen set, including either English or Spanish tests of Levels I and II or III and IV. $.75 for student booklets ($30.00 per package of 50). Examiner's Directions ($2.75 per copy), $25.00 per package of 100 answer sheets, $3.00 per scoring mask, $3.00 per norms booklet. New York City Board of Education. New York City Board of Education, O.E.A. Scan Center, 49 Flatbush Avenue Extension, 5th Floor, Brooklyn, NY 11201, USA, Attn: Grace Bijou, telephone: (718) 596-5226/7.

### Review

The Language Assessment Battery (LAB-82) was developed by the Division of Curriculum and Instruction

of the New York City Public Schools. Widely used in the Northeast, particularly New York City, New Jersey, and Connecticut, for student placement and program evaluation, LAB-82 should not be confused with earlier tests developed by the New York City Public Schools that bear the same name and are published by a commercial publishing company. The 1982 edition is substantially different from the earlier edition.

LAB-82 has Spanish and English versions. Each has two equated forms (A and B) and four articulated levels with a single scale covering Grades K-2, 3-5, 6-8, and 9-12. Level I (K-2) has a Listening/Speaking section (30 items), and a Reading and Writing section (28 items) for Grades 1 and 2. A new Beginning Reading test (28 items) to replace the Level I Reading and Writing section for Spring Kindergarten and Fall Grade 1 has recently been developed and will be available for the Fall 1987 administration. Level II has a Listening section (30 items), a Speaking section (26 items), a Reading section (36 items), and a Writing section (20 items). Levels III and IV have 38 items, 26 items, 55 items, and 20 items for Listening, Speaking, Reading, and Writing respectively.

Norms were based on representative samples of English proficient, limited-English-proficient, and Spanish-proficient students. Norms are reported by grade for both Forms A and B for Fall and Spring administrations.

The examination includes a variety of item types, such as question-answer in the Listening subtest, a listening cloze, reading cloze based on a systematic deletion procedure in the Reading subtest, structure items in the Writing subtest, and questions about pictures in the Speaking subtest.

For Level I, norms are available for the Kindergarten Listening and Speaking test and for the Grade 1 and 2 total test score, which also includes the Reading and Writing subtest. For Levels II-IV norms are published for English-proficient students on the English test and for Spanish-proficient students on the Spanish test for total test score, excluding the Speaking subtest (the only individually administered subtest). Norms for limited-English-proficient (LEP) students on the English test for subtest and total test scores (excluding Speaking in Levels II-IV) have been generated but are not in published form. Subtest norms for all tests and levels including the new Beginning Reading subtest but excluding Speaking in Levels II-IV, have also been generated but are not in printed form.

LAB-82 was an outgrowth of the Lau versus Nichols U.S. Supreme Court decision and the Aspira Consent Decree that mandated the education of students in an appropriate language environment. LAB-82 undertook the considerable task of developing both an instrument that could be used to measure a wide range of English skills in Grades K-12, and a parallel Spanish language version of the same test. The Spanish version is not a translation of the English version, but was developed concurrently with it.

Construct validity is crucial to the LAB-82, as it was designed to identify students for placement in appropriate educational programs. One way to demonstrate construct validity is to show that an instrument can distinguish LEP students from English-proficient students on the basis of an underlying English proficiency construct. To accomplish this, responses to the English version items by LEP (bilingual and English as a second language) students and English-proficient students were examined via Rasch analysis. Weighted mean square fit statistics were computed for test items. Misfitting items, those with mean square fits of one or more standard deviations above the average subtest mean square fit, were eliminated (O'Brien, 1985).

The criterion score for student placement in an entitlement program (ESL or bilingual) in New York City was set by the court at the 20th percentile based on an English-proficient student score distribution. This means that 80% of the English proficient students would pass the test. To accomplish this purpose appropriately, the test was constructed so that, at each level, the average percentage of English-proficient students answering an item correct would also be 80%. For maximum discrimination, items answered correctly by 50% of LEP students were selected. These dual criteria were applied to the selection of each item.

Grade KR-20 reliability for limited-English-proficient students on the English version ranged from .92 to .96 on total tests and from .80 to .95 on the four subtests (Listening, Speaking, Reading, and Writing).

One way to measure whether a test assesses the same trait among populations of different abilities is to determine whether the rank order of the difficulties of the item is the same for these groups. To determine whether the test measures the same underlying English language proficiency variable in the same way across the entire language proficiency continuum, a rank order correlation of the item difficulties for the English-proficient students and the limited-English-proficient students was performed at each level, for each form for both subtests and total tests. In 80% of the cases, correlation coefficients exceed .78, demonstrating that the test performs in the same way across levels of English language proficiency (Abbot, 1985).

A Rasch procedure similar to that used in the development of the English version was followed in the development of the Spanish version of the test. Items were selected based on mean square fit statistics and difficulty levels. Because the Spanish proficient students might have had their Spanish contaminated by residence in an English-speaking environment, it was reasoned that they would be somewhat less proficient in Spanish than the English-proficient students in English would be; therefore, the Spanish version was designed to have items that would be passed by 70% of the Spanish-proficient group on the average (as compared to 80% correct for English proficient students on the English version of the test). Grade KR-20 estimates (.86 to .96) were comparable to those obtained for the English version. A study by O'Brien (1985) suggests that the Spanish version of the test is also a measure of a single proficiency trait.

The availability of versions of the test in two languages makes it possible to determine language dominance and allows the use of the test in the evaluation of Spanish language programs. Using the English instrument for program evaluation is contingent upon the test's being sufficiently easy to discriminate among students of low-level English abilities and measuring the same trait over the whole range of English abilities (DeMauro, 1983). LAB-82 meets these two criteria. Furthermore, four articulated levels and two equated forms of the test permit its application for multiyear programs: Performances may be compared as the student progresses through the program and forms may be interchanged to prevent familiarity with test content. The availability of equated forms and levels is a property that is often overlooked in the evaluation of instruments that measure growth over many years.

LAB-82's use in program evaluation is facilitated by the availability of English-proficient and LEP norms. Fall and Spring norm groups may serve as proxy comparison groups as is common in Chapter I programs. Different models may utilize either the published English proficient norms or the LEP student norms available through the New York City Public Schools Office of Educational Assessment. Other criterion-related uses of the test have been suggested via use of latent trait models (DeMauro, 1985).

## Reviewer's References

Abbott, M. M. (1982). Language assessment battery (LAB)-1982. Paper presented to the Arizona State Department of Education, Phoenix.

Abbott, M. M. (1985, April). Theoretical considerations in the measurement of the English-language proficiency of limited-English-proficient students. Paper presented at the annual meeting of the National Council on Measurement in Education, Chicago.

DeMauro, G. E. (1983). The paradox of the proper norm for ESL evaluation. In S. Seidner (Ed.), *Issues of language assessment. Vol. II: Language assessment and curriculum planning* (pp. 45-57). Springfield, IL: Illinois State Department of Education.

DeMauro, G. E. (1985, April). Issues in the placement of limited-English-proficient students and in evaluation of their instructional programs. Paper presented at the annual meeting of the National Council on Measurement in Special Education, Chicago.

O'Brien, M. L. (1985, April). Psychometric issues relevant to selecting items and assembling parallel forms of language proficiency instruments. Paper presented at the annual meeting of National Council on Measurement in Education, Chicago.

# Language Assessment Scales

*Reviewed by*

**Mary McGroarty**
**University of California at Los Angeles**

## Synopsis

Language Assessment Scales. LAS. Grades 2-5 (LAS I); Grades 6 and up (LAS II). Designed to measure oral language skills in English or Spanish. Verbal or motor responses (i.e., pointing to a picture) are compared with expected answers or to previously determined standards of production. Total correct answers converted to weighted scored derived through procedures explained below and used to assign students to one of five proficiency levels. Level 1, nonspeaker, no control of the language skills; Level 2, nonspeaker with some isolated linguistic skills; Level 3, limited speaker; Level 4, fluent (proficient) speaker; Level 5, (highly articulate) fluent speaker.

Cut-offs are different for the two levels of the test.

| Total Score | | LAS Oral Proficiency Level |
|---|---|---|
| Level I | Level II | |
| 85-100 | 92-100 | 5 |
| 75-84 | 82-91 | 4 |
| 65-74 | 72-81 | 3 |
| 55-64 | 62-71 | 2 |
| 0-54 | 0-61 | 1 |

Individually administered. 20 minutes to administer the Long Form, 10 minutes for Short Form. 2 forms (A & B) for both levels. Student response forms are available in two formats: Multiple Copy Scoresheet (MCS) for hand or machine tabulation (SCAN-TRON) with a tear-off sheet for the teacher, administered with booklet of cue pictures; and individual test booklets that contain all cue pictures. $63.95 per Examiner Kit for MCS format and $63.95 per kit for test booklets format. Kit includes packet of 50 response forms, Administration Manual for all forms (1983, 25 pp.), Scoring and Interpretation Manual (1983, 58 pp.), and an audio cassette containing test items and two stories. All kit items available separately: 50 MCS test sheets, $28.95; 50 student test booklets, $37.50; Administration Manual, $5.50; Scoring and Interpretation Manual, $12.95; audio cassette, $9.50; cassette with additional stories, $9.50. Technical Manual for Form A, based on 7 years of LAS Research, $19.95 (1981, 134 pp.). Technical Supplement for Level I Form B, $5.50 (1982, 30 pp.). Technical Supplement for Level II Form B, $5.50 (1982, 26 pp.). Technical Supplement for LAS Short Form, $5.50 (1983, 27 pp.). Also available for computerized data management of LAS proficiency data: AUTOLAS for Apple, TRS-80 and IBM microcomputers; converts raw scores to converted scores and proficiency levels; lists, sorts and tabulates LAS and achievement data. Developed by Edward DeAvila and Sharon Duncan.

Published by Linguametrics Group, P. O. Box 3495, San Rafael, CA 94912-3495, USA, telephone: (800) 247-9436; in CA (800) 624-7373.

## Test References

Brainard, C. (1978). [Review of language assessments scales, LAS I for Grades K-5, English/Spanish]. *Modern Language Journal, 62*(7), 350-1.

Haber, L. (1985). [Review of language assessment scales]. In J. V. Michell, Jr. (Ed.), *The ninth mental measurements yearbook* (pp. 808-11). Lincoln, NE: Buros Institute of Mental Measurements & the University of Nebraska.

## Review

### Description

The LAS is a comprehensive oral language assessment measure that aims to provide "an overall picture of language proficiency based on a student's performance on four linguistic subsystems." The subsystems assessed are: the phonemic system (sounds); the lexical system (words); the syntactic system (rules for sentence construction); and the pragmatic system (ability to carry out tasks using language), according to the Test Manual. The latter subsystem is not in fact tested directly, rather a teacher or other adult rates a student's probable ability to carry out hypothetical speech acts. Designers specify that students are to be tested by qualified school personnel who speak "the language of the test as a first language."

The phonemic subsystem of language is tested by means of the student's ability to understand differences between minimal pairs (Section I, 30 items) and by ability to repeat the sounds of the languages (Section III, 36 items). These are unusual tasks in any language and do not particularly enhance the utility of the test. The lexical subsystem (termed "referential" by the authors), which is comprised of 20 items based on the Thorndike-Lorge Word List, requires the student to name an item pictured in the test materials. The syntactic subsystem is measured through two subscales, Oral Comprehension and Oral Production. Oral Production requires not only sentence-level comprehension and production, but also memory for connected discourse and ability to narrate as the section contains a story-retelling task. Storytelling is scored holistically according to one of five levels: Level 1, minimal; Level 5, "articulate native-speaker" proficiency. Sentence Comprehension (Section IV, 10 items) asks the child to select one of three pictures based on a taped stimulus sentence. The raw scores for all of these items are converted to weighted scores with the greatest weighting placed on the story-retelling task. The converted scores are added to provide a subtotal which is multiplied by 100 to give the student's total score.

The pragmatic aspect of language is assessed by the

optional Observation Form, consisting of 10 questions about the student's perceived oral language ability rated on -3 to +3 scale. It is intended for a teacher or other adult who knows the student well (someone other than the examiner) who must judge the student's ability to carry out several tasks using language. This subsystem is meant to be used only for comparison. The authors recommend that it be used only with students whose total score is within one standard error (2 points) of the cut-off point for a particular proficiency level. The authors refer to this range as the "gray area." The student's average rating is added to or subtracted from the total score. Supposedly, use of the pragmatic section as additional information on the student's language skills can reduce error of misclassification to proficiency level.

LAS I and LAS II are very similar. They are the same length. On both tests, Sections I and III (the sound system) and II (vocabulary) are nearly identical, while Section IV (comprehension) contains longer sentences with more embedding in LAS II. In LAS II, the stories used as the stimuli for retelling have been modified in subject matter to fit the presumed interests of the age group tested; for example, students might be asked to talk about the adventures of a rock band in LAS II, instead of the trial of a monster who drank pink ink, as in LAS I. In LAS II the retelling task can be adapted to assess written as well as oral production, and some relevant advice on scoring such production is then provided in the Test Manual.

## Technical Information

In the Test Manuals, particularly for LAS I, the developers provide several types of statistical reliability along with descriptive statistics (mean scores and standard deviations) for the age groups tested. More extensive information, based on larger samples, is available for LAS I. Depending on the statistics used, reliability was moderate to high. Interrater reliability for the storytelling task was high (interscorer correlations ranging from .86 to .95 for LAS I, an average of .80 for LAS II). Within each language, the subscales of the tests were moderately to highly intercorrelated (.38 to .69), with the exception of the weak correlations (.15 to .21) for vocabulary and comprehension as compared to total score. Internal reliability coefficients, available for LAS I but not LAS II, were moderate (.39) to high (.96) with most in the .60 to .80 range, thus indicating good internal consistency.

The authors present validity studies that compare student LAS test scores with teacher judgments of students who are, respectively, fluent or limited speakers of a language. For LAS I, the research showed that the test and the teacher judgments generally separated students similarly. The LAS II validity studies were based on the agreement between test results and the judgments of bilingual adults used to separate monolingual speakers of English versus Spanish. These results are encouraging, but the classifications are so broad that many questions about validity for the five levels of the test go unanswered.

The technical information provided shows that the test is reasonably reliable according to the usual criteria. Claims for validity based on agreement with adult ratings or intercorrelations of the subscales are not as strong. (See Merino and Spencer, 1983, for a detailed comparison of the LAS and other assessment instruments for determining oral language skills.)

## Additional Comments

The attempt to assess all the subsystems of language is theoretically interesting but not extremely enlightening from a practical point of view. The most valuable aspects of the LAS are the sections on Vocabulary, Sentence Comprehension, and Storyretelling. Exhaustive testing of phonemic discrimination offers intriguing research data but does not provide much guidance in gauging a student's ability to understand or produce natural language. The LAS has been used in several investigations of bilingual children's language proficiency (see Johnson, 1983, for an example of one such study). There is some evidence that the overall LAS score in English correlates moderately, as might be expected, with academic achievement in English verbal skills (see Merino & Spencer, 1983; Ulibarri, Spencer, & Rivas, 1981).

According to the experience of some practitioners, there is a perceptible developmental trend on the LAS I: Student performance tends to increase with age. LAS II is thought to be more difficult than LAS I. This is not surprising, since the comprehension and production tasks place greater demands on memory and discourse production skills as the student advances along the test's age norms.

A reading and writing component of the LAS is under preparation and will be available in 1987. Use of the new LAS Literacy test in conjunction with the Oral LAS may provide a more comprehensive assessment of overall language proficiency.

In sum, the LAS is an acceptable measure of oral proficiency in English or Spanish, suitable for use with students in elementary and junior high schools. While it could be used with older students to assess language skills, the subject matter does not seem appropriate for students over 16-years-old. As the test developers point out, the test is good, but not infallible. In cases of suspected error, a student's score on the LAS should be checked against other sources of information on student language skill before an individual placement decision is made.

## Reviewer's References

Johnson, D. M. (1983). Natural language by design: A classroom experiment in social interaction and second language acquisition. *TESOL Quarterly*, *17*(2), 55-68.

Merino, B. J., & Spencer, M. (1983). The comparability of English and Spanish versions of oral language proficiency instruments. *NABE Journal*, 7(2), 1-31.

Ulibarri, D. M., Spencer, M. L., & Rivas, G. A. (1981). Language proficiency and academic achievement: A study of language proficiency tests and their relationship to school ratings as predictors of academic achievement. *NABE Journal*, 5(3), 47-80.

# Listening Comprehension Picture Test

*Reviewed by*

**Phyllis Kuehn Abdelal**
**Georgia State University**

## Synopsis

Listening Comprehension Group Tests: Listening Comprehension Picture Test. LCPT. 1981. Beginning and intermediate adult students of ESL. Designed to measure listening comprehension of basic English structures without requiring reading or writing skills. Multiple-choice scoring. The examinee listens and answers questions by choosing from pictures or words *yes* and *no*. Score is number correct. Group administration. 30 minutes. Two forms of the LCPT are printed in the Student Picture Booklet, $2.95 (1981, 8 pp.). Examiner's Test Manual, $4.50 (1981, 15 pp.). Technical Guide, $5.95 (1981, 11 pp.). $5.95 per 50 LCPT answer sheets and 2 keys. Student Picture Booklet and Examiner's Test Manual by Donna Ilyin. Technical Guide by Donna Ilyin and Susan Rubin. Newbury House Publishers, 54 Warehouse Lane, Rowley, MA 01969, USA, telephone: (617) 948-2704 and (800) 343-1240.

## Test References

Newbury House. *Concerned about testing*. Rowley, MA: Author.

Richards, R. A. (1985). [Review of listening comprehension group tests]. In J. V. Mitchell, Jr. (Ed.), *The ninth mental measurements yearbook* (pp. 864-6). Lincoln, NE: Buros Institute of Mental Measurements & the University of Nebraska.

## Review

The LCPT measures listening comprehension of basic question words and structures and requires minimal literacy skills. Designed for use as a placement test in beginning and intermediate adult education ESL courses, the LCPT may be also used with low beginners in college intensive English programs.

The LCPT contains 33 multiple-choice items based on a series of pictures sharing a simple story line. The pictures are similar to those found in the Ilyin Oral Interview. The examinee looks at a picture (or series of pictures) and listens to a statement. The examinee hears questions based on the oral and visual information supplied. The examinee answers each question by choosing the letter representing one of five alternatives (the words *yes* and *no*, and three pictures) and marking the appropriate letter on an answer sheet.

The scores depend almost entirely on comprehension of interrogative forms: what, where, when, were, who, how, is, does, was, has. While the LCPT has the appearance of a five-choice multiple-choice test, in fact the first 16 items (half the test) may not be true five-option items. There are four questions asked about each of the first four stimulus pictures on the test. These include one yes/no question, using the first and second picture distractors, which are the words *yes* and *no*. A student who has any notion about these two question types can eliminate some inappropriate choices; for instance, a student who recognizes the rising terminal intonation of a yes/no question has a 50% chance of getting that question correct by guessing. Many basic level students recognize that *who, what, where,* and *how* do not require a *yes/no* answer and can eliminate those two choices. The practice items review both question types. The last half of the test involves more difficult language.

The published materials received in February, 1984, need more editing. Page 7 of the Student Picture Book labels two clocks *5:30* that are not drawn clearly. Page 6 pictures a clock that seems to show the time at *5:45*, but is labelled *6:45*. The Examiner's Test Manual contains errors in the Bill form script. On Page 10, the explanation referring to Page 8 uses *Tom* instead of *Bill*. Also on Page 10, Question 29, the script reads *women* instead of *woman*. These errors illustrate the necessity to have the test administrator carefully review the test before reading the stimuli to examinees.

With a naturalness of phraseology, the items test the ability to understand interrogatives without putting a premium on lexical knowledge. How such information can be used for placement must be determined by the construction of local norms in each individual ESL program. The Technical Guide (p. 11) includes tentative cut-off scores based on field trials conducted in the San Francisco Community College District (SFCCD). Users should not overestimate the measurement precision of this instrument or attempt to use it for other than general placement purposes.

### Validity

"Items were first generated from IOI items with high discrimination indices. Later, items were added, using results from studies made with STEL" (Technical Guide, p. 3). IOI, STEL, ELSA, and EPT are all ESL tests authored or coauthored by Ilyin. Correlations between LCPT and various forms of these tests ranged from .48 to .66. The only non-Ilyin test correlations reported were with the MTELP (form used was not stated), r = .19; the ELI-Aural, r = .39; and a composition, r = .50. Ilyin states that the MTELP and ELE-Aural were too difficult for students in the 100-500 level courses taught in the SFCCD, hence the low correlations.

Evidence of content validity is limited to the statement that "Instructors reported that the tests contained material that was taught in levels 100 to 400 and was appropriate for those levels." Any test is only a sample of a behavior domain, and any inference made regarding that behavior from the number of correct answers on a test requires evidence of test validity. An explanation of the rationale (Was there a test blueprint?) for the choice of item content, the weighting of the various content areas, and the dependency on interrogatives to test comprehension would be welcome.

Other evidence of validity is offered in the Technical Guide in the form of differences in means reported in levels 100-400 for students taking a 25-item developmental form of the test. These levels are not described in the Manual. However, information on them can be found in *Concerned about Testing* (p. 6), which now accompanies the test materials. The fact that the group means are different at the four levels is not sufficient evidence that the test discriminates well at these levels. There are overlapping distributions and small differences in means (3.54, .81, 1.48) between adjacent levels. An average difference of one or two correctly answered items does not seem sufficient to assume that the test is discriminating well at these levels. The 33-item version did not discriminate well for placement into levels 500 and 600 (means of 24.67 and 23.29, respectively). However, Ilyin admits that the test does not discriminate above level 400 (p. 9).

The Technical Guide also claims that the test is useful for diagnosing student problems. However, it seems questionable to make inferences about the comprehension of a particular grammatical structure from answers to only one or two items containing that structure.

One should also be cautious when using the test to measure achievement in the form of score gains, a use suggested in the Technical Guide and advertised by the publishers. The two forms (BILL and TOM) are called pre- and posttests, implying that they are alternate forms sampling the same domain. In fact, they are the same test (except for errors in the published version of the BILL form). The name *Tom* is substituted for the name *Bill*, and although the order of questions is reversed, the picture stimuli are the same, and the questions are exactly the same. If these forms are not considered exactly the same, then evidence supporting their equivalency should be present in the Technical Guide. If they are exactly the same test, then this must be taken into account when using them to measure gain. Individual gain scores have little reliability if the

two forms measure exactly the same factors. Mean gains of a group can only be loosely interpreted. The practice and memory effects can be large, especially with beginning students, if suitable time has not elapsed between pre- and posttests. Mean gains may only reflect greater familiarity with the test method and content. In the case of examinees placed in the lowest level classed by these test scores, retest gains may only reflect regression toward the mean. Unless such issues are explained in the Technical Guide, statements such as the following, "LCPT mean scores for 54 students in reference group C improved from 37% on the BILL form to 52% on the TOM form, showing a gain of 15% in a two-month period," (p. 9) can mislead the average ESL test user.

## Reliability

Reported KR-21 (in one case KR-20) reliabilities are high, ranging from .81 to .98. However, users should be aware of some administrative procedures that might affect test reliability. The Guide and Manual are explicit about most procedures, but leave some room for administrators to use judgment when answering student questions. In one field test study in which the LCPT was used, test procedures state that bilingual staff were used to translate introductions and test instructions whenever necessary. Pauses between questions are not timed. Examiners should allow students enough time to think and mark answers. These points illustrate why a tape is needed for a listening comprehension test like the LCPT.

Other errors may be introduced by the suggestion that when using the test for lower-level students, the examiner may choose to stop the test after 20 or 25 items, "if most students are frustrated and unable to do the test" (Technical Guide, p. 10). Reliability data are not given for a 20-item form, yet shorter tests are less reliable. Although the items are reportedly arranged in the order of increasing difficulty there is no reason to assume that all lower-level students will miss all later items.

After giving and scoring the first 25 items, it is suggested that students scoring above 40% correct be given the last 8 items. It is not clear if this is done at a different time or on a different day. If it is to be done on a different day, this could introduce another source of variation into the student's scores.

In summary, with appropriate caution the LCPT may be useful as a placement instrument in low and intermediate level ESL classes. When used as such, the examiner should study the materials carefully before administering the test, or preferably, make a tape of the test's instructions for use during the administration. The LCPT should not be used to diagnose errors or to show gains in achievement.

# Listening Comprehension Written Test

*Reviewed by*

**Lynn E. Thompson**
**Center for Applied Linguistics**
**Washington, DC**

## Synopsis

Listening Comprehension Group Tests: Listening Comprehension Written Test. LCWT. 1976-1978. Intermediate and advanced students of English as a second language (teenage to adult) who are able to read time, understand basic question words, and control basic sentence patterns. Designed to measure listening comprehension and writing skills in English for screening, placement, diagnosis of needs, and achievement. Scored by hand for appropriateness of information and structural accuracy: two points if the information is correct and appropriate; one point if information is correct and appropriate, but contains one or more grammar errors; zero points if information is incorrect and/or inappropriate, or errors prevent understanding. Total correct can be interpreted to classify examinees into four levels, which are based on San Francisco Community College District curriculum, but users are advised to establish their own cutoff scores. Group administration. 45 minutes. Two forms labeled Bill and Tom (1981) consisting of Examiner's Test Manual (1981, pp. 16-32) and Student Picture Booklet (1981, pp. 10-28) printed in conjunction with the Listening Comprehension Picture Test (LCPT). Technical Guide (1981, pp. 12-20) contains data and explanations of both tests. Technical Guide, $5.95. Examiner's Test Manual, $4.50. Student Picture Booklet, $2.95. $5.95 per 50 LCWT Answer Sheets. Technical Guide by Donna Ilyin and Susan Rubin. Student Picture Booklet and Examiner's Test Manual by Donna Ilyin. Newbury House Publishers, Inc., 54 Warehouse Lane, Rowley, MA 01969, USA, telephone: (800) 343-1240.

## Test References

Newbury House. *Concerned about testing*. Rowley, MA: Author.

Richards, R. A. (1985). [Review of listening comprehension group tests]. In J. V. Mitchell, Jr. (Ed.), *The ninth mental measurements yearbook* (pp. 64-66). Lincoln, NE: Buros Institute of Mental Measurements & University of Nebraska.

## Review

The Listening Comprehension Written Test represents an impressive effort to adapt the Ilyin Oral Interview (IOI) to a group listening test for the intermediate to advanced levels. Like the IOI, the LCWT assesses both receptive and productive skills, but with an altered focus: Responses are written rather than spoken in order to accommodate group testing. This allows the administrator to ascertain the examinee's ability to "understand questions and write sentences using basic structures taught in different ESL class levels" (Technical Guide, p. 12). A sample of written work for each student is collected. Besides serving as the basis for the three point (0-1-2) scoring of the test, the sample of written work permits the test user to analyze a student's control of basic grammatical structures and provides an attractive option for the teacher who needs a quick profile of student competencies. The availability of two forms of the test provides the possibility of using the test to measure achievement in a program of instruction. By its very nature, the test may serve to immediately identify those students needing additional assistance with writing, since the production of language requires a certain degree of ease with the written mode. In short, Ilyin has thoughtfully attempted to address not only the need for a listening comprehension test, but also some common concerns of ESL teachers and administrators.

The Technical Guide provides information on test development, some evidence of reliability and validity, instructions for test administration, scoring, and score interpretation. It is important to remember that the LCWT is still experimental. The present form of the test was developed through repeated administration and revision of a preliminary form of the test at the Alemany Center and the Mission Language and Vocational Center over a 2-year period for achievement and entrance purposes. This permitted the refinement of test items and the test administration instructions as well as the establishment of cut-off scores.

Preliminary results as reported in the Technical Guide point to the validity of the test as a means of distinguishing proficiency levels. Lower-bound estimates of internal consistency reliability (KR-21), based on field testing in 1975-76, are moderately good, ranging from .77 to .89 for four small and fairly homogenous samples of examinees. Content validity was established by asking instructors at the Alemany campus of San Francisco Community College District to examine the test and indicate tested material taught in their courses. Discriminant validity is demonstrated by presenting mean scores of examinees enrolled at different levels of ESL instruction, but there is no evidence of concurrent validity. It would be useful to compare the LCWT with other listening comprehension tests. The authors acknowledge that further studies are required to firmly establish reliability and validity of the LCWT.

Instructions for test administration, as outlined in the Technical Guide, are clearly presented with perceptive comments on the importance of a positive testing environment. A key factor to successful test administration is the person who administers the test. The author stresses the need for practicing the test script and being thoroughly familiar with the recommendations for successful test administration. Examination of the test confirms this. The test requires the examiner to follow a set routine and to assure the attention of all participants. Since the examinee must be initiated to the test procedure, it is vital that instructions be given clearly and care be taken that all students have understood. The testing process requires an examiner who is not only familiar with the test but experienced in dealing with students. Sufficient time to examine test materials and train test administrators should be calculated when considering use of the LCWT.

One additional consideration before administering the LCWT is to determine if all examinees are able to write sentences and to read clocks. The introductory stages of the test permits such screening but it would be less disruptive or embarassing to the student if the initial screening was conducted beforehand.

Procedures for scoring and score interpretation are not well defined. Student responses are judged first on the basis of communication. No comprehensive list of correct responses is available. Rather, the scorer is given a 3-point scale for judging the responses. Ilyin suggests that the scorer may find it useful to make a list of correct answers for each question. Of course, given the scoring criteria, there are a number of possible correct answers to most questions. It is assumed that this is to allow for variation of vocabulary and detail, while maintaining the focus on the grammatical accuracy and overall appropriateness of the response. Again, as with test administration, scoring should only be undertaken by trained staff, preferably ESL teachers. Future versions of the LCWT Technical Guide should provide more discussion of response variation. To her credit, Ilyin states that interscorer reliability studies should be done. Such studies would provide data on scoring consistency—vital data given the variety of possible responses.

The interpretation of scores is not well explained in the Technical Guide. Cut-off scores, established for the course levels at the Alemany campus, are the only basis for score interpretation given in the Guide. However, these levels and the skills taught in each are described in a pamphlet that accompanies the test (*Concerned about Testing*, p. 6). This information should be available in the Technical Guide. Ideally, score interpretation should be related to a description of skills rather than a course level.

A useful component of the Technical Guide is the diagnostic checklist. It allows the examiner to recognize patterns of student error. The checklist is not a complete error analysis, but for those teachers who have the time and inclination, it can be a helpful diagnostic tool.

Examination of the test materials themselves yields a generally favorable impression. The two forms appear roughly equivalent and should be pleasant for the student given the author's efforts to contextualize the test forms, that is, students follow the activities of either Bill or Tom.

A few of the stimuli seem a little awkward, particularly the solicitation of the conditional. There are also a few spots where the script is confusing for the examiner, which stresses the importance of being familiar with the script. Pictures in the student booklet are small and at times ambiguous. This needs to be taken into account when grading student responses. The student answer sheet is straightforward, although the presence of level cut-offs at the bottom could be unnerving to a sensitive examinee.

*Conclusion*

The LCWT materials clearly represent consistent efforts to develop a good intermediate level test of listening comprehension and writing. The test provides interesting and useful data for student placement and evaluation. When considering use of the LCWT, it is necessary to allow for the assessment of other skill areas not covered by the test. In this regard, the Technical Guide (p. 12) and sample brochure (p. 2) contain the following potentially misleading statement. "The LCWT tests receptive and productive English language skills . . . " It tests, however, only a limited domain of listening (understanding questions/commands) and only one productive skill (writing). Aside from this, the test appears professional and well designed.

Overall the LCWT is a successful test; however, the basic question of validity plagues all writing tests. Are we really testing what we say we are? In the case of the LCWT one wonders if it is really appropriate to assess two skills with the same instrument. An unacceptable response on the test could reflect (a) failure to comprehend the picture, (b) inability to write correctly rather than a lack of comprehension of the aural stimulus, or (c) failure to comprehend the aural stimulus rather than the inability to write correctly. Further studies of the LCWT may perhaps dispel this concern.

Despite the preliminary nature of the present forms, the LCWT seems to be a well-intentioned step toward the development of a useful new instrument. The authors of the Technical Guide describe the test appropriately: "This edition is being made available so that others may use it, study and document its characteristics and share that information with the profession, which does need the continual development of useful ESL proficiency tests" (p. 15).

# Maculaitis Assessment Program

*Reviewed by*

**Jose E. Cruz-Matos**
**City University of New York**

**Clara V. Velazquez**
**City University of New York**

**James Kalfus**
**Hawes Elementary School**
**Ridgewood, New Jersey**

### Synopsis

Maculaitis Assessment Program. MAC. 1982. K-12 Designed to select, place, diagnose, and determine the proficiency and achievement of school-age, nonnative speakers of English enrolled in Grades K-12. Raw scores are converted into one of the following proficiency levels: Beginner (basic, intermediate, advanced), Intermediate (low, intermediate, advanced), and Advanced (low, intermediate, superior). Individual and group administered sections. The batteries and testing times are: MAC Basic Concepts Test (BCT), 15 minutes; MAC K-1, 25 minutes; MAC 2-3, 83 minutes; MAC 4-5, 119 minutes; MAC 6-8, 109 minutes; MAC 9-12, 109 minutes. Examiner's Manual (1982, 124 pp.). Technical Manual (1982, 276 pp.). K-12 Program Set includes, one BCT Examiner's Kit, one K-1 Examiner's Kit, one 9-12 Examiner's Kit, one K-12 Technical Manual, and one K-12 Examiner's Manual. Complete program set is $195.00. If "30-day approval" is indicated on order, you may keep or return part of set for credit. 6% extra for postage and handling. Jean D'Arcy Maculaitis. Alemany Press, 2501 Industrial Parkway West, Hayward, CA 94545, USA, telephone: (800) 227-2375 or (415) 227-2375.

### Review

The six Maculaitis Assessment Program (MAC K-12) batteries are appropriate for testing a variety of student populations whose home language is other than English. These norm-referenced and criterion-referenced assessment instruments measure students' communicative performance. According to their author, they can be used to:

Determine whether or not a nonnative student should be selected to participate in the district's English as a second language, limited English proficient or bilingual education (ESL, LEP, BE) programs.

Provide specific diagnostic and placement information about the students with regard to his or her competence in the four major language skills, that is, listening, speaking, reading and writing.

Provide an indication of an LEP student's global as well as specific English language proficiency.

Provide an indication of the student's potential academic achievement in his or her second language (English).

Assist in providing exit criteria for a program.

The MAC batteries are basically four-skills tests. The MAC BCT involves only listening and speaking; the MAC K-1 and MAC 2-4 involve listening, speaking, and reading; and the remaining three tests involve listening, speaking, reading, and writing. The MAC BCT is a test of cognitive development that one might use to assess readiness for further learning. These include the identification of colors, shapes, numbers, letters, and spatial relationships. The other tests focus on the traditional components of language tests (phonology, vocabulary, and syntax), on functions, and other discoursal aspects of language (asking questions, answering questions, comprehending statements or dialogues, or filling out an application form for a school trip).

The MAC Technical Manual (TM) presents a thorough discussion of all data, including conversion tables by grades/forms. A summary of the reliability data (Cronbach's alpha) for the MAC batteries is as follows:

| | | |
|---|---|---|
| (green) | MAC BCT | - .98 |
| (pink) | MAC K-1 | - .94 |
| (blue) | MAC 2-3 | - .95 |
| (orange) | MAC 4-5 | - .96 |
| (ivory) | MAC 6-8 | - .96 |
| (tan) | MAC 9-12 | - .94 |

Reliability is excellent.

The types of validity reported reflect the specified aim(s) of the assessment program. The groups that participated in the standardization of the six test batteries are described in the MAC TM. Members of numerous cultural groups were included in the standardization sample, and every effort appears to have been made to make the MAC fair for all test takers. The MAC batteries permit one to obtain normative comparisons (percentile ranks, stanines, and normal curve equivalency [NCE] data) on such dimensions of language as fluency, pronunciation, writing style, grammatical structure, vocabulary, aural comprehension, and visual recognition.

As evidence of validity, data relating to the ability of the test to predict grades in English is included in the TM for each subtest. Multiple regression coefficients based on the various parts of each battery range from .23 to .34 for the six batteries. These coefficients are not as high as one might hope. Internal statistics on each respective battery and the MAC as a whole support the instruments' validity. The correlations between each item and the part in which it appears are generally quite good. Considerable information relevant to conent validity is also presented in the MAC TM. All major and minor linguistic skills tested are defined and test blueprints for all batteries also appear in both the Technical and Examiner's Manuals. The appropriateness of the content domain was established over a 10-year period over 19,000 subjects. The TM defines the domain of behaviors tested and the procedures used by the author to sample those behaviors. A helpful explanation of the ingredients of a good test, namely reliability, validity, and practicality is also included in the Appendix.

Because the characteristics of the sample population participating in the field studies on which the reliability data were obtained are fully described in the TM, the test user can judge whether the MAC is appropriate for his or her specific student population. The description is based on nationality, native language, gender, grade level, length of time studying ESL, and so forth. Numerous difficulty and discrimination indices indicate that the test items and the testing program as a whole are appropriate in difficulty for low and middle income non-English proficient (NEP) and LEP students attending urban and suburban elementary and secondary schools.

In order to facilitate storage and handling, the manuals, test batteries and collateral materials are color coded by grade level. Because the Examiner's and Technical Manuals were also written to teach the reader about assessment, they help ensure staff preparation for assessment and adequate interpretation and reporting of test results.

Sample test material is provided for students above Grade 1. This feature is particularly important for LEP learners who often lack test sophistication and experience. The Examiner's Manual (EM) contains adequate instructions for test administration. Even the handling of unexpected emergencies and cheating during testing are discussed.

One EM suffices for administrating all MAC subtests. The major headings found in the EM Table of Contents are: Part I, Description; Part II, Preparation; Part III, Directions; Part IV, Technical Data; Part V, References, General, Battery, numerous appendices, and a list of tables. The Table of Contents for the TM presents the following major headings: Part I, Description; Part II, Validity; Part III, Standardization; Part IV, Scores and Reports; Part V, Understanding and Using Test Results; Part VI, Conclusions; Part VII, References, appendices, and tables.

Although the scoring procedures are more complex than those found in many other available ESL testing instruments, the Oral English and Writing Ability Rating Sheets reduce the subjectivity of rating assigned to productive skills.

English writing ability is measured through (a) a multiple-choice test of grammar and (b) two realistic and appropriate writing samples for each battery above Grade 3. This allows test takers an opportunity to express themselves and to demonstrate special talents, needs, and strengths. Thus, the test samples both creative and informational writing styles.

The illustrations that compose part of the stimulus material are appropriate to the designated age groups and sensitive to the population being tested. Primary type is used for those test items and passages that are read by children in Grades 2 and 3. Unlike most commercially available ESL tests, the MAC requires students to listen to appropriate responses and not read responses printed in test booklets when testing listening comprehension.

The reviewers recommend that school districts using the MAC K-12 offer an examiners' workshop prior to initial testing. Familiarity with the various test components, scoring procedures, and manuals is essential. It would also be desirable to develop alternate forms of the MAC. These would facilitate its use for both pre- and posttesting. Finally, the inclusion of an index in both the Technical Manual and the Examiner's Manual would facilitate their use.

The Maculaitis Assessment Program seems to be an excellent developmental second language testing program for use at the K-12 levels. The various batteries can provide a more valid, reliable, and practical means of assessing the students' L2 proficiencies in listening, speaking, reading, and writing that is available elsewhere. The MAC, the MAC Examiner's Manual, the MAC Technical Manual, and all other collateral materials represent highly professiona' efforts. The MAC may be more expensive and take longer to administer than other tests for NEP/LEP students; however, in the long run it may be more efficient and more useful.

# Michigan Test of English Language Proficiency

*Reviewed by*

**Frederick Jenks**
**Florida State University**

### Synopsis

Michigan Test of English Language Proficiency. MTELP. Pre-university and university. Designed as part of a battery to estimate student's linguistic readiness to pursue academic study at the university level. Multiple-choice scoring on answer sheet by examiner using a scoring stencil overlay, number of correct answers (raw) leads to a converted score by using a conversion table, scores range from 15-100. Individual or group administration. 75 minutes plus administrations time. Forms E-L (minus I) and P-R may be administered locally. Publication dates: 1968-79 Forms E-L, P-R. Administration/Technical Manual (1977, 18 pp.). $14 per set containing 20 test booklets, 100 answer sheets, Administration/Technical Manual and scoring stencil. Specimen set containing one unofficial form, answer sheet, scoring stencil and Manual is $5. English Language Institute, Testing and Certification Division, The University of Michigan, Ann Arbor, MI 48109, USA, telephone: (313) 747-0456.

## Test References

Carroll, J. B. (1965). [Review of the Michigan test of English language proficiency]. In O. K. Buros (Ed.), *The sixth mental measurements yearbook* (review no. 360). Highland Park, NJ: Gryphon.

Cervenka, E. J. (1978). [Review of the Michigan test of English language proficiency]. In O. K. Buros (Ed.), *The sixth mental measurements yearbook* (pp. 189-190). Highland Park, NJ: Gryphon.

## Review

The MTELP, a widely used proficiency test, contains sections pertaining to structure (40 items), vocabulary (40 items), and reading comprehension (20 items). A multiple-choice test, MTELP requires that examinees read the questions in a test booklet and select the best answer from four responses; this selection is then indicated (*a*, *b*, *c*, or *d*) on a standard answer sheet by darkening a circle with a pencil. This test for nonnative English speakers is used in determining whether the examinee has a recommended language proficiency to commence degree-earning study at the college level.

Commercially available MTELPs are retired components of the old Michigan battery. Users are often confused by the similarity in names and mistakenly believe the MTELP is the battery. The MELAB is a secure test battery that is administered at The University of Michigan and at 400 test centers in 120 countries. It also includes a written composition and a measure of listening skills that is different from the MTAC. (See this volume for a review of the MTAC.)

The examiner's qualifications are not mentioned in the MTELP Manual. I recommend that the examiner be familiar with material in the Manual and have experience in supervising timed examinations. No special equipment is required to administer the MTELP, and the instructions for grading the test are clear. Score interpretation information in the Manual permits the examiner to make placement recommendations. However, the reader should be mindful that a standard error of measurement exists on MTELP and might be considered when making admission decisions.

Retired forms of the MTELP have been available for nearly 20 years. Many of the earliest test forms are still in use at numerous schools. Test security has become a major issue since so many forms of MTELP have been loosely guarded by some testing sites. Thus, as recently as March 1985, the MTELP headquarters released a memorandum stating that "the test materials (Forms E-L minus I) are retired, nonsecure components of the Michigan Test Battery." These forms, then, must be used with discretion since their high accessibility combined with the lack of a centralized recordkeeping headquarters for MTELP permit students to take the same form several times or to obtain copies of MTELP, in some instances.

The paucity of current research on MTELP and the lack of design information for past research reported in the Manual are major weaknesses at this time. A number of studies reported in the Manual are based on results of the Michigan Test Battery and not the MTELP exclusively. Also, a key study in the Manual is based on data collected in 1956-57, a time when international student profiles and university curricula were significantly different from today's. Though a more recent study conducted in 1967 reports predictive validity, users should be aware that the MTELP is designed to measure language proficiency, and that many other factors besides language ability will affect academic performance. Throughout the Manual, one is conscious of the gaps in research-design information. No evidence is provided for validity of MTELP results as a placement/proficiency measure; the placement recommendations do not seem to be founded on solid longitudinal research. (See "Standards for Educational and Psychological Tests," APA, 1974, p. 45.)

It is questionable how MTELP has managed to maintain its prominence in light of its lack of security and questionable validity (content, construct, and predictive). For example, content and construct validity are claimed on the basis of presumed relationships between MTELP reading selections and university reading, and the premise that "vocabulary and structural knowledge are necessary—although not sufficient—for integrated communication skills" (Manual, p. 14). Finally, predictive validity is based on 1956-57 data and 1967 data (Manual, pp. 16-17), which may have become obsolete.

No evidence is reported to indicate that age, sex, race, or other personal variables were/are taken into consideration when revising or preparing MTELP. Reported data indicate that native language background and MTELP scores have been examined.

An examination of the content of grammar questions and choices, and the types of reading comprehension questions, indicates that MTELP is based on a structuralist approach to language. However, no efforts are made in MTELP Manual to reflect or justify any particular approach to L2 learning or testing.

MTELP's major strength is its wide availability via unofficial forms and its maturity, the latter permitting many institutions to have gathered their own database from years of using the test. Offsetting these strengths are some major weaknesses: (a) lack of test security; (b) outdated information, that is, the reported correlation between MTELP and TOEFL of .896 has not been reexamined since TOEFL shifted to a 3-section format; (c) vocabulary choices based on Thorndike-Lorge word lists that are 40-years-old; (d) some disagreement on my part as to whether reading selections are really non-technical in content; and (e) many aspects of research design of the studies that have been done at The University of Michigan are open to question and/or difficult to ascertain.

*Reviewer's Summative Comments*

It is surprising that institutions put faith in MTELP scores, given the paucity of studies that support its validity and reliability. One could argue that it measures little of relevance. This is not to say that it does not have reliability or validity. Rather it does not scientifically demonstrate either, due primarily to the lack of studies which take into account changes in other tests to which it had been previously correlated, changes in research design strategies during the past 20-30 years, and shifts in language teaching/learning theory since most MTELP research was completed. MTELP scores from unofficial tests should not be used for college or university admission purposes according to the Publications Division of the English Language Institute. Furthermore, the Proficiency Recommendations reported in the Manual do not appear to be founded on a solid database, rather they are more akin to estimates based on experience gained at The University of Michigan. Until MTELP research is updated or prior research is more fully explicated, it is difficult to say for what an MTELP score can be used.

# Michigan Test of Aural Comprehension

*Reviewed by*

**Stan Jones**
**Carleton University**

### Synopsis

The Michigan Test of Aural Comprehension. MTAC. 1969. Post-secondary. Designed to test knowledge of English structures presented orally. Multiple-choice test for group administration. 30 minutes for complete administration. 3 forms of the test, but one examinee test booklet serves for all three versions (1969, 5 pp.). Administration Manual (1972, 16 pp.); no technical manual. $17.00 for a package of 20 test booklets, 100 answer sheets, and Administration Manual; the tape is an additional $15.00, but the user can prepare a tape or read the prompts directly from the Administration Manual. John Upshur, Mary Spaan, and Randolph Thrasher, Publications Division, English Language Institute, The University of Michigan, Ann Arbor, MI, 48109, USA,

telephone: (313) 747-0456, cable: ELIUM.

### Test References

Carroll, J.B. (1978). [Review of Michigan test of aural comprehension]. In O. K. Buros (Ed.), *The eighth mental measurements yearbook* (p. 188). Highland Park, NJ: Gryphon.

### Review

This is one of many tests developed by the Testing and Certification Unit of the English Language Institute at The University of Michigan. MTAC is part of a series that includes the Michigan Test of English Language Proficiency (MTELP).

MTAC is an oral grammar test as its high correlation with written grammar tests (see below) makes evident. It does not appear to be designed to test phonological discrimination or, indeed, any feature of language that might be specifically oral. Consideration of the first example question demonstrates the grammatical emphasis of this test. The examinees hear "Are you busy?" and are asked to choose one of these three phrases as the correct answer:

a. Yes, I am.

b. Yes, you are.

c. Yes, he is.

It seems to me unlikely than any failure of auditory discrimination would lead to the choice of either *b* or *c*.

Unfortunately, the Manual does not include any statistical data that would permit us to assess what components of language proficiency this test measures. However, there are some descriptive statistics on the MTAC included in the 1977 MTELP Manual. These show healthy KR-21 reliability estimates ranging from .88 to .96 for different samples. The MTAC showed a correlation of .77 with the MTELP and a correlation of .52 with a 30-minute impromptu composition. It is unfortunate that these statistics have not been included in the MTAC Examiner's Manual.

The only other published data on the test are from a study by Madsen (1979). In developing a new test, Madsen compared the scores his subjects obtained on his test and on the MTAC with those they obtained on the three components (grammar, vocabulary, reading) of the Michigan Test of English Language Proficiency (see review in this volume). It is interesting that there is a high correlation between scores on the MTAC, a listening test, and the grammar component of the MTELP: a correlation of .78 in one group of students (n = 72) and of .76 in another group (n = 73). The correlations with the vocabulary component (.61 and .58) and with the reading component (.64 and .48) are lower, suggesting that the MTAC/grammar correlation is more than a method (all items use the multiple-choice format) effect. Because the grammar section is a major component of the MTELP, whole test correlations between it and MTAC are high: .80 and .74. These data confirm the grammatical basis of MTAC.

Test users seeking data specifically about listening comprehension might well consider other listening tests, such as the listening component of the CELT (Comprehensive English Language Test) or the listening section of Michigan's own English Placement Test, as scores on MTAC are so closely related to scores on written grammar tests. MTAC's sole advantage over either of these is that it provides multiple forms.

These multiple forms are one of the more unusual features of the test, as the same answer booklet serves for each of the three forms. Each item contains three options; each choice is correct for one form of the test. For example, if the three choices were:

    a. I am almost finished.

    b. I just finished.

    c. I just started.

Choice *a* would be correct on one form where the cue might be "I'm nearly done"; *b* would be correct on a second form with the cue "I just completed it"; and *c* on the third, "I've just begun". Although each grammatical structure tested on one form is also tested on the other two, it is not always tested by the same question. Thus, if item 20 on Form 1 tests the phrase *had little*, that phrase might be tested by item 15 on Form 2 and item 63 on Form 3. Item 20 on Form 2, with the same choice of answers as item 20 on Form 1 might test What-questions. Thus, the forms were constructed to be parallel, but no data has been published by the authors to validate this assumption.

The test is a secure test (all examples are drawn from the example questions used in the test booklet), and purchasers must sign an agreement to respect the test's security. Users must also agree not to use the test for admissions purposes (preventing competition with another Michigan test). The spoken prompts are provided in the Administration Manual so that users can make their own tapes rather than using the tapes provided by Michigan. There are 90 questions on each form.

## Reviewer's References

Madsen, H. (1979). An indirect measure of listening comprehension. *Modern Language Journal, 63,* 429-435.

# University of Oxford Delegacy of Local Examinations
# The Oxford Examinations in English as a Foreign Language

*Reviewed by*

**Clive Bruton**
**The British Council**
**London**

### Synopsis

University of Oxford Delegacy of Local Examinations: The Oxford Examinations in English as a Foreign Language. Preliminary Level (PL), 1978-1984. Higher Level (HL), 1982-1984. All foreign students of English studying in U.K. at two levels: the Preliminary Level (PL) and the Higher Level (HL), both for any age. PL is designed to measure a candidate's writing and reading skills for survival in English, HL aimed at students who have reached higher intermediate or advanced stage. Both examinations separate performance and receptive skills (as far as is possible) and concentrate on authentic writing and reading tasks, using nonliterary material. Written responses centrally assessed by appointed examiners according to criteria specified to them. Group administration. PL, two papers: Paper 1, 2 hours; Paper 2, 2 hours, plus 10 minutes reading time. New papers compiled for each series of examinations. Two scheduled PL examinations per year in March and November, one scheduled HL examination in May. University of Oxford, the Oxford Certificate in English as a Foreign Language (pamphlet, undated, 6 pp.), EFL timetable 1984, the University of Oxford Delegacy's Examination in English as a Foreign Language, Preliminary Level (photocopied sheet, undated, 2 pp.), The University of Oxford Delegacy's Examination in English as a Foreign Language, Higher Level (photocopied sheet, undated, 2 pp.). Examinations available to Delegacy's Centres, ARELS member schools, and institutions approved by the Delegacy. Charge per candidate £10.00 for PL, £12.00 for HL; past examination papers available at 10 pence per copy, postage extra. Oxford Delegacy of Local Examinations, Ewert Place, Summertown, Oxford OX2 7B2, England, telephone: 0865 54291.

### Review

The Preliminary Level Examination is principally concerned with assessing performance by means of test items selected from among the reading and writing tasks candidates might be expected to have to perform in real life. It is intended to test the candidates' ability to cope with practical reading and writing tasks at a level below that of the Cambridge First Certificate in English. Paper 1 tests writing skills. Among the items tested are the writing of formal/informal letters and the ability to write connected prose on topics relevant to a candidate's situation in the form of messages, notes, notices, signs, and so forth. Paper 2 tests reading skills. These include the use of a dictionary, the ability to fill in forms, follow instructions, read for the general meaning of a text, and read to select specific information. Throughout the examination, receptive skills are tested at a higher level than productive skills. Candidates are allowed to use an English dictionary for both papers.

The Higher Level Examination is intended for candidates who are reasonably competent at a level between that of the Cambridge First Certificate in English and the Cambridge Certificate of Proficiency in English. As in the Preliminary Level, nonliterary material is used to provide authentic tasks in reading and writing. Paper 1 tests productive skills and includes a realistic writing task (e.g., a report, a curriculum vitae, etc.) of about 400 words; a selection of letter writing tasks to test handling of register; summary/expansion exercises; and functional writing tasks, similar but more sophisticated to those in the Preliminary Level examination. Paper 2 tests receptive skills and includes the ability to fill in a form based on complex information, "jigsaw" comprehension, scanning and skimming tests, a directory question, and comprehension and response-in-depth questions. Candidates are required to have a good English dictionary for use during the examination.

The grading system for both examinations is that candidates are placed in one of the grades: Distinction, Credit, Pass, Fail 1, Fail 2. In the Higher Level examination candidates must pass in both papers, whereas in the Preliminary Level examination candidates are only required to pass overall (i.e., weak performance in one paper can be compensated by a stronger performance in other paper).

The primary attraction of these examinations lies in the nonliterary authenticity both of the texts presented and of the tasks that candidates are required to perform on the texts. In Paper 2 of the Preliminary Level examination for March 1984, candidates are presented with a catalogue list from a mail order firm and are required to fill in an order form for certain items that they are told they wish to send to a friend. In Paper 2 of the Higher Level examination for May 1983, candidates are presented with a timetable of trains between Oxford and London and other information taken from an Oxford newspaper and required to revise or prepare a schedule.

The papers that test primarily productive skills also require candidates to perform authentic tasks. In Paper 1 of the Preliminary Level examination for March 1982, candidates are required to write an advertisement to be put in an English newspaper for a radio they wish to sell. In Paper 1 of the Higher Level examination for May 1982, candidates are given the instruction: "You and some friends are going out for an evening on the town. One of the group can only join you later. Write a note to tell him where to find you."

The face validity of the examinations is enhanced by the fact that the Oxford Delegacy holds a yearly meeting for each examination to which teachers who have submitted candidates are invited. At these meetings teachers review the latest examination(s) and make suggestions for future papers and questions. In this way close contact is maintained between the teachers and the testers.

However, such a fluid approach can cause problems. First, the examinations do not as of yet have a defined syllabus; in fact there is very little information available on the test specifications and content, assessment criteria, or allocation of marks.

Secondly, the emphasis given to authenticity in all the publicity is not always reflected in the test items. For example, in Paper 1 of the Preliminary Level examination for March 1984, one of the options for candidates in Question 1 is "Write a dangerous situation."

Third, since the examinations are intended for students studying in Great Britain, many of the materials and tasks are culture specific. Thus, in Paper 1 of the Preliminary Level examination of March 1984, one of the pictures presented to candidates is of a cricket match, while in Paper 2 one of the questions concerns the opening of a budget account in Selfridges.

The confusion between the skills being tested in the two papers in each examination is a fourth potential problem area. Given that it is not always possible to isolate a particular skill to be tested—candidates will usually be required to read, for example, before they are given a writing task—it seems unnecessarily confusing to include letter-writing tasks in a paper designed to test primarily receptive/reading skills.

Finally, the procedures for pretesting and posttest follow-up are also unsatisfactory. At present there is no formalized mechanism for pretesting items before they are included in the examination. Once the examinations have been administered, follow-up analysis appears to be limited to an analysis of how many candidates (in terms of numbers and percentages) have been placed in each of the passing and failing grades.

In sum, the examination materials and tasks have a refreshing nonliterary face validity for students studying in Great Britain. But they suffer from the fact that no attempt appears to have yet been made to specify their content and the criteria for assessment nor to ensure that test items are performing satisfactorily.

# Oxford Placement Test

*Reviewed by*

**Diane Wall**
**University of Lancaster**

**Synopsis**

Oxford Placement Test. OPT. Original version, 1982

(known as Version 1 since 1985); versions 2 and 3, 1985. Nonnative students in any English-teaching institution, age unspecified. Designed to ensure efficient, reliable, and accurate grading and placing into classes at all levels from elementary to postproficiency; to establish which coursebooks and teaching materials are suitable for particular groups; and to determine realistic examination targets for groups or individuals. Multiple-choice. Individual or group administration. One hour. Part A, Reading and Listening, 100 items, 10 minutes. Part B, Grammatical Structure, 100 items, 50 minutes. A Guide to the Oxford Placement Test (3 pp.), contains suggestions for administration and placing of students, and Teacher's Introduction (2 pp.), introduction and administrative guide printed on inside cover of Marker's Kit (1983). Available from 1985: Testpack for each version of the test (containing 40 copies of Parts A and B, with Teachers' Introduction and key to all three versions on inside of wrap-around cover), £6.50; cassette for Part B of each version, £2.20. Dave Allan. Oxford University Press, Walton Street, Oxford OX2 6DP, England.

## Review

The Oxford Placement Test aims to solve the problem of dividing a large group of students into several smaller groups of people whose language ability is roughly equal. Publicity for the test and accompanying information stress how effortlessly this task can be carried out; much of the Guide to the OPT is devoted to a detailed account of how the test can be administered and scored for as many as 200 students in 90 minutes. The ease with which the test can be given is perhaps its most valuable selling point. Its next most attractive feature might well be its claim that Part A is a highly sophisticated and refined measure of communicative performance. If the handiness of the test will not sell it, the idea that it might fit in with current notions of language teaching certainly will. Two new versions of the OPT went on the market in 1985, not only in Great Britain but in places as far afield as Sweden and China.

Unfortunately, in the attempt to provide something convenient for the greatest number of consumers, the publishers have not addressed in print some important questions.

Is the OPT really communicative? As the publishers claim that this a highly sophisticated and refined measure of communicative performance, it is necessary to examine its contents before commenting. Part A consists of 100 items which are based on real-life "slips of the ear." The student is given a sentence like the following: What do you think of the new (teachers, T-shirts)? and must underline the word he or she hears when the sentence is read on a cassette recording. Each sentence is read aloud once, and there is no connection between one sentence and the next.

In order to merit the label "communicative," a test should be able to meet these conditions:

1. Items should be in contexts similar to spoken language. Understanding the context can help listeners and readers to determine meaning, The fact that in these 100 items the context never helps the testee suggests that the context may as well not be present. It would be foolish to suggest that context will always help the listener (this would prevent slips-of-the-ear occuring in native speakers), but a test which presents context which contributes nothing to understanding appears more like an elegant phoneme discrimination test than a highly refined and sophisticated measure of communicative performance.

2. The task the student needs to do should reflect activities in the target situation. In the real world a student might have to choose between two sounds, but how often is this choice accompanied by a reading decision as well? It is possible in this test for the listener to hear the correct answer but not be able to indicate it because of reading difficulties. Therefore, the test may be more difficult than the task in the target situation.

This is not a call for a more discrete listening component, one which would eliminate reading altogether, but for one in which reading does not play such a critical role. This is especially important when working with students who wish to prepare for some of the major listening exams, such as the ARELS of RSA Communicative Listening, and have not yet strengthened and may not need to strengthen their reading skills.

Another way in which the test might reflect the real world more would be by testing something more than the ability to distinguish between sounds. Whereas current approaches to teaching emphasize listening for gist, for relevant details and for intelligent inferences, this one asks students to do nothing with their listening except discriminate phonemes.

In sum, Part A, in spite of its novel appearance, does not seem to have any special reason to be considered communicative. The fact that many textbook writers and methodologists use this term loosely does not mean that it is right to do so.

The second half of the OPT looks very familiar: 100 multiple-choice items containing structures culled from well-known textbooks and examinations. There are two parts to the Structure test and teachers are informed that even though results will be more reliable if the complete test is given, either half can be given in lieu of the whole for administrative convenience. One would assume that both parts of the test would test roughly the same thing, but this is not the case. The second half for example, contains 10 question-tag items in a row, while the first half does not test this point at all (Version 1).

Each half is further divided into subsections of 10-30

items, 3 of which form passages of continuous prose. The idea is to force the testees to read longer portions of text in order to select the correct response. Here we find the context that was missing in the Reading and Listening test, and its inclusion provides an interesting challenge for the testees.

Unfortunately, the layout of the test does not make it clear, either in terms of paragraphing or separating the columns, where one text ends and another begins. Another problem exists in the way the multiple-choice distractors are laid out on the paper, making it hard to see that the middle distractor is not the natural continuation of the sentence in question.

The OPT claims to be the result of many years of research, but potential users are not shown the necessary data to enable them to decide for themselves whether test claims are actually valid. It is difficult for some examining bodies to provide this information (when, for example, two or three versions of an exam are published each year); however, in OPT's case, especially since its claims are so varied and so strong, it seems reasonable to expect that the publisher should provide more detailed accounts of the test's rationale, validity and reliability.

Nevertheless, if the OPT is used only for placement there is probably no permanent damage done by using it to make first decisions and letting time sort out subsequent problems.

The Teachers' Introduction does state that "the test offers a reliable basis for the initial assessment of students of English" and allows that teacher judgment will often be the best long-term means of evaluating whether students are correctly placed. This goes some way towards admitting that the OPT may not solve everyone's problems, but it does not explain why this test should be used (except for the fact that it is already there) rather than something from within each particular institution.

It is a commonplace that in marketing the buyer must beware - he/she should not accept all claims of sellers at face value. However, one would hope that in an educational setting publishers would feel more responsible than other sellers to their buyers, making fewer claims and more efforts to substantiate the claims they have made.

# PRE-LAS

*Reviewed by*

**Patsy Jaynes**
**Jefferson County Public Schools**
**Lakewood, Colorado**

## Synopsis

PRE-LAS. PRE-LAS. 1976. Grades K-1. Designed to measure expressive and receptive abilities in three components of oral language: morphology, syntax, and semantics. Discrete-point items in Sections I-IV are marked in test booklet if the examinee does not answer correctly; Sections V-VI are transcribed to test booklet and scored holistically. Individual administration. 10 minutes. Test booklet, Forms A and B (1986, 4 pp.). How to Administer PRE-LAS (1986, 15 pp.). Scoring and Interpretation Manual (1986, 28 pp.). Cost: $68.95 for Examiners Kit containing Administration Manual, Scoring and Interpretation Manual, cue picture book, 50 student test booklets, and cassette. Sharon E. Duncan and Edward A. DeAvila. Linguametrics Group, PO Box 3459, San Rafael, CA 94912, USA, telephone: (415) 459-5350.

## Review

The PRE-LAS was designed to measure general oral English language ability of children from ages 4-6. Six subtests measure expressive and receptive abilities across the linguistic areas of morphology, syntax, and semantics. Like the Language Assessment Scales (LAS) for older children (see review this volume), the PRE-LAS examines overall English language performance, rather than concentrating on a single aspect of oral language.

There are two forms available, A and B, which makes it possible to pre- and posttest students with alternative forms. There is only one Spanish language form available.

The PRE-LAS package includes students response booklets, a cue picture book, an Administrator's Manual, and a Scoring and Interpretation Manual. These are all conveniently bound in a three-ring notebook for ease of administration. An audio cassette tape of the entire test, as well as audio cassette tapes of the mini-stories, are available as optional material.

Statistical data on the test is provided in the PRE-LAS Technical Report, which is available from the authors. The data is based on the administration of the test to approximately 850 students at nine sites in the southwestern United States and Hawaii. However, the report contains statistical tables without interpretive information. Based on the data in the report, PRE-LAS appears to be highly reliable. Although no reliability figure for the total test is given, the reliabilities of the separate parts range from .69 to .93, with the listening parts being less reliable than the speaking parts.

Examinees are asked in the first subtest to perform a

total physical response to the stimulus of "Simon Says." They are asked to identify a picture that matches an oral stimulus from the test administrator; given a large drawing of a house, the examinee is asked to point to ten different items identified by the examiner. Part 4 asks test takers to repeat what they hear, thus checking on their ability to repeat target phonemes embedded in phrases and single words. These four subtests constitute 55% of the total score.

The remainder of the test constitutes 45% of the score and involves more creative use of language. Subtest V is an oral cloze exercise where the examinee supplies a missing word or words to finish a story; similar to the LAS, in Part VI the test taker retells a story immediately after hearing it while looking at stimulus pictures. PRE-LAS stories are shorter and more interesting than are LAS stories. Two stories are needed for the scoring system to function properly.

The PRE-LAS is individually administered and requires a minimum of 10 minutes for completion. Raw scores must be converted to weighted scores using a variety of different tables and both the Finishing Stories and Let's Tell Stories subtests are compared to transcriptions of sample responses at each score level. These samples are presented in age-related groupings so that a 4-year-old's production is not compared to a 6-year-old's.

The time factor is a positive aspect of the PRE-LAS. Ten minutes is an appropriate length given the young child's ability to concentrate. The decision to make the use of the cassette tape optional was also a very practical one, as children this age relate better to people than to machines.

A serious practical consideration with the PRE-LAS, as with all levels of the LAS, is that the scoring system requires a sophistication that some people may find confusing. For the most part, computation with decimals has been eliminated, but the conversion of raw scores remains a potential source of error. Extensive in-service training is needed for any staff member who is responsible for administering the PRE-LAS. The subjective nature of scoring the final two subsections of oral production is a potential problem, yet the authors provide considerable information on how to interpret scores while taking into account the standard error of measurement. Additional language information is suggested for those children whose scores fall in "grey" areas or within the standard error between levels 3 and 4, which represents the division between limited English proficient and proficient.

The PRE-LAS is recommended for measuring the oral English proficiency of young children. Its strength lies in its ability to assess oral language in an environment that is enjoyable for both child and test administrator. Its attempt to assess across a child's morphology, syntax, and semantics is commendable. More importantly, the total physical response and cloze attributes of this measure incorporate recent theoretical developments in second language acquisition/assessment and make the results more meaningful. Still, research is needed on the validity of the PRE-LAS.

For children this young, the PRE-LAS subtests can be very helpful in determining differing levels of English comprehension in a preschool setting of listening, following directions, and learning language in context.

# Quick Language Assessment Inventory

*Reviewed by*

**Kathryn Singh**
**Cooperative Learning Implementation Project**
**San Ramon, California**

## Synopsis

Quick Language Assessment Inventory. 1974. No specific grade level is given as an examinee population. Designed to determine the need for instruction in English as a second language, number of special classes needed, number of households requiring Spanish translations of school-related literature, candidates for Spanish as a second language, population information requested by school board, and/or State Department of Education. The test is administered individually by any school employee to the parent/guardian. Examinees receive points based on language experience, parents' birthplace and education, and language used at home. Points are tallied (possible total of 11), deducting one point for each year examinee was enrolled in U.S. schools. A final score of 0-2 indicates *Mainly English Speaker* (Category I); 3-5, *Transitional English Speaker* (Category II); 6-8, *Beginning English Speaker* (Category III); and 9-11, *Mainly Spanish Speaker* (Category IV). Approximate administration time is 1 minute, with instant scoring. Total packet includes Administration Manual (1974, 4 pp.) and 50 student inventory sheets. No Technical Manual, but Administration Manual provides some information on test item descriptions, validity, reliability, interpretation of scores and possible use of results. Cost is $10.00 with additional inventory sheets available at .15 each. Steven Moreno. Moreno Educational Company, PO Box 19329, San Diego, CA 92119, USA, telephone: (614) 461-0565.

## Review

The Quick Language Assessment Inventory (Inventory) claims to provide school personnel with an assessment of a child's language abilities in both English and Spanish within 1 minute. Unlike other assessment tools, this instrument does not test a child's ability to use discrete grammatical and lexical items. Instead, it offers a summary of language exposure opportunities made available to the child through parents, schooling, and length of time in the U.S. The main purposes of the inventory are to determine the need for English as a second language instruction and to gather information on the district's bilingual population.

The use of the term *language assessment inventory* may be misleading. Although the tool does provide information that might offer some insight into a child's opportunity to learn English, it does not necessarily provide an accurate rating of the child's actual proficiency in either English or Spanish. This task would, in fact, require the tester to speak directly with the child in order to determine his/her degree of comprehension/fluency. Exposure to a language does not always lead to its acquisition.

The Manual indicates that any school employee may administer the Inventory. No specific training or language background is needed. Ideally, proficiency testers should be bilingual in English and the language of the child, and at least familiar with the stages of language acquisition. A bilingual examiner, required by law in many states, can ease the child and parent/guardian into the assessment situation by using the primary language for greetings and preassessment explanations. Knowledge of language acquisition stages would allow for a more complete interpretation of results, and a more accurate placement.

The time required for administering and scoring is 1 minute, according to the author. One major setback is that the Inventory is only available, it seems, in English. Translating each question, recording responses, and tallying points would certainly take more than 1 minute, unless the district prepared a translation and had it readily available.

Indicators used in the Inventory as measures of language ability may not be valid in all cases. The following assumptions were made when the instrument was designed:

1. Birth and education outside the U.S. detract from the potential to acquire English.

2. Birth and education inside the U.S. guarantee successful acquisition of English.

3. All young children (K-3) have an advantage over older children in the language acquisition process.

4. *Mainly Spanish* indicates little or no English proficiency and *Mainly English* indicates little or no Spanish proficiency.

Obviously, all four assumptions may be challenged. Second language learners vary from individual to individual. Current language acquisition theory tells us that there are a variety of factors that affect a person's ability to acquire a second language; aptitude, age, motivation, stress level, previous language experience, and attitude toward self and others. Adding or deducting points for the above mentioned indicators may be valid in some cases but not in others.

The categories offered for interpretation of the Inventory are very general. What is the difference between Beginning, Transitional, and Mainly English? *Interlanguage*, the stage between nonfluency and fluency, is very fluid and difficult to break into specific, absolute categories solely on the basis of previous language exposure. Depending on linguistic demands presented by communicative and academic situations, a second language learner may fluctuate from one category to another. A student may be *Mainly English* in social vocabulary and *Beginning English* in academic vocabulary. Placing students into neat categories may not be appropriate in assessing language strengths and weaknesses, and determining the need for ESL instruction.

The results of two studies related to the validity of the Inventory are very briefly described in the Administration Manual. In a study of 1,855 southern California students, Grades K-6, the multiple correlation coefficient between 11 categories of sociocultural information and classroom language was .893. The Inventory questions were developed, presumably based on this sociocultural information, but the author gives no further information on how or why particular items were selected.

When classroom teacher ratings of 943 students, Grades K-6, were compared with Inventory ratings, the Inventory was successful in predicting 93% of the classroom language for all students. There appears to be a strong relationship between the sociocultural information and classroom language ability, but important details concerning the information, the language, and the data from the studies are missing. There is no data given to justify placement in the four specific language proficiency categories outlined in the Manual.

There are no studies reported on the reliability of the Inventory. According to the Administration Manual, "the reliability is 100% accurate since the Inventory is based on objective data from parents and guardians." No evidence is given that the internal consistency or information gathered at different times by different scores is reliable. The fact that the information gathered by the Inventory is self-reported data does not insure that it is a reliable instrument.

This Inventory, when first created in 1974, was most likely a welcome addition to the still developing field of second language education. At this time however, its role must be reduced from that of a language assessment tool to that of a home language survey or exposure inventory. Information provided by the instrument may offer an overall picture of the student's past experiences, but should not be used to determine current language proficiency in either first or second languages. The author of the Inventory recognizes this fact and suggests the use of the Oral Language Proficiency Test for more complete information.

# The Second Language Oral Test of English

*Reviewed by*

## Hollis G. Stein
Prince George County Public Schools
Greenbelt, Maryland

## Synopsis

The Second Language Oral Test of English. SLOTE. 1983. Grades K-Adult. Designed to assess the ability of nonnative English speakers to produce 20 standard English grammatical structures. Verbal responses to pictures are scored *correct* or *incorrect* with one point awarded for each correct answer. Sample correct and incorrect responses are given in the Test Manual. Points are scores 0-3 per subtest, 0-60 overall. Individual. 15 minutes. One form. SLOTE Test Manual (1983, 60 pp.). $15.95 per Test Manual which contains test pictures, Student Score Sheet, Class/Group Score Sheet, administration procedures and technical data. Ann K. Fathman. Alemany Press, 2501 Industrial Parkway West, Hayward, CA, USA 94545, telephone: (800) 227-2375 or (415) 887-7070.

## Review

The Second Language Oral Test of English (SLOTE) is a very useful test instrument for assessing the oral language skills of nonnative English speakers. Numerous strengths of SLOTE will be discussed in this review; however, two are particularly valuable. First, SLOTE can be used to assess oral proficiency of students of any language background, as it is not designed to diagnose errors common to only one language group which is the case with many available ESL tests. Secondly, it has a Class/Group Score Sheet on which teachers can make group profiles of student errors. The SLOTE has some shortcomings, which will also be discussed in this review; however, the strengths outweigh the shortcomings. The SLOTE is a test which many ESL teachers and programs should use as a part of their test battery.

One strength of the SLOTE is that it is an easy test to administer and score. A single publication contains the Test Manual, warm-up pictures, practice pictures, and 60 test items divided into 20 subtests, each testing a separate structure. The Test Manual contains a clear explanation of administration procedures as well as a chart detailing correct and incorrect responses for each test item. The tester is told how to sit in relation to the student and how to place the booklet so that the student can read the stimulus for each item that is printed on the pages facing the tester and opposite the test pictures. Because of the clear instructions in the Manual, testers are easily trained.

Students' oral responses are scored *correct* or *incorrect,* with one point awarded for each correct answer. There is space on the Student Score Sheet to record incorrect responses for later error analysis. Points are totaled both for subtests (0-3) and for overall score (0-60). Total score cut-offs for ESL level placement are provided in the Test Manual.

By analyzing subtests, the teacher can quickly determine a student's knowledge of specific morphemes and/or syntactic patterns. Phonetic, syntactic, and semantic variants of a pattern are tested within the subtests. Articles, pronouns, plurals, simple verb tenses, negatives, and questions are just some of the areas included in the subtests. The Class/Group Score Sheet is extremely valuable in this analysis and allows the teacher to compile error data not only for individuals, but for whole classes or groups of students. With the score sheet, the teacher can identify those structures that a group of students have mastered and those structures that pose the greatest difficulty. This greatly assists the teacher in planning a meaningful curriculum.

Some physical aspects of the SLOTE design add to ease of use. Test illustrations are simple, clear, and uncluttered. Students have no trouble recognizing what is being represented. In most instances, there is only one test item per page; however, even when there are three questions on one page, the item numbers are printed clearly on the student's illustrated page and on the examiner's page, and they correspond clearly with the item numbers on the Student Score Sheet. In addition, the correct, or desired, response(s) is printed below each test item stimulus.

The Test Manual contains the technical data on the test's development reliability and validity. The reported test-retest reliability (.98) and interrater reliability (.97) are excellent, although these coefficients are based on a sample of only 40 students. The internal consistency reliability (KR 20), based on a national sample of 1,100 students, is .95.

Data on construct and criterion-related validity are also presented in the Manual. The correlation between correct usage of English structures tested on the SLOTE and correct usage of the same structures in free speech is .62 (N = 150). The correlation with teacher ratings of overall grammatical proficiency in the classroom for the same group of students is .68. Data on concurrent validity with a number of other language proficiency tests including TOEFL, the Bilingual Syntax Measure, and the Ilyin Oral Interview are also presented. The pattern of correlations supports the validity of SLOTE as a pragmatic oral test of grammar. The data presented on test bias suggests that differences in language background, student age, native language, and school district do not significantly affect SLOTE Test Scores.

There are some shortcomings to the SLOTE that should be pointed out. The 20 subtests are not organized to be progressively more difficult. As a result, beginning students with knowledge of few structures struggle through the test, or the tester moves through the test selecting the commonly known imperatives and regular plurals. Proceeding through the entire 60 questions to test knowledge of these easier areas is frustrating for both the student and tester.

The wording of some stimuli needs improvement. For example, use of the word *son* to begin Yes/No questions is awkward. The tester should be told to use the testee's name instead. The method employed to elicit the *'s* ending for possessives as in *the cat's ball* is cumbersome, with the result that the structure is rarely elicited. Finally, it is often difficult to distinguish between a student's pronunciation of *two man* or *two men* in the irregular plural section. These, however, are only minor problems in administering the test.

A more serious shortcoming is that SLOTE does not test some advanced structures that speakers of English need to know. Based on the SLOTE alone, students may score at the High Intermediate/Advanced level, or even place out of an ESL program, yet the teacher will not have assessed knowledge of structures such as future tense, past progressive tense or reflexive pronouns. While these structures may not be essential for elementary school students in the lower grades, they will be essential for older elementary school students, secondary school students, and for adults. In addition, the fact that there is only one form of this test is a drawback. There should be a limit to the number of times students are given the same form.

In summary, the SLOTE is highly recommended when used as one of a battery of tests to obtain an individual language profile. This test provides useful information about the oral language proficiency of beginning LEP students of any language background and age. It is quick and easy to administer and is well received by the students. SLOTE is not, however, as valuable a test for assessing the oral language skills of older students of high intermediate or advanced proficiency, as it is for elementary school students.

# Secondary Level English Proficiency Test

*Reviewed by*

**Janice I. Brecher**
**Centennial School District**
**Warminster, Pennsylvania**

## Synopsis

Secondary Level English Proficiency Test. SLEP. Grades 7 - 12. Designed to measure ability in understanding spoken and written English. Scored with plastic stencil provided with test materials. Group administered. Three scores: Section 1, Listening Comprehension, 40 min-

utes; Section 2, Reading Comprehension, 45 minutes; Total 85 minutes. Two forms: Form 1, 1981, 38 pp.; Form 2, 1984, 38 pp. SLEP Test Manual (1984, 40 pp.). 1986 prices: $85 per complete kit (either form) containing cassette tape, 20 test booklets, 100 answer sheets, 2 scoring stencils and Manual. $30 per 20 test booklets, $25 per 100 answer sheets, $5 per pack 5 stencils, cassette, or Manual. Educational Testing Service/TOEFL Program and Committee of Secondary School ESL Teachers. Educational Testing Service, Secondary Level English Proficiency Test, CN 6158, Princeton, NJ 08541-6158 USA, telephone: (609) 734-5264.

## Test References

Lloyd, B. H. (1985). [Review of secondary level English proficiency test.] In J. V. Mitchell (Ed.), *Ninth mental measurements yearbook* (pp. 1335-6). Lincoln, NE: Buros Institute of Mental Measurements & the University of Nebraska.

Subkoviak, M. J. (1985). [Review of the secondary level English proficiency test.] In J. V. Mitchell (Ed.), *Ninth mental measurements yearbook* (pp. 1336-7). Lincoln, NE: Buros Institute of Mental Measurements & the University of Nebraska.

## Review

SLEP is helpful in making decisions regarding assignment to ESL classes, placement in a mainstream English program, exemption from a bilingual program, exit from an ESL program, and ESL program evaluation (ETS, 1984b, p. 5). SLEP is not a predictor of academic success, a measure of academic achievement, or a test of cultural adaptability.

SLEP is a four-option multiple-choice test. The 150 items are divided into two sections, Listening Comprehension and Reading Comprehension, with 75 questions in each section. There are four parts in each section. The number of questions in each part is indicated below.

| Listening Comprehension | Reading Comprehension |
|---|---|
| Part 1, Single Picture Stimulus (25) | Part 5, Cartoon (12) |
| Part 2, Multiple-Choice Dictation (19) | Part 6, Line Drawings (16) |
| Part 3, Map-Related Questions (11) | Part 7, Cloze (39) |
| Part 4, Extended Conversations (20) | Part 8, Literary Passage (8) |

The uniqueness of the tasks to be performed in the SLEP has been highlighted in other reviews. Parts of both subtests are rated as "excellent" for assessing "functional understanding more directly than tests that use written oral passages and comprehension questions. Note also that no judgment of grammaticality is required." (DeBoe, 1983, p.14) Another reviewer has described SLEP as "different from the usual standardized, objective, non-real" test. It uses "real language, presented in a relatively comfortable format" (Robinson, 1984, p. 28). Both reviewers praised the clear voices speaking at normal speed on the tape as precise examples of standard English spoken on radio and television.

## Scoring

The SLEP is a norm-referenced test. The Manual contains tables to show how norming groups performed. The tables are arranged by type of remedial program in which students in the norming groups were enrolled and by grade, length of time spent in English instruction, and length of time in the United States, rather than by native language.

For Forms 1 and 2 raw scores on each form have been statistically equated and placed on a common scale. This compensates for inevitable differences in difficulty from form to form and ensures comparable scores across forms. This allows for alternate forms to be suitable as both a placement test and exit test. Because the forms are scored locally, the results can be obtained quickly and inexpensively.

## Manual

The revised Manual provides a comprehensive overview of the SLEP Program including the purposes and use of the test and a description and history of its development. Adequate information is also given on administering and scoring the test and the interpretation of scores. Statistical information is included also.

The most interesting part of the Manual can be found near the end where advice is given on how to set exit criteria for mainstreaming purposes and how to carry out local validation studies. This section shows how the scores fit into the total picture, rather than allowing scores to stand as isolated statistics.

## Validity and Reliabilty

Validity studies indicate that SLEP is a valid test of English language proficiency. According to a study in Oregon, involving 484 subjects, native speakers of English perform very well on the SLEP, thus supporting the claim that SLEP is a valid test of ESL because it is psychometrically unable to distinguish between native speakers. (ETS, 1984a, p.2) Another validity study of the SLEP Test in Florida concurred that the SLEP does not discriminate among native speakers. It concluded, moreover, that the test discriminates validly among nonnative speakers based on the length of time they have studied English—the longer the period of English instruction, the higher the scores. (Holloway, 1984, pp. 2-3).

The publishers conducted a study of the criterion-related validity of the test involving 1,239 students representing 68 schools in 20 states. The results indi-

cate that SLEP scores showed low to moderate but statistically significant correlations with years of English study both within and outside the United States, time enrolled in school, and length of time the student has lived in the United States. (Stansfield, 1984, pp. 8-10).

Largely due to its multiple-choice format, the reliability of the test is quite high. The reliability (KR-20) of the total test is .96, while the reliability of the listening comprehension section is .94, and the reading comprehension section is .93. (Stansfield, 1984, p. 7).

## Difficulty of Test Parts

The three most difficult parts, in increasing order, are Extended Conversations (Part 4), Cloze (Part 7), and Literary Passage (Part 8). They are more difficult because they require a global understanding of context as well as recognition of discrete elements of language. (Stansfield, 1984, p. 6).

Conclusions from a validation study by Holloway (1984, p. vi) also address this issue. He reports that SLEP is not, on the whole, inappropriately difficult for non-native speaking population; however, the appropriateness of the Literary Passage (Part 8) as a measure of non-native proficiency is highly questionable due to poor performance on this part by even native speakers. His tables support that both native and nonnative groups performed better on the listening section than on the reading section due to lower scores on the Cloze (Part 7) and Literary Passage (Part 8) parts. Native speakers averaged above 90% correct on 6 out of 8 test parts, but only 81% correct on Part 7 and 64% correct on Part 8. These were the most difficult parts of the test for both nonnative and native populations. Regarding the Literary Passage, Holloway (1984, p. 48) asks: "How is this part supposed to be a measure of non-native English proficiency if the native models scored so poorly?"

## Limitations

The obvious missing parts in this test are components to evaluate students' production of speech and writing. It was the only limitation cited in a SLEP User Survey taken by ETS. (ETS, 1984a, p. 2) On the one hand, it can be said that SLEP produces limited results by testing only listening and reading comprehension. On the other hand, any test should be considered to be part of a total evaluation program, a point which ETS makes in the Manual. (ETS, 1984b, p. 36) The SLEP test should not be used as the only determiner of any of its stated goals. A school district could easily supplement the test with an oral interview and writing sample.

Another question that could be asked is whether an oral production section is really a necessary component of a test used for mainstreaming at the secondary level. Most of the language activity in the secondary school classroom is listening and reading, and these are the skills required to understand the teacher and the text. Therefore, it could be left to individual school districts to determine whether tests of productive skills are necessary for placement.

ETS reports that the revised answer key, which permits the scorer to place a mark beside each incorrect answer on the examinee's answer sheet, facilitates the diagnostic analysis of responses. (ETS, 1984a, p. 1). However, the ability of the test to diagnose the problem areas of a student's language skills is limited to the ability of the teacher to analyze the test item. In order for the test to be truly diagnostic, the Manual would need a section indicating the feature tested in each item.

## Summary

The SLEP Test has two sections (eight parts) to measure listening and reading comprehension for the junior and senior high school student. The test results can help educators make decisions about student placement in language programs. The test parts utilize unique tasks to elicit student responses. The Manual provides information to equate Forms 1 and 2 on a common scale and provides scales for converting scores. It appears from the literature that the SLEP is a valid and reliable test of English language proficiency. The one major area of concern is the difficulty of the Literary Passage, which needs to be reconsidered. Although the test does not measure language production, this is not a major weakness because it does measure the major language skills needed in the secondary classroom. However, ETS' claim about the test's diagnostic value is moderated by the teacher's ability to analyze the problematic nature of an incorrectly marked test item. Within the limitations discussed in this review, the SLEP is recommended as a test that meets its objective of measuring ability in understanding spoken and written English.

## Reviewer's References

DeBoe, M. (1983). Secondary level English proficiency (SLEP) test. *The ORTESOL Newsletter, 6*(3), 14.

Educational Testing Service. (1984a, May). *SLEP bulletin board, 1*. Princeton, NJ: Author.

Educational Testing Service. (1984b). *SLEP test manual*. Princeton, NJ: Author.

Holloway, D. M. (1984). *Validation study of SLEP test*. Unpublished master's thesis, University of Florida, Gainesville.

Robinson, T. (1984). [Review of SLEP test]. *Teachers Texts and Technology Review, 1*, 28.

Sloan, S. (1982). Let's look at SLEP. *Secondary school SIG newsletter, 5*(1), 2.

Stansfield, C. W. (1984). Reliability and validity of the secondary level English proficiency test. *System, 12*(1), 1-12.

# Short Selection Test

*Reviewed by*

**Pamela M. Riley**
**University of Sydney**

## Synopsis

Short Selection Test. SST. Students aged 16+ outside of Australia. Designed to measure overall English language ability required for study in Australia. Listening comprehension, multiple choice, credit for one correct answer to each question; dictation, replication of original passage; cloze reading passages, exact word scoring; essay, post-matriculation candidates entering tertiary studies scored by comparison with native-speaker written production in both content and expression. Results interpreted in terms of estimated number of months of full-time English language instruction required before candidates can undertake studies in Australia, with a limit of 12 months maximum. Results assessed at three levels: secondary students entering years 11, 12, or certificate courses in Technical and Further Education; students entering undergraduate institutions; and students pursuing postgraduate degrees and diplomas. Administered to groups in Australia and overseas by Australia-based personnel, returned to Australia for assessment in Canberra. 1 1/4 hours for first three sections, 1/2 hour for essay. 10 parallel forms. First prepared, 1979. Administration guidelines in Australian development training manual. Short Selection Test: Information for Candidates, (1983, 7 pp.). Secure, not available commercially, developed and administered by Language Education Branch, Department of Education and Youth affairs, PO Box 826, Woden ACT 2606, Canberra, Australia, telephone: 89 1333.

## Review

### Purpose

The Australian Short Selection Test (SST) is prepared by the Language Education Branch of the Commonwealth Department of Education and Youth Affairs. Overseas students from non-Commonwealth Africa, Asia, Latin America, the Middle East, and Southeast Asia who plan to study in Australia during the last 2 years of secondary school or at any formal postsecondary educational institution, take the SST unless they have had an English-medium education. It is a test of general English proficiency intended for prospective students 16-years-old or over, which purports to assess both aural and written skills, receptively and productively.

### Range

The range of the examinees, from upper secondary

students through technical and vocational students to postgraduates is so wide that the SST is criticized as being inappropriate, not assessing the academic skills in English needed by the postgraduate in specific disciplines at one extreme, and focusing on literacy skills that are unnecessary for some forms of technical education at the other. The majority of examinees are at the postsecondary level. They plan to undertake undergraduate or certificate level courses, and the SST aims to focus on the language skills they will need. Results are assessed on three levels for postgraduates, graduates, technical, vocational, and upper secondary school study.

## Description

There are four sections to the SST: listening comprehension, dictation, reading comprehension (cloze procedure) and a short essay, the latter being taken only by those intending to take postmatriculation studies.

The Listening Comprehension test is intended to test the skills needed for education in Australia—listening and comprehending a prepared informative talk. As students outside of Australia often report that their initial difficulties with spoken English are the speed of delivery and the Australian accent, the aural sections of the test are recorded at normal pace by speakers with markedly Australian accents. The test consists of three short—about 3 minutes and 250-300 words in length—academic lectures which have been read onto tape and an answer book, available before the lecture, with about six questions and three or four multiple-choice answers on each lecture. Each question is stated in the form as an incomplete statement, and the examinees choose the option that best completes the statement according to what they have heard. Although this is intended as a listening test, performance depends in part on the examinees' ability to read the stimulus and options. Completion of a task after listening instead of multiple-choice question-answer has been suggested as a more realistic test.

Dictation assesses the skills of intensive listening and accurate recording. The two short dictation passages (60-80 words each) in the SST are heard three times, once without pause so listeners can get the gist of the passage, once with appropriate pauses (approximately every six words) for them to write, and a third time without pauses to enable them to correct. Although the second reading is at normal speaking pace so listeners have to reconstruct the portions of language, the fact that the passage is given a third time reduces effectiveness as a measure of integrated language skills. The whole exercise is recorded on tape for world-wide consistency. It is scored on a verbatim basis, with a mark deducted for every deviation from the original.

The reading comprehension test uses a rational deletion cloze procedure, with 8-10 words between deletions. These are two passages with 20 deletions in each, scored on an exact-word basis. Cloze procedure has been said to produce integrative tests of overall language proficiency for both first and second language speakers.

The essay, on general topics such as pollution or conservation, is necessarily short, and only 1/2 hour is allowed. The examinees' lack of familiarity with the demands of sustained writing beyond the paragraph, together with very slow writing skills, makes this test difficult for most students. The essay is assessed by comparing its content and form with native English speakers' essays written in the same amount of time.

## Results

Scores on the three (or four) sections are summed, and the evaluation is expressed in terms of the length of preparatory English instruction the students are estimated to require to reach the proficiency deemed necessary for the level of the selected course: secondary, tertiary or technical-vocational. This instruction is given at designated Australian institutions. Assessments range from no precourse English to 12-month requirement. These "guesstimates" are based on the measured progress that students have shown in English language courses in these institutions averaged over several years, but overlook factors such as effective teaching/learning strategies and techniques of both teaching institutions and individual learners. The SST has not been used experimentally to monitor the progress of students attending courses of their choice with or without supporting English language instruction. Score users sometimes complain that results are summed, and that assessments are given globally in broad bands such as 2-week or 5-month precourse English requirement, without detailed results of sections of the test. For students in a particular course, one subsection of the test may be much more important than others, and tertiary institutions in particular have expressed dissatisfaction with the lack of information on English proficiency they receive. A breakdown of results, at least into oral, written and reading skills, would enable institutions to provide remedial and developmental support courses in English language tailored to student needs from the beginning of formal courses.

## Administration

Most students take the SST in their own countries where it is administered by Australian missions. In 1983, over 9,000 students attempted the test. Two major problems are ensuring consistency of administration and scoring, and maintaining test security.

The physical conditions under which the test is taken vary greatly from air-conditioned laboratories with individual booths and ear phones, to open halls with candidates crowded together and the aural section broadcast over loudspeakers. Common complaints include the poor quality audio equipment that distorts the tapes, interference from traffic and other outside noises, and poor lighting. Where there are large numbers of candidates, such as in Jakarta, tests can be administered by trained, experienced staff, but in centers located outside of capital cities the tests are sometimes given by inexperienced supervisors. Completed papers are marked in Canberra, so consistency of scoring is maintained.

## Security

Security is a major difficulty in a test of this nature given over such a wide geographical area. There are ten parallel forms used randomly in an attempt to maintain security. The test would be more secure if subsections were given in different combinations, for example, each listening, dictation, and cloze passage were administered from a different form of the test.

## Reliability and Validity

Test reliability has not been assessed. Neither has there been research on validity nor a study comparing the SST with TOEFL or ELTS, both of which are also used to screen students coming to Australia.

## Conclusion

The effectiveness of the SST in screening students is difficult to assess, as there has been no systematic follow-up of students in their studies in Australia nor any follow-up of those who "fail" by being assessed as needing more than 12-months preliminary English. Weaknesses are the lack of information on reliability, the listening section, the summation of results on all sections, assessment in terms of preliminary English requirements, and the lack of information available to Australian educational institutions about the English proficiency of applicants. Strengths are the consistent scoring system, and the inclusion of integrative tests of language, cloze procedure, and an essay for tertiary-level applicants.

Even critics concede that although the SST does not always predict accurately, it is much more effective than the test used previously, which contained discrete items on syntax, vocabulary, and multiple-choice reading assessments.

# Structure Tests-English Language

### Reviewed by

### Jon Jonz
### East Texas State University

### Synopsis

Structure Tests-English Language. STEL. 1976. Junior high and above. Designed to measure knowledge of syntactic structure and vocabulary in English. Multiple-choice format scored with the use of an acrylic scoring stencil; raw scores converted to one of six placement levels. Group administration. 30 minutes. 3 levels, 2 forms per level (all 1976, 4 pp.). Directions for administering are printed on every test booklet (no manual available). Technical data are printed on every test booklet (no manual available). $9.00 (prepaid) per test package containing 20 tests (ten copies each of Forms 1 and 2) and 20 answer sheets. $10.00 (prepaid) for two answer keys (one each for Forms 1 and 2). $7.25 (prepaid) for 20 additional answer sheets. Jeanette Best and Donna Ilyin. Harper & Row Publishers, Keystone Industral Park, Scranton, PA, USA, telephone: (800) 242-7737.

### Review

The STEL is a fast, easy, inexpensive multiple-choice test of selected syntactic structures and verb forms in written English. It is available in three difficulty levels and two alternate forms at each level. The purpose of the test is to provide rough-and-ready placement information with minimal investment of testing time. It can also be used in pre/post or post-only applications; the authors recommend 90 days intervening between administrations.

Each test consists of 50 items in which the examinee is to select the correct response of three alternatives presented. The test takes 30 minutes to administer and approximately one minute per examinee to hand score. The test booklets are well planned; the front page contains directions for the student, and the back page contains directions for test administrators. Once the test is underway, no test pages need be turned because the 50 test items are printed on facing pages.

Available data indicate that STEL is reliable and that it has two claims to validity. Reliability data for each form at each level are reported on the back page of the test booklet. Reliability coefficients range from .86 to .90, and though the method by which these coefficients were calculated is not specified, they can be interpreted tentatively as indicating acceptable stability, especially in view of the brevity of the tests. Parallel form reliability is also reported on the last page of the test booklet. The Beginning level forms correlate (product-moment) at $r = .81$ ($N = 106$), Intermediate level forms at $r = .87$ ($N = 69$), and Advanced level forms at $r = .89$ ($N = 33$). These indices are somewhat depressed from the internal consistency reliability reported for single forms. The conditions under which these data were collected are not reported.

STEL also has claims to validity. In addition to acceptable parallel form reliability, which is a special sort of concurrent validation, one can also document the validity of STEL in relationship to the content of the various levels of ESL courses taught at Alemany Adult School in San Francisco, California, the home institution of the tests' authors. Additionally, the STEL authors conducted a criterion-related validity study using the judgment of experienced ESL teachers as the criterion. One of the authors (Ilyin, 1975, p. 133) reports that "On pretests . . . I asked teachers to group students in the top 25%, middle 50%, before the students took the tests. A t-test showed differences were in the expected direction and probability was in every case better than .01."

The principal reservation that must be expressed is that very little technical information is readily available about STEL. The most comprehensive treatment of the development of the tests is available in Ilyin (1970). It is not clear, however, that the procedures and technical data reported in that document refer to the published test or only to its precursors. The tests described in an attachment to Ilyin (1970) (Forms L, M, N, O, R, S, T, U, and Trial Tests A, B, C, D for each level) became the published STEL, but exactly how the transition was accomplished is not documented.

The top portion of each acrylic scoring stencil offers "Placement Information." From this chart one learns that a raw score of 28 on Form 2 of the Beginning Level test would place a student in the higher section of a beginning course. That is exactly the information that would help one make placement decisions. However, what if one's ESL program does not follow the grammatical agenda that the Alemany Adult School course of studies does? Is the placement information still usable?

Ilyin (1975, p. 135) cautions "The tests' usefulness will not only depend on programs having similar objectives and using similar materials, but also on the way the tests are administered and secured." Certainly a responsible disclaimer; however, it was published with reference to the STEL's precursor, the EPT 100-200-30, and does not appear along with other test information on the test booklets. The enterprising consumer, however, using both the Table of Equivalency Scores of Students in Adult Program ESL, a part of the STEL sample package available free from the publisher, and the Newbury House Linguistic Grading Scale, printed on pages 6 and 7 of the publisher's current catalog, *Concerned about Testing*, can get an idea of what the raw score of 28 and "placement in higher section of beginning course" mean. One learns from the Table of Equivalency Scores that the score accords with a TOEFL score below 350.

From the Linguistic Grading Scale one learns that higher sections of the Beginning level involve a basic vocabulary of 600 base words in addition to the use of the following verb forms: simple present, present continuous, simple past (regular), future (going to), imperative, simple future, present perfect, simple past (irregular), and past continuous. But one should not need to refer to so many diverse sources for information; the test's publisher should produce a technical manual for STEL that collects all information about test development and test-score interpretation in one easily accessible place. Another Ilyin co-creation, the English Language Skills Assessment in a Reading Context (ELSA), also available from Newbury House, comes with a nicely developed technical manual. In fact, considerable STEL technical information is scattered throughout the ELSA Manual. Other widely used Ilyin tests (e.g., Ilyin Oral Interview) are also accompanied by technical and administrative information, but not STEL. This lapse should be remedied at the earliest possible time.

In summary, STEL provides a quick, reliable, inexpensive way to gather initial placement information for adult and adolescent ESL programs. However, the user of STEL does not have immediate access to the broad range of technical information that one normally expects to have accompanying a standardized test.

## Reviewer's References

Ilyin, D. (1970). Developing a placement test for adults in English-second-language programs in California. (ERIC Document Reproduction Service No. ED 036 766)

Ilyin, D. (1975). Structure placement tests for adults in English-second-language programs in California. In L. Palmer and B. Spolsky (Eds.), *Papers on language testing 1967-1974* (pp. 128-36). Washington, D.C.: Teachers of English to Speakers of Other Languages.

Pack, A. C. (1977). [Review of structure tests-English language]. *Modern Language Journal, 61*, 427.

# Test of Ability to Subordinate

*Reviewed by*

**Karen A. Mullen**
**University of Louisville**

### Synopsis

Test of Ability to Subordinate. TAS. 1978. Intermediate and advanced ESL students. Designed to identify strengths and weaknesses in writing sentences in English. Written responses scored as *correct* or *incorrect* by comparing them with suggested responses. 45 items divided into nine 5 item subgroups, each representing a different subordinate structure. Standard of mastery set at passing 80% of items of each structure. Incorrect responses to be examined for particular problems and used in designing a writing program to remedy errors. Group administration. 35-40 minutes. One form (1978, 45 questions). Teacher's Manual (1978, 12 pp.). $12.00 per test package (60 answer sheets, 1 Teacher's Manual, 30 test booklets). $2.00 for 100 additional answer sheets. David M. Davidson. 639 West End Avenue, New York, NY 10025, USA, telephone: (718) 636-2104.

74

## Test References

Davidson, D. M. (1976). Assessing writing ability of ESL college freshmen. (ERIC Document Reproduction Service No. ED 135 247)

Kunz, L. A. (1980). [English as a second language]. In A. S. Trillin (Ed.), *Teaching basic skills in college* (pp. 145-207). San Francisco, CA: Jossey-Bass.

Perkins, K. (1982). [The test of ability to subordinate: predictive and concurrent validity for attained ESL composition]. In T. Culhane, C. Klein Braley, & D. K. Stevenson (Eds.), *Practice and problems in language testing* (Occasional Papers No. 26, pp. 104-112). Colchester: University of Essex, Department of Language and Linguistics.

Saitz, R. L. (1979). [Review of the test of ability to subordinate.] *Modern Language Journal, 53*(5&6), 305.

Weaver, J. E. (1979). [Review of the test of ability to subordinate]. *TESOL Quarterly, 13*(2), 268-70.

## Review

TAS assesses the writing maturity of ESL students by means of sentence combining tasks requiring subordinate structures. The test materials include a test booklet, an answer sheet, and a Teacher's Manual. In the test booklet, the subject first reads and responds to four examples under supervision and then reads 45 items, each consisting of two or three kernel sentences and an accompanying sentence frame:

> a. Luis lived in the Dominican Republic.
>
> b. Then Luis came to New York.
>
> Frame: _____ came to New York, he lived in the Dominican Republic.

On the answer sheet, the subject sees the frame again and is expected to fill in the missing words, in this case *Before Luis*.

The Teacher's Manual contains a short introduction; a statement of purpose; a list of subordination structures, their specific representation in test items, and the requisite kernel changes; statistics on validity, reliability, standard error of measurement, and mean score; and directions for administering the test, including the script of directions to the student, a guide for grading and interpreting the results, and a list of acceptable responses, previously determined from sampling native speakers. Nine subordinating patterns are represented: adjectival modifier in a noun phrase (includes possessive nouns and pronouns); adverbials of time, place, manner, degree, and frequency; prepositional phrases; infinitive phrases; participial phrases; gerund phrases; relative clauses; and noun clauses. There are five items in each set. Correct responses to four out of five items in each set represents mastery of the pattern in question. The Manual reports a Spearman-Brown split-half coefficient of .90 (a measure of reliability), a Kuder-Richardson inter-item reliability of .88, a standard error of measurement of 2.83 and a mean score of 27.78, based on a sample of 219 students.

Information on the procedure for structure and item selection and the statistical data associated with test development are not reported in the Teacher's Manual. For this one must consult Davidson's monograph, *Assessing Writing Ability of ESL College Freshmen*. Here the method for establishing content and construct validity is presented. The sentence-combining technique is an established procedure for measuring writing maturity. Selection of the nine structures and their representation in actual test items was based on a survey of nearly 40 composition texts (ESL and non-ESL) and 100 randomly selected native-speaker, college-freshman writing samples, all on the same topic and judged to be college-level by their instructors. The particular items of each structure were determined by a combination of text citation, actual use in writing samples, and adaptability to the test format. The items were submitted to several dozen linguists, English teachers, and ESL teachers for verification of content and anticipated responses, and then tested on native and nonnative speakers. Thus, the test was constructed so that it contains structures which are expected to appear and do in fact appear in the writing of proficient, native-speaker, college-freshman writers.

It is important to consider the technique by which these structures were determined. First, the author assumes that writing texts will cover all types of a given structure indicating mature writing. For ESL texts, this is not necessarily true. For example, a text may discuss relative clauses in general and show the principle by which relative clauses are formed, using subject and direct object focus as examples of the process. The intricacies of indirect object focus as examples of the process. The intricacies of indirect object and object-of-the-preposition focus may be omitted for reasons of difficulty. However, a native-speaker writing text will discuss these last two structures more fully since they have levels of formality associated with them.

> For example: I recognized the person that John gave the message to.
> *versus*
> I recognized the person to whom John gave the message.

It is interesting that neither of these two types are included in the inventory of relative clause structures, although advice on these two abounds in native-speaker writing texts.

Secondly, it is assumed that structures that function differently can be grouped together into one category. A look at prepositional phrases will serve to illustrate the problems of such an assumption. Both the adjectival prepositional phrase (e.g., the mayor of New York) and the prepositional phrase as a major sentence constituent (e.g., He gives a lot of money to his children) are grouped together. There is one instance of the former and four instances of the latter. If the student misses the one adjectival prepositional phrase, he or she is still considered proficient in the use of prepositional phrases, although his or her understanding of the function of prepositional phrases is limited to one type.

Thirdly, it is assumed that structures that function in a similar way can be considered members of different structural patterns.

> Consider: Have you ever heard of parents not (loving their children) I am tired of (her asking for money).

Because *parents* is part of the frame in the first item, the response is considered to be a participial phrase. Because *her* is not part of the frame in the second item, the response is considered to be a gerund. Yet, an appropriate syntactic analysis will admit both a gerundive and participial reading, that is, each sentence is syntactically ambiguous. Both should be included in the same item-set because of their inherent similarity. In addition, they should be distinguished from participles that cannot be read as gerunds (e.g., Carefully [following] directions, they found our house.) and from gerunds that cannot be read as participles (e.g., Instead of [walking], they took the bus.)

Some subordinate structures are less complex than others; they may require subordination of a word (e.g., The Persian rug was stolen.), or a phrase (e.g., the mayor of New York.), or a clause (e.g., I have friends that might help us.) But, no means is provided by which to assess the level of syntactic maturity according to the level of structural complexity mastered. In addition, the two major functions of subordinated units are not distinguished. In the examples above, the structures, whether word, phrase, or clause, function as modifiers. Compare that to sentences where the word, phrase, or clause function as a major sentence constituent.

> For example: I thought the idea interesting (object complement). He speaks Spanish with an accent (adjunctive adverbial). We don't know if the train arrived (object).

If students are able to show evidence of mastery of one function and not the other, there is no system of evaluation to show it.

Davidson provides evidence of concurrent validity by correlating scores on TAS with scores on a writing sample. A correlation coefficient of .65 is reported on a sample of 219 ESL students from New York University and City University of New York, 62% of whom are Spanish speakers. The testing sample should be larger and more representative of ESL learners in various post-secondary programs. Furthermore, the correlation coefficient should be adjusted by taking into account the interrater reliability of the writing sample and the interitem reliability of the TAS. In addition, the procedure for establishing concurrent validity could be refined. It is not clear that if the students were tested, found lacking in control over these subordinate

structures, and given the necessary instructions, that the compositions which these students write would be appropriately evaluated with high scores by giving them the test again. First, students might be able to perform well on these sentence-combining tasks and not be able to execute them in spontaneous writing. Secondly, the compositions might contain abundant examples of the correct use of these subordinate structures and yet show defects beyond the sentence level, resulting in a low rating. A more realistic procedure for establishing concurrent validity would be to examine the structures written in compositions in order to ascertain the number of spontaneously attempted subordinate structures in each category and to establish a ratio of correctly attempted ones. These ratios could then be correlated with scores in each of the nine subgroups. In this way, the validity of the test as a measure of the ability to subordinate in writing would be more clearly evidenced.

Evidence for predictive validity, on the other hand, is based on the premise that if a student cannot do a problem in the test, he or she cannot do it in spontaneous writing. Notice that this argument is different from the previous one which states that if a student could do a problem on the test, then he or she could do it in spontaneous writing. It would be fruitful to examine the compositions of low-achieving students to see what percentage of subordinate structure attempted were performed correctly. One would expect there to be no significant difference in the coefficients of variations in the two sets of scores, one set the scores of low achievers on the TAS and the other set their average percentage of correctly formed structures in spontaneous writing in contrast to those attempted. In addition, one would expect the correlation between the two sets of scores to be high.

The Teacher's Manual does not report any study of item difficulty nor item discrimination. The background research on a different group of subjects (reported in the ERIC document cited earlier) indicates that some structures are easier than others and that a hierarchy of difficulty might be used in order to arrive at an overall assessment of writing maturity. This information should be reported for the sample of 219 students cited in the Teacher's Manual, as well. In addition, there is no analysis of items to determine if examinees with high scores get the items correct and examinees with low scores miss them. This kind of study is important if the test is to be used to place students into levels of instruction.

Strengths in TAS's favor are its base in current linguistic theory and ease of administration and correction. Further, TAS is easily adapted for diagnostic purposes, provides students sufficient time to demonstrate their syntactic ability, and appears to correlate with evaluations of student writing. However, there are a few weaknesses which must be kept in mind. There is no way to determine significant differences in student scores for purposes of determining level of proficiency, some items do not correctly or adequately represent the intended structure, and the various functions of a structure are not distinguished. In addition, the test statistics are minimal. No norming exists, no investigation of item statistics is evident, and the validating studies are limited in concept, size, and population representation. The test might be used to satisfy one's curiosity about whether given students might be able to do the items correctly, and it might prove useful in designing an instructional syllabus whose focus is that of subordination. However, it will not fully answer the question of the extent to which subordination needs to be taught. It will also not give any assurance that these structures, once taught, will appear correctly in spontaneous writing.

# Test in English (Overseas)

*Reviewed by*

**Don Porter**
**University of Reading**

### Synopsis

Test in English (Overseas). TEO. Candidates 16-years-old and over, resident in Britain for less than 5 years, whose native language is not English and who have been educated outside of Britain. For university admission. Written paper and aural paper. Continuous writing scored subjectively against qualitative criteria exemplified in sample texts, rest of test scored as *correct* or *incorrect*, against lists of correct responses. Totals translated to descriptions of proficiency levels. Group administered. Written English, 2 1/2 hours plus 15 minutes reading time; Aural, 40 minutes. Two new forms of each paper each year (in March and June), Written question paper (8 pp.), answer book (12 pp.), Aural test (5 pp.). No administration manual. No technical manual, but "Tests in English (Overseas), The Position After Ten Years." P. L. McEdowney (1976, 52 pp.). Test is available only at approved centers, test kits are not available; however, past papers are available from JMB. 1984 entry fee of £8.60 per candidate. Joint Matriculation Board, Manchester M15 6EU, England, telephone: 061-273-2565.

### Review

This review is based on the June 1983 form of the test, together with the booklet "Test in English (Overseas): The Position After Ten Years" (McEldowney, 1976, Joint Matriculation Board).[1]

The Test in English (Overseas) is designed to provide evidence of the proficiency necessary for pursuing a course of higher study in the medium of English, and is accepted by many British universities, in particular the universities of Manchester, Liverpool, Leeds, Sheffield, and Birmingham, which cooperate in the Joint Matriculation Board. The test constructors aim to produce a test based on (students') actual future requirements (p. 5) and recognize the consequent need to establish the types of English involved in English-medium study. These are stated to be "competence in understanding and production within five broad language functions involved in the spoken and written modes of expository English" (p. 12), the five being: description, process, narrative padding, narrative, and instruction. These five are arrived at, however, not by formal observation and analysis of actual language use in academic contexts, as in the British Council ELTS or the Associated Examining Board's TEEP, but, apparently, by introspection. The importance of these five is expressed in terms of belief: "The test is set in the belief that . . . " (p. 5). For a test which places a premium on its appropriacy to students' requirements, this is a surprisingly relaxed approach to content.

As the five core functions are felt to be appropriate across a wide range of candidates, they are assessed through texts and activities that are not restricted to any one discipline, and which are designed not to favor any particular subject. Thus, topics are chosen "from central, neutral, semi-technical sources like encyclopedias . . . sources of semi-technical writing for the educated layman" (p. 13). The written texts chosen have the appearance of genuine academic writing, and clearly exemplify the range of core functions. The Aural test consists of a radio interview and a short lecture, both of which are immediately repeated in the form of a short summary. Both recorded texts have a moderately academic flavor, but both have the appearance of having been written in order to be spoken, rather than of normal unscripted speech. This suggests a certain lack of validity: If we want to know a student's ability to cope with natural, appropriate speech, why test him or her on something else? The interview format is particularly open to this objection. Under what circumstances does the university student have to listen to radio interviews?

The student is required to engage in a variety of activities through language. In the Written test, the student writes half-a-page about a process illustrated by a diagram or a sequence of pictures; one-and-a-half pages describing a second visual; indicates where necessary words are missing and what they might be in a passage from which single words have been deleted and the gaps closed; matches the words in a passage to a set of definitions; matches definitions to parts of a diagram; and uses information from passages to complete and label tables and diagrams. In the Aural test, the student takes notes while listening and uses them to label diagrams. Seven out of nine tasks involve pictures, diagrams, or tables. Thus, "it is not the candidate's knowledge of the subject that is being tested, the basic factual information (being) provided in some nonverbal form, using techniques typical of normal expository English where verbal and nonverbal information are constantly used to support each other" (p. 14). The use of visuals has two purposes: to isolate the writing from the reading skills and to conform to the conventions of academic writing. However, the word constantly in the quotation is overdone, as visuals are not exploited in academic writing to the extent they are here. Neither are they exploited in the same way. Indeed, they are usually employed to aid text comprehension rather than, as in the case of the TEO, being separated from the text, which makes them and the texts, more difficult to process.

The variety of activities makes for an interesting test, but the test constructors appear to assume that the nature of the test activity does not need to be appropriate to students' actual future requirements in the way the core functions are. Thus, the variations on diagram labelling do not appear to have any great relevance to students. More importantly, students will rarely have to write on the basis of exclusively visual input; and it is not at all clear what the deleted words task will actually succeed in measuring in relation to students' needs.

Although new forms of this test are generated twice a year, no statistics are amassed on the performance of each form and then presented in a technical manual; in fact no statistics are publicly available. Apparently, the test is constructed primarily in the belief that test content and activities will be valid (and therefore automatically reliable) as they attempt to assess in some direct manner aspects of language and language use that relate to students' requirements; and secondarily, in the belief that if a second test is constructed closely on the model of the first, it will in fact assess the same abilities with the same precision. It is unfortunately the case, however, that the intention to assess given abilities does not guarantee that those abilities will be assessed, even if the test functions reliably, which also needs to be demonstrated. Moreover, test forms are not necessarily parallel simply because they are nearly identical in structure and content. Such tests need to be analyzed and modified, and scoring needs to be adjusted, until the forms are genuinely parallel; then the statistical evidence for their parallelness must be made known.

In sum, this is an interesting test for the testee, and one which is widely accepted in British universities, but there are a variety of doubts about its validity in relation to its expressed general purpose, doubts that can only be dispelled by providing further theoretical argumentation and supporting statistical data.

### Footnotes

[1]Page references cited in this review are from McEldowney's booklet.

# Test in English for Educational Purposes

*Reviewed by*

**Pauline M. Rea**
**University of Lancaster**

### Synopsis

Test in English for Educational Purposes. TEEP. For nonnative speakers of English wishing to study at tertiary level institutions in the U.K. To provide, by means of individual profiles for the four language skills, information on students' understanding and use of written and spoken English in academic situations. Two compulsory sections, Papers I and II, and one optional section, Paper III. Paper I (2 hrs. 15 mins.) is a general paper testing reading, writing, and listening abilities. Paper II (2 hrs. 25 mins.) tests the same skills, but is broadly subject specific with two parallel tests available: IIA for arts/social/administrative/business, or IIB for science/engineering students. Paper III (time unspecified) assesses speaking skills and candidate responses are recorded on tape. The assessment criteria for writing subtests are relevance and adequacy of content, composition organization, cohesion, adequacy of vocabulary for purpose, grammar, punctuation, and spelling; for oral responses, relevance and adequacy of content, intelligibility, appropriacy, adequacy of vocabulary for purpose, grammar, and fluency. Three administrations per year, closing dates for entry applications are given in parentheses: January/February (20 December), May (20 March), September (20 August). Individual applications are made through a registered Associated Examining Board (AEB) or AREL-FELCO center. Centers wishing to register should contact the Secretary General at the AEB. Papers I and II are conducted on the same day with Paper III administered at any time within the same week. Cost details are provided at the time of entry applications. Information Manual (1984, 55 pp.). Cost: £12 per paper plus £5 per examinee. Cyril Weir. Associated Examining Board, Wellington House, Aldershot, Hampshire, GU11 1BQ, England, telephone: Aldershot (0252) 25551.

### Test References

Weir, C. (1983). The associated examining board's test in English for academic purposes: An exercise in content validity. In A. Hughes & D. Porter (Eds.), *Current developments in language testing* (pp. 147-53). London: Academic Press.

### Review

The TEEP has been recently introduced (May 1984) and was motivated by the need for a more suitable screening mechanism for students from overseas and an examination which provided "receiving institutions in tertiary education with a comprehensive picture of the English language proficiency of students for whom English was not the mother tongue" (Information Manual, p. ii). Broadly, the TEEP is comparable in its overall aims to the TOEFL and to the ELTS but it differs from both these proficiency measures in two important respects: (a) the extensive research program undertaken at the initial planning stage and (b) its format and overall design. Unlike the TOEFL, it does not report candidate performance in terms of test scores. Rather, it provides profiles of candidates' performance, a feature shared by the ELTS.

What is especially noteworthy about the TEEP is the way in which it was researched during the preparatory stages. A considerable corpus of information was gathered about candidates' target language use situations, relating in particular to the nature and extent of the language demands faced by overseas students in the most frequently studied subject areas. Although there is no guarantee that the data obtained through the observational visits and circulation of a national questionnaire (returned by 940 overseas students, 530 British students, and 559 staff members) accurately reflects what actually takes place in the target study situation (i.e., linguistic demands on students, marking criteria applied, threshold levels of acceptability, etc.), this test represents a nearly unique attempt to address key issues of test validity and design from an empirical perspective.

As one of the best examples of large scale communicative testing, the TEEP is an innovative measure of performance abilities in an academic context. Making full use of empirical data from the observational and postal survey (Weir, 1983), this examination includes relevant testing activities that reflect the demands placed on students when studying through the medium of English. For example, Paper I (with three subtests) is based on a study cycle that focuses on lectures. It attempts to simulate the situation in which students' preliminary reading leads into a lecture, the information from which is subsequently employed in a written answer. Paper II is focussed on a seminar. Thus, the TEEP addresses the construct of communicative competence by presenting candidates with discourse-based language processing tasks that assess both the "constituent-enabling skills underlying abilities in reading, listening and writing" (Information Manual, p. iii) and the product of language proficiency through thematically and causally related assignments in which input from a reading and/or listening task are integrated in the performance of a global writing task.

Due to differential language proficiency requirements across subjects and departments in tertiary institutions, no overall test score is reported. Instead, individual descriptors of performance are provided in terms of five bands from Beginner to Approaching Native Speaker Proficiency. The main purpose for such scales is to provide more readily interpretable information for the receiving institution and useful diagnostic input for those involved in subsequent English language training. While it is clearly desirable to provide student profiles, one wonders (in the case of both the TEEP and the ELTS) whether this data will be used by those for whom it is intended in a way that maximally exploits the information elicited by the various examination components.

Tests frequently come under fire for the shackling influences they exert on the teaching and learning process. However, in the case of the TEEP the most likely outcome is positive washback to the teaching and learning situation given the availability of (a) a detailed specification of test objectives and the evaluation criteria, (b) a full sample Paper I and IIA (IIB is in preparation), and (c) the intrinsic authenticity of test format and content to the academic context. Further, the use of banded scales in the reporting of student profiles should stimulate greater interest in individuals' strengths and weaknesses and the need to enhance student performance in the domain of enabling (process) and global (product) skills.

Three main limitations to the TEEP emerge. The first relates to the validity of the subject-specific division: non-science and science/engineering. The research of Alderson and Urquhart (1984) lends some support for the importance of background discipline and the need to provide specialist area testing modules. However, no evidence is provided by the AEB for the two existing thematic distinctions of the TEEP. Secondly, the examination is very long. The length for Papers I and II alone is 4 hours 35 minutes. (No indication of the speaking component time allocation is given in the Informational Manual.) Given the apparent overlap in skills assessed in Papers I and II, it would be useful to know if test reliability would be unacceptably reduced if the test were shortened, or whether the information provided by both Papers is indeed complementary, with each containing unique variance, essential to the validity of the performance profiles.

The third criticism relates to the Information Manual circulated by the AEB. Although excellent with respect to the information it includes, there are certain important omissions. There is very limited information on interpreting and using test results. The initial research, we are informed (p. ii), investigated levels and discipline areas in which students most frequently enroll, but no indication is given on the way in which these factors influence the interpretation of results. Which courses are the most/least demanding? Is a Grade 5 crucial for students of law and linguistics, whereas a Grade 2 would suffice for administrative studies? A second omisssion relates to validation data for the TEEP. Conventionally, test manuals include a certain amount of evidence in support of the reliability and validity of the measure in question. Although "a great deal of internal and external validation" has been undertaken (p. iii) no data from these investigations are provided. In what way, for example, are Papers IIA and IIB parallel in terms of task format or task difficulty? How was the content selection of the texts controlled? Or, since it is a crucial issue in the validation of communicative tests, against which yardstick(s) has criterion-related validity been established? Since it is fairly widely known that the TEEP is a very well researched examination (Weir, 1983; Emmett, 1983) it is unfortunate that these details are not available in the Manual.

In conclusion, a thorough specification of test objectives offers no guarantees for a good test but, in the case of the TEEP, there is very impressive match between the planning, construction and implementation stages of the examination's development. A variety of test formats from controlled to unguided open-ended tasks are included, the task types are discourse-based involving language processing authentic to the construct of language proficiency in an academic context, and information relating to both the process and product of language proficiency performance is derivable from the test battery. These factors also have wider implications, beyond the immediate testing context, and are likely to have a positive backwash effect on the teaching and learning of English for academic study purposes.

### Reviewer's References

Alderson, J. C. & Urquhart, A. H. (1984). ESP tests: The problems of student background discipline. In T. Culhane, C. Klein Braley, & D. K. Stevenson (Eds.), *Practice and problems in language testing* (Occasional Papers, No. 29, pp. 1-13). Colchester: University of Essex.

Emmet, A. (1983, October). *The test of English for educational purposes.* Paper presented at IUS Conference, University of Essex, Colchester.

*Test in English for educational purpose (TEEP).* (1984). Information manual. Aldershot, Hampshire: Associate Examining Board.

Weir, C. (1983). *Identifying the language problems of overseas students in tertiary education in the U.K.* (Vols. I and II). Unpublished doctoral dissertation, London University, London.

# Test of English as a Foreign Language

### Reviewed by

### Douglas K. Stevenson
### University of Essex

### Synopsis

Test of English as a Foreign Language. 1964-1986. TOEFL. Nonnative speakers of English, recommended for students at 11th grade level or above. Designed to evaluate English-language proficiency of individuals whose native language is not English, most often those wishing to study in North American universities and colleges. Separate answer sheets are computer-scored, or manually with a $15 fee, or manually scored through the Institutional Testing Program. Group administration or individual (nonstandard administration for examinees with visual, aural, or physical impairments). Administered under International Testing Program six Saturdays per year on scheduled dates at more than 1,100 centers in 170 countries and areas; under Special Center Testing Program six Fridays per year; under Institutional and Overseas Institutional Testing Programs, given at dates and in locations convenient to participating universities, colleges, and institutions (for internal use). 105 minutes (approx. 180 minutes total administration). Since 1976, three-section form yielding three section-scores and total score. New, equated form each month; 12 new equivalent forms each year. TOEFL publications and research information include: Manual for Administering TOEFL (1985, 16 pp., revised biannually); video tape for training supervisors and staff (30 minutes); Preparing for a TOEFL Administration; TOEFL Test and Score Manual (1985, 39 pp.); ETS/TOEFL test analyses and statistical reports (for each equivalent test form). The TOEFL Research Report series as of July 1986 consisted of 21 research reports (e.g., No. 19, 1985, 153 pp.). Additional TOEFL publications include Bulletin of Information (1986, 32 pp.); Testing American Style (1981, 16 pp.). Understanding TOEFL: Test Kit 1 (1980, $11 U.S., $15 overseas); Listening to TOEFL: Test Kit 2 (1984, $11 U.S., $15 overseas); sample TOEFL Test (1980, $3); as well as North American, and overseas editions of TOEFL Bulletin of Information, a Computer Tape Score-Reporting Service, an Examinee Identification Service, a Public Use Data Service (1983, $60). Cost of International Program per examinee is $27 U.S. and $35 overseas (includes Examinee Handbook, two copies of Examinee's Score Confirmation Record, and official score reports sent directly to up to three designated institutions), Special Center Program is $2 additional. North American and overseas institutional (internal use) testing also available. Jointly sponsored by the College Board, the Graduate Record Examinations Board, and Educational Testing Service. Test of English as a Foreign Language, Educational Testing Service, Princeton, NJ 08541, USA, telephone: (609) 921-9000.

### Test References

Hale, G. A., Stansfield, C. W., & Duran, R. P. (1984). *Summaries of studies involving the test of English as a foreign language* (Research Report No. 16). Princeton, NJ: Educational Testing Service.

Loyd, B. H. (1985). [Review of TOEFL]. In J. V. Mitchell, Jr. (Ed.), *The ninth mental measurements yearbook* (pp. 1568-9). Lincoln, NE: Buros Institute of Mental Measurements & University of Nebraska.

Oller, J. W., & Spolsky, B. (1979). The test of English as a foreign language. In B. Spolsky (Ed.), *Papers in applied linguistics: Advances in langauge testing: Series 1. Some major tests* (pp. 92-100). Washington, DC: Center for Applied Linguistics.

Phillips, S. E. (1985). Test of English as a foreign language. In D. J. Keyser & R. C. Sweetland (Eds.), *Test critiques: Vol. III* (p. 655-8). Kansas City, MO: Test Corporation of America.

Tatsuoka, K. K. (1985). [Review of TOEFL]. In J. V. Mitchell (Ed.), *The ninth mental measurements yearbook* (pp. 1569-70). Lincoln, NE: Buros Institute of Mental Measurements & University of Nebraska.

## Review

The Test of English as a Foreign Language (TOEFL, pronounced "toe-full") is a highly secure, internationally administered, standardized, multiple-choice test. TOEFL seeks to estimate the proficiency of nonnative speakers of English as a second or foreign language with the major purpose of providing impartial, comparative, and current information on the language proficiency of foreign students. TOEFL is administered to individuals from hundreds of language and cultural backgrounds, who seek admission at the undergraduate or graduate levels to some 2,500 universities and colleges in the U.S., Canada, and other countries for study in a wide variety of academic subject areas. TOEFL results are also required by a number of certifying boards or agencies and academic and governmental groups in the U.S. and other countries. The TOEFL is one part of the larger TOEFL program, which includes the Test of Spoken English, the Test of Written English, the Secondary Level English Proficiency test (see reviews in this volume), and the English tests administered by the Education Commission of Foreign Medical Graduates and the Council of Graduates of Foreign Nursing Schools.

Since 1976, TOEFL has consisted of three sections, each separately timed. A test booklet consisting of a multiple-choice four option format and a separate answer sheet are used with all sections. As TOEFL is a universal test by necessity, that is, one that can be administered to examinees from any and all language backgrounds, all instructions and examples are in English. The three sections are Listening Comprehension, which measures the examinee's ability to understand English as spoken in the U.S.; Structure and Written Expression, which measures mastery of important structural and grammatical items in standard written English; and Reading Comprehension and Vocabulary, which tests the examinee's ability to understand the meanings and uses of words in written English, as well as the ability to understand a variety of written materials. The instructions and stimuli for the Listening Comprehension section are on audio tape.

Listening Comprehension (35 minutes) has three parts. In the first part, the examinee selects the written option that most closely corresponds to a statement spoken once on audio tape. In the second part, short conversations are heard, followed by a question. The best response is chosen from the four printed options (15 items). In the third part, several brief talks, lectures, public announcements, and so forth, held to be representative of academic or student contexts in the U.S., are presented. Each is followed by spoken questions (15 items).

The Structure and Written Expression section (25 minutes) has two parts: (a) incomplete sentences, with words or phrases as options (15 items); and (b) sentences in which some words or phrases are underlined. In the second part (25 items), the examinee must identify the words or phrases in each sentence that are not appropriate to standard, formal written English.

The third section, Reading Comprehension and Vocabulary (45 minutes), also has two parts, consisting of 30 items each. In Part 1, a word or phrase in a sentence is underlined. The examinee chooses the option which when substituted best preserves the original meaning of the underlined word or phrase. In Part 2, short reading passages are presented, followed by questions requiring either informational or inferential responses.

Raw scores (number of questions answered correctly) are converted to 20-80 scaled scores for the three sections, and 200-800 scaled scores for the total score. However, the actual distribution of obtained scaled scores is more restricted than these two scales imply. Section scores on each form usually range from 22-67; the total score usually ranges from 227-677. No pass/fail scores are given in the Manual for Score Users. Rather, the Manual contains information on various reference groups (e.g., percentile rank by graduate, undergraduate, male/female, professional license, native language and area), and the results of a biannual survey of how various institutions use TOEFL scores. The point is made consistently that individual institutions must determine whether or not TOEFL is appropriate for their individual needs, and must establish levels of acceptable performance. Score users are cautioned in the Test Manual against misuse, or even unwarranted reliance upon TOEFL.

Reliability estimates are substantial, well within the desirable range for this type of test. For example, average reliabilities for 12 forms (administered in 1981-1982) are .89, .87, and .89 for the three sections, and .95 for the total score. As expected, estimates tend to vary among form and groups, but generally cluster around or above the .90 level.

Among the standardized ESL/EFL tests now in use around the world, whether commercial or institutional, TOEFL is unusual for two reasons. First, it is by far the most researched of all foreign language tests. Secondly, it is, without a doubt, the most widely used. In 1985 over 450,000 examinees took TOEFL at 1,000 test centers in 135 countries. And more than 2,500 universities and colleges in North America, as well as many other institutions elsewhere, made use of TOEFL scores. As a result, TOEFL's information and databases are without parallel among EFL tests and measures. Ironically, it is much easier to be critical with so much data and so many studies available, than it is with many other tests whose main claim to validity is often an appealing, (or trendy title) and the promise of "future studies."

The content validity of TOEFL ultimately rests, as with all proficiency measures, on the degree to which experts perceive it to be valid. The content validity of the TOEFL is the responsibility of a Committee of Examiners composed of linguists and specialists in English language·pedagogy. One could easily ask if the tasks and content are representative of those encountered by nonnatives in academic contexts, or why a particular vocabulary item or grammatical feature was chosen. And so on. Realistically, however, neither contrastive analysis nor error analysis techniques are adequate to guide the selection of content, given the variety of populations and target language-use situations. Also, no validated list exists that specifies by weight and degree the linguistic and communicative abilities necessary for given sociolinguistic situations. That TOEFL does agree that content is best specified by experts, and does rotate membership in this group often to avoid stagnation or the dominance of one view, leads to the reasonable conclusion, if not demonstration, that the content of TOEFL in general, is representative.

TOEFL has been included in a large number of criterion-related studies that tend to support its validity. It correlates well with other instruments claiming to measure similar abilities and less well with those that do not. In particular, three points related to these studies should be remembered. First, despite the frequency with which TOEFL has been castigated as a discrete-point test, it has shown moderate to high correlations with direct or integrative measures such as cloze tests (written and oral), oral interviews, and essay ratings. Second, over the years TOEFL has gained the stature of commonly being used as a criterion for the validation of other tests; that is, they are considered valid to the extent they agree with TOEFL. Finally, although studies of TOEFL as a predictor of grade-point average are now considered inappropriate, teachers' ratings of English proficiency or readiness to study in English have been included in predictive studies with encouraging results.

Construct validity studies of TOEFL are naturally constrained by our present inability to specify exactly what is meant by English-language proficiency and to verify it empirically. Factor analyses also tend to support the belief that the TOEFL is measuring several major, if interrelated, language proficiency areas. It should be noted that TOEFL, much more than any other test of a similar type, has been most conscientious in attempting to demonstrate that it measures all that it proports to measure.

It is unfortunate that so little attention is paid to a great strength of the program of which TOEFL is a part. It offers at a modest cost a service that would otherwise be lacking to hundreds of thousands of examinees and to the cooperating institutions. None of these alone could support the hundreds of testing centers, and very few even the construction, design, pretesting, analyses, and score distribution tasks for even one or two new forms each year. TOEFL also most closely approaches the professional testing standards established for psychological and educational measures. Critical research studies are carried out regularly in house and made public. Support has been given to external studies as well. Stringent standards for administration, score reporting and interpretation are set forth, and followed. Warnings of misuse are conspicuously posted. Commendable efforts are made to familiarize examinees with the test and test type; sample kits and tests are available.

Given its purposes, examinee populations, and multiple uses and considering the attendant limitations on test content, tasks, and predictive specificity, TOEFL remains the best of its breed. Beyond those practical limitations that are necessary to its purposes and scope, TOEFL's weaknesses largely reflect the state of the language testing art.

# Test of English for International Communication

*Reviewed by*

**Kyle Perkins**
**Southern Illinois University**

## Synopsis

Test of English for International Communication. TOEIC. Adult nonnative speakers of English in commerce and industry. Designed to assess the English language listening and reading abilities of adults whose command of English ranges from minimal to near-native and who need or expect to use English in their work. Multiple-choice. Components: Part I, Listening Comprehension, single picture, four spoken descriptions, 20 items; Part II, Spoken Utterances, three spoken responses, 30 items; Part III, Short Conversation, four printed answers, 30 items; Part IV, Short Talks, four printed questions and answers, 20 items; Part V, Reading Comprehension, incomplete sentences, 40 items; Part VI, Error Recognition, underlines, 20 items; Part VII, Reading Comprehension Passages, 40 items. Raw scores are converted to a common scale by score equating. Total scores range from 10 to 990; the subscores from 5 to 495; the total score is not directly related to the total number of correct answers. Group administration. 2 1/2 hours. First administered in 1979, three new forms of the test are prepared each year. (Form 3BIC, 1980, 41 pp.). Bulletin of Information (1985, 27 pp.). Test Analysis (1980, 15 pp.). Cost and administration information available from Director, TOEIC, International Office, Eduational Testing Service, Princeton, NJ, 08541, USA; in Japan: Mr. Akira Ito, World Economic Information Services, World Trade Center Building, No. 4-1, 2-Chome, Hamamatsu-Cho, Minato-Ku, Tokyo, 105, Japan; in Korea: Mr. M. K. Kim, The Si-sa-yong-o-sa Publishers, 5-3 Kwanchol-Dong, Chongro-Ku, Seoul, 110, Korea; in Taiwan: Mr. Anthony Y. T. Wu, The Language Training and Testing Center, 2-1 Hsu Chow Road, Taipei, 100, Taiwan, Republic of China; Educational Testing Service, Princeton, NJ, 08541 USA, telephone: (609) 921-9000.

## Review

The purpose of the TOEIC is to assess attained English language proficiency of candidates in the context of a work environment of international trade. According to an ETS flyer, various corporate, governmental, and private agencies use TOEIC results as a criterion for hiring, assignment to overseas posts requiring English language proficiency, assignment to or promotion within departments where English is needed or desirable, identification of employees who know English sufficiently well to benefit from corporate training programs abroad, determination of the effectiveness of English language-training programs, and assignment to, placement within, or exit from company-sponsored English language training programs.

The unique aspect of TOEIC which sets it apart from ALIGU, MTELP, or TOEFL is the content. The 20 picture stimuli for Part I include objects that one would encounter in industry and commerce: a welder, a factory building, a work station in a vocational shop, two machinists operating a lathe, an architect's model of an office complex, a bridge girder, and a printed circuit. Part VII contains as stimuli a page from an appointment calendar, an airline schedule, a telephone message form, a hotel registration form, a fare schedule for taxis, a letter of recommendation, a tariff schedule for a shipping company, and a secretarial help-available advertisement.

All questions in Parts III and IV are WH-questions; the options include phrases, clauses, and complete sentences. The items assessed in Parts V and VI include idiom chunks and collocations, for example, *starts at, out of stock, unconditionally guaranteed,* passives, degress of adjectives and adverbs, the form and function of the parts of speech, *ago* marking a point in time, duration adverbs, tense sequences, count versus noncount determiners (*much* and *many*), number agreement, and word order. Part VII includes items testing paraphrase, literal comprehension, evaluation/judgment, main idea, supportng ideas, single-string inference, multiple-string inference, and various combinations of the preceding.

The TOEIC is an integrative test in the sense that it engages different modes and language components. For example, in the Listening Comprehension section, the subject reads the options in English, choosing the correct answer based on what was heard on tape.

The TOEIC has impressive test statistics: KR-20 reliability coefficients of 0.916 for listening comprehension, 0.930 for reading, and 0.956 for the total test (Woodford, 1982, p. 66). The maximum possible validity coefficients for the two parts and the total are 0.9571 for listening comprehension, 0.9644 for reading, and 0.9778 for the total test (assuming the criterion measures were perfectly reliable and taking the square root of the reliability coefficient).

The Bulletin of Information reports the results of empirical concurrent validity studies conducted on the TOEIC. Independent direct measures of listening and speaking were correlated with the TOEIC. For a direct measure of listening, 15 short statements or questions and 10 dialogues in English were played to the subjects. Each exercise had three questions which were asked in Japanese by a Japanese examiner, and the subjects were encouraged to answer in Japanese. The TOEIC Listening Comprehension section and the direct measure of listening correlated at 0.90 for these Japanese subjects.

The Language Proficiency Interview (LPI), a face-to-face interview, was the direct measure of speaking. The subjects were rated on a 0-5 scale. The TOEIC listening comprehension and LPI correlated at 0.83.

For a direct measure of English rating, the subjects were asked 30 questions based on different reading tasks, such as reading tables of contents, labels, and advertising copy in English. The questions were asked in Japanese, and the subjects answered orally in Japanese. The correlation between TOEIC and the direct measure of reading was 0.79.

The direct measure of writing consisted of three components which resulted in a composite writing score. The subjects were asked to reconstitute 10 "dehydrated sentences," to write a 25-40 word letter to a company complaining about a shipping delay, and to write the English translation of 10 Japanese sentences. The TOEIC and the direct measure of writing correlated at 0.83.

In sum, the TOEIC is a standardized, highly reliable and valid measure of English, specifically designed to assess real-life reading and listening skills of candidates who will use English in a work context. Empirical studies indicate that it is also a valid indirect measure of speaking and writing. The items assess major grammatical structures and reading skills and, in addition to being an integrative test, the TOEIC also appears to tap communicative competence in that the items require the examinee to utilize his or her sociolinguistic and strategic competence.

## Reviewer's References

Cowell, W. R. (1980). *Test analysis: Test of English for international communication.* Princeton, NJ: Educational Testing Service.

Educational Testing Service. (1982). *Test of English for international communication bulletin of information.* Princeton, NJ: Author.

Woodford, P. E. (1982). The Test of English for international communication (TOEIC). In C. Brumfit (Ed.), *English for international communication* (pp. 61-72). New York: Pergamon Press.

## Test of English Proficiency Level

*Reviewed by*

**Helen Jorstad**
**University of Minnesota**

### Synopsis

Test of English Proficiency Level. TEPL. 1985-86. Secondary-Adult. To determine a student's instructional level for placement in an ESL program. Oral responses (30 items, one section) marked correct or incorrect by comparing them to suggest responses and scoring criteria. Written responses for the Structure, Reading, and Writing sections may be transferred to optional Scantron sheets and scored electronically or manually. Totals in each section suggest placement in one of seven proficiency levels: A, Zero English; B, Low Beginning; C, High Beginning; D, Low Intermediate; E, High Intermediate; F, Low Advanced; and G, High Advanced. Oral section individual (5-20 minutes), Written sections group (60 minutes). One form available in Manual (1986, 61 pp.) No technical manual. $49.95 per Examiner's Kit including Manual and testing materials, which are reproducible line masters. TEPL Scantron answer sheets, 500 for $49.95. George Rathmell, The Language Teachers' Center, PO Box 98, The Sea Ranch, CA 95497, USA. Alemany Press, 2501 Industrial Parkway West, Hayward, CA 94545, USA, telephone: (415) 998-7070 or (800) 227-2375.

### Review

According to the Manual, the Test of English Proficiency Level (TEPL), is a multi-skill test designed to place students in appropriate levels of instruction in school programs. It includes sections that test literacy as well as functional oral proficiency.

While the Manual indicates that the test meets the criteria for a test of communicative competence, such

as those delineated by Savignon (1983, p. 245), it seems to conform to her criteria only marginally. It is especially difficult to see how the TEPL assesses dynamic negotiation of meaning, since the Oral section, which contains context-free items requiring a one-sentence answer, supports only correct or incorrect responses. The instructions for scoring indicate that students may be given credit for nongrammatical responses that reflect the natural language of their peers. Still, negotiation of meaning is clearly not involved.

In effect, the Oral section is a discrete-item test. Its 30 items give the student a single opportunity to show mastery of a given grammatical/functional category. An item is correct "only when (1) it is appropriate, (2) it is syntactically and grammatically correct, and (3) it contains the 'key element'" (p. 15). To its credit, the Manual indicates that informal usage and incorrect pronunciation are usually not considered in scoring responses. The Oral section continues until the student misses four or more items from six contiguous questions.

The Written section of the test is in a single booklet, which alternates Structure, Reading, and Writing sections in five parts, arranged according to order of difficulty. The 30 Structure items are situated in single context-free sentences rather than in a meaningful passage; the student is asked to choose one of five elements to complete each sentence. The preliminary edition used for this review (not published by Alemany Press) contained some unfortunate typographical errors: commas were omitted and one word was omitted in a stem, making the item almost impossible to complete correctly. Each item in this section usually has only one clearly correct completion.

The Reading section consists of cloze passages with five possible choices for each item. Because the cloze blanks test contextual appropriateness beyond the sentence level, several can be completed with more than one choice, including the first item of the first passage, for which any of the five choices might be a defensible completion if considered solely in terms of its immediate environment. The meaning of part of the fourth reading passage is confusing. It states that redwood is often used for outdoor construction because insects do not like its taste; yet the next item speaks of weak wood which may be destroyed by bugs—a case of questionable logic, since wood that tastes bad may be either weak or strong. Still, it is true that some textbooks require students to make similar logical inferences. A spelling error in the distractor of another item is also frustrating, as is a missing word in the final passage.

The last section of the test is Writing. The student is asked to write five short compositions: (a) a three-sentence description of a picture, (b) a short personal data form and a description of a place, (c) a description of a person, (d) a narrative paragraph about past events, and (e) a contrast of one aspect of the student's native country with the U.S. Clearly, having to complete a personal data form is a real-life writing task. The writing samples are scored holistically and placed into one of three categories: clear and correct (no more than three errors in grammar, usage, and spelling); minimally acceptable (the message is communicated despite errors); and unacceptable (the message is not conveyed). Examples of compositions in each category are provided as scoring models.

There is no measure of listening comprehension included in the test. Listening is tested indirectly in the Oral section.

A unique feature of the TEPL is the fact that no raw scores are reported. Instead, performance on each section is related to one of several proficiency levels. The Manual includes a set of instructional materials appropriate to students at each level.

The Manual includes one and one-fourth pages describing how to use TEPL for placement and devotes slightly more than a page to "Technical Reports," which provides some basic descriptive statistics. These parts of the Manual seem very preliminary. The multiple-choice structure and reading portions of the test were administered to 254 students in a single junior high school in Oakland, California. While a reliability of .94 is cited, there is no indication of how reliability was determined. No data are available either for the oral test or for the rating of the writing sample. Inter/intrarater reliabilities are not discussed. As for validity, a table compares the seven TEPL levels with seven other tests, but gives no statistical information. Although the Manual indicates that studies are in progress with more students, it seems unfortunate that more were not completed prior to publication. Little data are reported even for the one study indicated. Hopefully, more information will be provided on how to use the test for placement purposes, as well as on the ability of the test to predict success in placement, given that this is the main aim of the test. The TEPL will probably be useful only in conjunction with other testing procedures for placement. In particular, test administrators should be aware of TEPL's limitations, which are both technical and theoretical. Since it is inexpensive, some administrators may wish to try using it experimentally, along with other measures, recognizing that except for the Writing section it is essentially a discrete-item test.

## Reviewer's References

Savignon, S. J. (1983). *Communicatve competence: Theory and classroom practice*. Reading, MA: Addison Wesley.

# Test of Spoken English

*Reviewed by*

**Kathleen M. Bailey**
**Monterey Institute of International Studies**

## Synopsis

Test of Spoken English. TSE. Adults, especially graduate students and professionals whose native language is not English. Designed as a semidirect measure of oral English skills. Examines verbal responses to tape recorded and written stimuli. Scored by trained raters at ETS on an overall comprehensibility scale (0 to 300 points) and subscales of pronunciation, grammar and fluency (0.0 to 3.0 points). Group administered nine times annually—January, March, April, May, June, August, September, November, December—at TOEFL testing centers worldwide. New forms created annually. Approximately 20 minutes. Examinee Handbook and Sample Questions (1986, 19 pp.); Supervisor's Manual (1986, 27 pp.); Manual for Score Users (1982, 32 pp.). Administration and scoring done by ETS (or its representatives) at no cost to the user agencies (score recipients), but at a cost of $54 to the individual examinee. SPEAK, which contains a retired form of TSE and rater training materials is available for purchase by institutions for $300. Additional forms of SPEAK are $75 each; Educational Testing Service (ETS) TOEFL Program, Princeton, NJ 08541-6157, USA, telephone: (609) 921-9000.

## Test References

Clark, J. L. D., & Swinton, S. S. (1979). *An exploration of speaking proficiency measures in the TOEFL context* (TOEFL Research Report 4). Princeton, NJ: Educational Testing Service.

Clark, J. L. D., & Swinton, S. S. (1980). *The test of spoken English as a measure of communicative ability in English-medium instructional settings* (TOEFL Research Report 7). Princeton, NJ: Educational Testing Service.

Powers, D. E., & Stansfield, C. W. (1983). *The Test of Spoken English as a measure of communicative ability in the health professions: Validation and standard setting* (TOEFL Research Report 13). Princeton NJ: Educational Testing Service.

Subkoviak, M. J. (1985). [Review of test of spoken English]. In J. V. Mitchell, Jr. (Ed.), *The ninth mental measurements yearbook*. Lincoln, NE: Buros Institute of Mental Measurements & University of Nebraska.

Tatsuoka, K. K. (1985). [Review of test of spoken English]. In J. V. Mitchell, Jr. (Ed.), *The ninth mental measurements yearbook*. Lincoln, NE: Buros Institute of Mental Measurements & University of Nebraska.

## Review

The Test of Spoken English (TSE) was developed by Educational Testing Service to meet a general need for an international standardized test of oral English proficiency. Like the TOEFL, the TSE is administered at testing centers around the world by ETS or its representatives. One advantage of this system is that TSE scores can be used in admissions or screening decisions prior to the candidates arrival in the country. For example, the test is currently used by North American universities employing nonnative speakers as teaching assistants and by agencies certifying or licensing foreign trained professionals in certain health-related fields. A retired form of the TSE, which is called SPEAK, is available to those wishing on-site administration and scoring.

The TSE is considered a semidirect test of oral proficiency, since it involves tape recorded speaking tasks rather than face-to-face conversational interaction. As a semidirect test, it has greater face validity than paper-and-pencil tests (indirect tests of speaking skills) and greater administrative convenience than direct measures (e.g., the Interagency Language Roundtable Oral Proficiency Interview).

The cost of the TSE is absorbed by the examinee, who must pay $45.00 to register, designate where the scores are to be sent, and complete the test individually. Approximately six weeks after the test date, the designated user institutions receive an official score report from ETS. It includes the examinee's overall comprehensibility score, reported on a scale of 0 to 300 (in increments of 10), and scores for fluency, pronunciation and grammar, which are reported on a scale of 0.0 to 3.0 (rounded to the nearest decimal of 10). The four scores are each the average of scores awarded by two trained raters. Initially, pairs of TSE raters were reported to have an average interrater reliability of .88 (ETS, 1982, p. 20); however, Bejar found a slight increase in average interrater.

When a person registers to take the TSE, the registrant receives a copy of the examinee handbook, complete with a small floppy disc, which explains the parts of the test and provides sample questions. The booklet provides a clear description (in English) of the TSE, including samples of the picture stimuli the examinee will encounter. It also explains the scoring system and gives verbal performance descriptors related to the levels of the scoring system.

The TSE begins with a series of simple, unscored warm-up questions (about the candidate's reason for taking the test, for example), which are designed to put the candidate at ease and familiarize him or her with the recording apparatus. In subsequent sections, the examinee must read a paragraph aloud, describe a single picture, narrate the events depicted in a series of line drawings, complete several partial sentences, and verbally elaborate on a schedule of activities (provided in outline form), as if the candidate were speaking to a group of students or colleagues. A sample of more creative language use is elicited by asking the candidate to express his or her opinion on a controversial topic or to describe a familiar object, such as a bicycle. These varied tasks elicit speech samples ranging from highly controlled to relatively open-ended. (It should be noted that the user agencies do not hear an individual candidate's tape recorded speech samples; these are only used to generate a set of numerical ratings, which are then reported to the user agencies.)

Criticisms of the TSE frequently center on its nature as a semidirect test, rather than on the content of the test itself. Many people point out that they have difficulty speaking into a tape recorder in their native language. Indeed, face-to-face conversation with a live interlocutor providing nonverbal feedback and negotiating for meaning is quite different, in some respects, from responding to oral and written stimuli, alone and on tape. For this reason, research documenting the performance of native English speakers on the TSE would be helpful.

Another complaint that is sometimes heard deals with the extended discourse task in which the examinee must describe an object or express his opinion. The specific nature of these tasks is changed slightly from one form to another in order to ensure test security. The objective is sometimes raised that few people have to describe a bicycle in real life. However, the task of identifying an object and explaining its functions is common in many disciplines; describing a bicycle is only one realization of this speech act. A sample tape, which is available to user institutions, contains excerpts of examinee responses to both the sentence completion task and the bicycle description, and shows how rich the latter task can be in revealing individual differences among examinees. If potential user agencies need a more discipline-specific speech sample, they should consider administering a face-to-face oral interview tailored for the candidate. However, the variety of speaking tasks on the TSE clearly elicits ratable speech samples in the categories of pronunciation and grammar. Whether or not the candidate's fluency or overall comprehensibility scores are influenced by the examinee's familiarity with the topic is an empirical question that has not yet been addressed. The availability of the Examinee Handbook and Record should at least alert the candidate to what to expect on the test itself, thereby potentially reducing anxiety and some error in the measurement process.

A final comment has to do with the scoring system and the score reports. ETS does not set standards. Individual user agencies must do this themselves. Setting score standards is a very important activity, and institutions would do well to either base it on research or conduct follow-up research on the appropriateness of the standard.

The first form of the TSE was retired from the operational program in 1982 and published for institutional use as part of the Speaking Proficiency English Assessment Kit (SPEAK). SPEAK is designed for postarrival testing of candidates. It contains a set of rater training materials, including eight rater training tapes and six rater testing tapes, as well as test booklets, scoring sheets, and the test recording. Two additional forms of the TSE, called SPEAK 2 and SPEAK 3, have now been incorporated into the program. Together TSE and SPEAK provide the capability to test candidates both prior to arrival and on-site (Stansfield & Ballard, 1983).

The TSE is a valuable addition to the tools available for testing oral English proficiency. However, like most exams, it should be used judiciously. Under the present system of administration, the cost to the examinee is moderate to high, depending on his financial circumstances, although there is no cost to the user agency. Such organizations must determine their own local standards for admission and placement. Having information on oral English skills prior to a candidate's arrival in the country can be very beneficial to both the examinee and the user agency.

### Reviewer's References

Bejar, I. I. (1985). *A preliminary study of raters for the Test of Spoken English* (TOEFL Research Report 18). Princeton, NJ: Educational Testing Service.

Educational Testing Service. (1982). *TSE manual for score users*. Princeton, NJ: Educational Testing Service.

Stansfield, C. W., & Ballard, R. J. (1984). Two instruments for assessing the oral English proficiency of foreign teaching assistants. In K. M. Bailey, F. Pialorsi & J, Zukowski/Faust (Eds.), *Foreign teaching assistants in U. S. universities*. Washington, DC: National Association for Foreign Student Affairs.

# Test of Written English

*Reviewed by*

**Holly Jacobs**
**University of Alabama-Birmingham**

### Synopsis

Test of Written English. TWE. College and other institutional applicants from non-English language countries. Designed to provide direct measure of nonnative English speaker's ability to perform academic writing tasks. Scored holistically by trained readers using a criterion-referenced scale of 1 to 6. Offered at three regular administrations of the Test of English as a Foreign Language (TOEFL) during 1986-87. 30 minutes. One or more new forms are used at each administra-

tion. Administration instruction included in TOEFL Supervisor's Manual. No technical manual. Price included in regular TOEFL fee of $27-$35 per student; fee includes reporting of scores to the examinee and three colleges. TOEFL. Educational Testing Service, CN 6656, Princeton, NJ 08541, USA, telephone: (609) 921-9000.

### Review

The Test of Written English (TWE) was developed by the Educational Testing Service (ETS) as a new component of the Test of English as a Foreign Language (TOEFL), in response to the general trend toward direct, functional tests of communicative competence and to indications that most TOEFL users wanted a writing sample to be included in the exam administered worldwide to nonnative applicants seeking admission to English-medium colleges and other institutions (Stansfield, 1986). During 1986-87, the writing test will be a required component of the TOEFL. (See review of TOEFL in this volume.) There has been no indication whether the writing test will be included in all, more, or fewer administrations of the TOEFL in the future.

The test requires examinees to write one essay on an assigned topic. Examinees are advised that they will have 30 minutes to plan, write, and correct their esssay. Prewriting activities such as thinking, note taking, or outlining are recommended, and workspace is provided. Overall quality of the writing is emphasized over quantity, but examinees are advised to cover the topic adequately and to support their ideas with examples. Approximately 1 3/4 pages are provided on the redesigned TOEFL answer sheet for writing the essay.

Initially, or until a procedure is found for equating different forms of the test and placing them on the TOEFL scale, the TWE results will be listed separately on the ETS score report rather than being incorporated in the scaled total score reported to TOEFL users (Stansfield & Webster, 1986). As with other tests of this type, the TWE is not available to individual users such as classroom teachers, although presumably it may become available in the future to colleges and other institutions in North American through the ETS Institutional Testing Program.

#### The Writing Question.

Great care is exercised in the development of writing prompts. As described by Stansfield and Webster (1986), potential essay topics are first prepared, reviewed, and revised by a team of writing specialists who also coordinate reading of the essays. The questions are then reviewed by ETS editors and revised as necessary, before being pretested both outside and within North America. To maintain test security, a new essay topic will be used for each administration, and different topics may be used for different parts of the world.

Any particular administration of the TWE will require examinees to perform one of two types of writing tasks: (a) to compare/contrast two opposing points of view and defend a position, or (b) to describe and interpret a chart or a graph. This choice of topic types was based on a survey of 190 academic departments by Bridgeman and Carlson (1983) which indicated that faculty tended to favor these two writing tasks as most appropriate for such an exam. The same study indicated, however, that the ability to argue for a position was considered a relatively unimportant writing skill by a majority of departments (except for undergraduate English and graduate management departments), while the ability to describe an object or a procedure and to organize arguments from one to several sources were considered among the most important writing skills by a majority of departments. Although it is thought that the TWE will "provide an opportunity for the examinees to do the kind of writing required in many college courses" (Stansfield, 1986), additional research is needed to demonstrate that these writing tasks, particularly the chart/graph topic, will elicit writing of the type that most nonnative applicants are expected to produce in their English-medium academic programs.

### Scoring Procedures.

Essays are scored holistically, on a scale of 1 to 6, for the examinee's overall demonstrated competence in writing, rather than for particular features such as structure, spelling, punctuation, or word usage. Each essay is scored independently by two readers, with the final score based on the average of these two ratings. When the two scores are discrepant by more than one point, the essay is scored by a third reader. To help maintain common standards and good reliability, readers use a criterion-referenced scoring guide that defines each point on the scale in a single statement, followed by several short descriptions of certain features of writing at each level. A copy of the scoring guide, which was developed and validated during TWE pretesting, is provided to examinees and institutional score recipients.

Readers are experienced teachers in English or ESL at the secondary school or college levels who have previously demonstrated reliability and received training in using the TWE scoring procedures. An effort is made to use nearly equal numbers of teachers from both groups. Extensive safeguards are followed to produce and maintain reliability during scoring sessions, including scoring and discussion of sample or rangefinder papers, to establish standards, use of the scoring guide, continuous monitoring of standards after scoring begins, and periodic rescoring of new benchmark essays.

### Statistical Characteristics

Since this is a new test, reliability and validity information is quite limited. Preliminary statistics from the July 1986 administration of the test to 10,800 examinees at TOEFL centers throughout the world indicate that the test had an average uncorrected reliability of .74 if based on the scores of only one reader, and an average reliability of .85 when adjusted with the Spearman-Brown correction for two readers. These findings are consistent with expectations for direct tests of this type, but the relatively low single-reader reliability suggests that ETS should continue to use at least two readers for scoring each essay.

Similar, but slightly lower interrater reliabilities are reported by Carlson, Bridgeman, Camp, and Wanders (1985) from an ETS-sponsored study involving an experimental version of this test that was administered to 638 applicants to U.S. universities as undergraduate and graduate students in business, engineering, and the social sciences. Carlson et al. also found relatively high reliabilities across topics, suggesting that TWE scores may be quite consistent from topic to topic for both readers and writers. Additional research is needed, however, into the questions of (a) whether only one writing task will generally provide a sufficient sample of writing performance, and (b) whether a given score on this test (regardless of the topic) will always represent the same degree of writing performance as measured by the test.

The Carlson et al. (1985) study also offers some preliminary evidence of construct validity for the TWE. Correlations of .72 between holistic scores on the experimental writing test and total scores on the TOEFL suggest there may be a fair degree of overlap in what is measured by the TWE and the TOEFL, but that each also probably measures some aspect of English proficiency that is not assessed by the other.

### Summary

The Test of Written English represents a significant advance in the standardized test information available to those using the TOEFL as a basis for decisions that affect the academic careers of thousands of nonnative speakers of English. While reliability and validity of the writing test are yet to be demonstrated, preliminary evidence based on an experimental version is promising. Also to be resolved is the problem of statistically equating different forms of the test and placing them on the TOEFL scale. Unfortunately, the name chosen for this new test may create confusion among many users accustomed to dealing with the Test of Standard Written English (TSWE), which is a multiple-choice test for native speakers. Nonetheless, ESL practitioners should rejoice and the test developers are to be commended for this bold step which should further stimulate greater emphasis on performance in second language classrooms and testing programs.

### Reviewer's References

Bridgeman, B., & Carlson, S. (1983). *Survey of academic writing tasks required of graduate and undergraduate foreign students* (TOEFL Research Report No. 15). Princeton, NJ: Educational Testing Service.

Carlson, S. B., Bridgeman, B., Camp, R., & Wanders, J. (1985). *Relationship of admission test scores to writing performance of native and nonnative speakers of English* (TOEFL Research Report No. 19). Princeton, NJ: Educational Testing Service.

Stansfield, C. W. (1986). A history of the Test of written english: The developmental year. *Language Testing, 3 (2)*, 224-34.

Stansfield, C. W., & Webster, R. (1986). The new TOEFL writing test. *TESOL Newsletter*